CW00375409

THE COATI SABLE

THE COATI SABLE

by

PETER GWYNN-JONES

The Memoir Club

© Peter Gwynn-Jones 2010

First published in 2010 by
The Memoir Club
Arya House
Langley Park
Durham
DH7 9XE
Tel: 0191 373 5660
Email: memoirclub@msn.com

All rights reserved.
Unauthorised duplication
contravenes existing laws.

British Library Cataloguing in
Publication Data.
A catalogue record for this book
is available from the
British Library

ISBN: 978-1-84104-205-3

Typeset by TW Typesetting, Plymouth, Devon
Printed by J F Print, Sparkford, Somerset

Dedicated to

My mother and my stepfather and Banny
who were only to know half the story

to English Nicola

to Texan Ginny

to Indian Tanisha
and in memory of her mother and grandmother

to Gurneys

and

to pets and ponies

Contents

List of Illustrations

umbrellas. As head, standing in the centre and pointing to a notice board. Nicholas Tyacke in a white jersey stands in the background.

13. My sister Alexandra.

14. First appearance in a tabard as Bluemantle Pursuivant (standing) after the Garter Service, June 1973, with Theo Mathew, Rouge Dragon Pursuivant (sitting).

15. As Lancaster Herald on the steps of the College of Arms painted by Dominic Ramos assisted by his father Theo.

16. My mother and stepfather in 1978.

Between pages 196–197

17. The map of the United States of America showing lectures and adventures between 1980 and 2005, including Alaska, Hawaii and the key to the city of Cochran, Georgia.

18. Virginia Clegg, 'Ginny', being literary in my bush hat.

19. After receiving the CVO in 1998 with (far left) Nicola Harker (née Beaumont), (left) Stephen Dickinson and (right) Mary Dickinson (née Gurney).

20. Into the jungle for birdwatching and bughunting at La Selva, Costa Rica.

21. Kavas Jehangir in his Muslim cap and an angry Raj Mullah. The elephant had recently been parted from her calf. Kavas was able to overcome his fear and establish a bond of friendship with the elephant. In spite of this, Raj Mullah subsequently became a man-killer.

22. The stalwarts of Garter House: Judith Hardy (centre) adviser on Peerage and Baronetcy claims, legal matters and genealogist; Gillian Barlow (left) my personal heraldic artist; Julia Hett (right) research assistant.

23. Out riding in India with Siasp Kothavala, accompanied by Louise, canine daughter of Victoria.

24. Heraldry is fun. The Princess Royal in Garter's Office 2008.

Acknowledgements

I am greatly indebted to all who have contributed to the contents of this book, in particular Peter Dare for the photograph on the dust cover.

Jennifer Long, my secretary for typing the original manuscript.

Sally Acloque and Peter O'Donoghue for proof reading.

CHAPTER 1

Birth and the Whitwell sisters

I DO NOT KNOW WHERE IN 1939 I was conceived. My mother was not one to allow a pregnancy to interfere with her life, although notes she left me state somewhat testily that she whipped in for the Essex foxhounds in 1939 'but had to give up owing to child'.

At the beginning of March in 1940 my mother was in London where she had an interest in the United Hunts Club then run by Evan Skey and his wife. The Second World War had broken out; and the Skeys had turned part of the Club premises, I believe a squash court, into a wine cellar in anticipation of wartime alcohol shortage. Evan Skey and my father, both in the Royal Artillery, were good friends and were now busy with wartime activities. Life as far as their wives were concerned went on as usual, and the United Hunts Club and its West End wine cellar were a high priority; my birth was not. In consequence I was nearly born on the Great North Road; but my mother was able to drive back in a hurry to her mother's house at West Tanfield in North Yorkshire where I was born almost immediately on the same day. My birthplace, Tanfield House, was a pleasant enough Georgian-type residence on the banks of the River Ure.

I am told I was a difficult birth. Perhaps under the circumstances this is not surprising. A Yorkshire midwife was called in together with a doctor. My mother always told me that she could remember my birth with the doctor saying that 'the child has had it, try and save the mother'. The Yorkshire midwife, being a good Yorkshirewoman, did not accept the doctor's comment. She smacked me on the bottom; and so I survived. My mother remained considerably ill for some time afterwards.

Control of the situation was taken over by my grandmother, Gladys Harrison, who was responsible for registering my birth. She therefore ensured that her first grandchild was born very firmly on her own birthday. At the time there seems to have been some uncertainty as to the exact date of my arrival as it was around midnight. The 12th of March therefore became an important day in my family. Years later my grandmother's sister Muriel was to die on it. She also recruited Nanny and instructed her uncle, Ted Leatham, to put me down for Eton and the Marylebone Cricket Club, better known as the MCC. My christening took place in May at West Tanfield Church with four godparents, assorted small dogs and my grandmother's great friend Lilias Hill-Walker, who is reputed to have bent over the font and said something like 'poor child, with parents like yours you have no chance in life'. My father was present, posing jauntily in military uniform. He gave me the nickname of Bumps and likened my nose to a robin's egg with its freckles. Others referred to me as Peter Llewellyn. Eventually the Llewellyn was to be dropped by all except my mother's youngest sister, Bobby, and I became simply Peter. Significantly, my other two living grandparents did not attend my christening, although my paternal grandmother, Edith Gwynn-Jones, was kind enough to send a christening robe and a cuddly panda. The christening robe is still in a drawer, waiting, probably in vain, for the next generation; and the panda has remained thereafter a constant companion.

Life was to revolve around my maternal grandmother for the next six years. As I learnt to talk I had difficulty in pronouncing 'Granny' and she therefore accepted my efforts, which were interpreted by the family as 'Banny'. Banny she remained thereafter, and by that she was to be known by her five grandchildren, myself and my four first cousins.

My own early life was therefore much influenced by my grandmother, the family matriarch, and this inevitably reflected her own background. She was born Gladys Rachel Whitwell at Barton Hall, near Darlington on 12 March 1882, being the youngest of the five children of Edward Robson Whitwell and his wife, Mary Janet Leatham, both from North Country Quaker families.

My grandmother had in turn been much influenced by her own father to whom she was very close. She kept a diary from 1 January 1893 until 21 April the same year. During that period the diary makes frequent references to her father but only one to her mother, on 18 April:

We went to Seaton today, I enjoyed myself. We went into Stockton this morning to get a lot of things but not very nice. We have to go again on Monday to get our dresses tried on it is a bore. We got crowds of new shoes and boots etc. I am so glad Mother is going to dress us disently for Winsor.

Her mother was an accomplished watercolourist and woodcarver and it may be significant that my grandmother wrote in her diary during a term at school that: 'Some of the girls are going to learn woodcarving, <u>I am not</u>.'

If relations between mother and daughter were not good, the mother's relations were much in evidence, and this was something that I too was to inherit. I grew up to know many of the Leatham clan.

My great-grandparents brought up their five children at the Friarage in Yarm. In about 1890 Quakerism was abandoned; and the children were put into a gig and driven off to be baptized *en masse* in the Church of England. However, Quakerism was to linger on in the family, as those of Quaker extraction remained a closely knit social circle; and from the religious aspect there remained a deep-seated disapproval of being told by clergy how to behave. This manifested itself long afterwards in the family tradition of walking out before a sermon. Sitting as we often did in one of the front pews, it must have caused some surprise when the family, led by my grandmother, walked out of the church as the Anglican parson mounted the pulpit.

My grandmother's diary as a child at Yarm also reveals endless house parties with the children staying up late for dinner and smoking cigarettes in the library far into the night. There were dances and lawn meets of hounds, the breeding of exotic pigeons in the Friarage's pigeon house, which I believe is now a scheduled monument. There were plenty of pet rabbits and a cockatoo. There were apple-pie beds and varied pranks; but above all my grandmother revealed a typical generosity and a lack of responsibility with her pocket money. Throughout her diary there remains an enduring affection for her father which was clearly reciprocated. Ted Whitwell seems to have allowed his children to enjoy themselves, presumably to the despair of nannies and governesses. Much of this childhood was to influence my own, with my grandmother as a matriarchal figure trying to graft it onto her first and much spoilt grandchild.

The bond which I was to develop with my grandmother Banny and she with her father, Ted Whitwell, had in turn been influenced by a similar bond between Ted and his own mother Anne Backhouse Robson. This earlier matriarch had married Henry Whitwell, a Quaker civil engineer, who was shot in Madrid in 1848 at the age of thirty. Photographs of a portrait which was later stolen show Henry Whitwell as a good-looking Byronic young man. Banny always told me that he was a boyfriend of the Empress Eugenie, which had been the cause of his death. I am certain that this is typical of many exaggerations that during my career as a Herald I have so frequently encountered among family traditions. Nonetheless there is often an element of truth around which such fantasies are built. In this case, it is certain that Henry Whitwell died of gunshot wounds in Madrid. He had probably gone on business involving engineering but totally unconnected with any philandering. He had a stammer and may have been unable to provide the relevant password to the Spanish guards. This stammer was inherited by his son Ted who in consequence is reputed as a result to have given up prayers at the Friarage. Prayers were replaced by racy poems from Swinburne. Why anyone with a stammer should find Swinburne of all poets easier to recite must remain inexplicable!

Henry Whitwell and his wife Anne Backhouse Robson had two children, Ted and his sister Maria Jane who married William Lucas, a director of Barclays Bank. The pretty Maria Jane was said by my grandmother to have suffered badly from asthma and to have been mistreated by her husband. Her daughter Helen was to play a part in my life. Anne Backhouse Robson married, as her second husband, David Dale, a Scottish industrialist, who had been involved in a serious coach accident outside Darlington. He was nursed back to health by my Quaker Robson forebears and subsequently married the daughter. Thereafter he involved himself in Quaker business and banking activities and was made a baronet.

Anne brought up both her sons, Ted Whitwell and his half-brother Jimmy Dale, at the White Lodge in Darlington, imparting to both a love of horses and dogs which was ultimately to play such a part in my own life. It is said of her that every time she lost one of her dogs or horses the whole of Darlington went into mourning.

My great-grandfather, Ted Whitwell, was therefore of Quaker

stock, descended from worthy tradesmen, industrialists and bankers. This middle-class background was somewhat lost to later generations such as Banny who regarded trade as anathema and insisted that we were all descended from the knights who accompanied William the Conqueror. When I later became interested in family history, I pointed out to her that her great-grandfather was a grocer in Kendal in Westmorland. The reaction was typical. There was a pause in the conversation, she took a deep breath, puffed at her small du Maurier cigarette and admonished me, 'Peter, you must realize that grocers then were not what they are now. Please give me another glass of sherry.' I told her she was outrageous but poured out the Amontillado sherry notwithstanding.

My great-grandparents, Ted Whitwell and Janet Leatham, were married in 1873. I have their somewhat grand marriage certificate which was hand engrossed on vellum, sporting bogus heraldry and witnessed by some sixty Quaker relatives. These included a number of Liberal Members of Parliament among whom was my great-great-grandfather Edward Aldam Leatham, the bride's father, and Member of Parliament for Huddersfield, and his brother-in-law John Bright the Member of Parliament for Rochdale and one of the nineteenth century's most prominent politicians. John Bright played no part in my background and was never mentioned by the family. Edward Aldam Leatham was rather different and was well remembered. He purchased Misarden Park in Gloucestershire, and his second wife, 'Auntie Mattie', may possibly have been my earliest memory, thus linking me with John Bright and his involvement with the Corn Law problems of the early nineteenth century. John Bright, heavily involved with these national matters, seems to have been largely ignored by the family, perhaps because he had a less racy attitude to life, which many of the Quaker families were then adopting. He was teetotal.

After marriage my great-grandparents settled at Barton Hall before moving on to the Friarage at Yarm. Whether or not Ted Whitwell and his wife had a happy marriage is beyond my knowledge. She went around the world with her paintbrush painting hundreds of pictures, which continue to fill the walls of her descendants' homes. In addition there was her woodcarving and the writing of books. Dominating and tall, she would arrive in a room with great presence and immediately become a focus of attention. My uncle and mother, her grandchildren, regarded her as a frightening relative who had to be endured. Neither my mother nor my uncle were musical; but my great-grandmother insisted that they play on the piano while she sung in a high squeaking voice. Many Edwardian ladies were great travellers, but possibly my great-grandmother was one of the few that arrived at the Taj Mahal and refused to go inside because taking off her shoes was, in her opinion, an attempt by the Indians to humiliate the Empire.

In the meantime her husband, Ted Whitwell, and his half-brother Jimmy Dale and various cousins and relations of the ubiquitous Pease family were subscribing to the Old Raby Hunt. North Country though Ted may have been and was to remain, there was a sudden interlude in his life, when at the age of nineteen with the Hertfordshire, under Lord Dacre, he first learned to ride with hounds. Up North in 1899 the Old Raby Hunt reported that:

> There is no harder rider to hounds with the four or five local packs than Ted Whitwell. His hunters which are usually high class e.g. Grenadier, Gorgon and Galleon are not considered to be slow at their fences.

The Old Raby Hunt's biographical account goes on to report that Ted Whitwell:

> Appears to have climbed all the principal heights in Switzerland and the Tyrol, beside being a pioneer in first assaults of five mountains, including Aiquille de la Blaitiere (Mont Blanc range) and Dent Blanche from Zermatt, direct up the face of it, instead of the easier and more roundabout way. He would vary the monotony of all this climbing by driving scratch teams along the Riviera and in Italy.
>
> His hobby is roses. Both he and Mrs Whitwell were great rose growers during their stay at Barton Hall, having secured one hundred and sixty pounds worth of prizes, besides winning the sixty guineas Challenge Trophy exhibited at Crystal Palace and elsewhere (North Country roses are, as a rule, too late for the Crystal Show). They always showed in the largest classes and were scarcely ever beaten.
>
> He is a great cigar smoker and even when hounds are running!

Ted Whitwell was Chairman of the Horden Collieries which would seem to have been something of a sinecure job left over from the part his forebears had played in the industrialization of the north. It is not part of my story to embark on nineteenth or twentieth century social history, particularly that of Quaker families. I can only say that he was a very popular and much respected figure.

Settled at Yarm with his wife and five children, Ted Whitwell's life focussed on hunting during the winter and taking his yacht, the *Vanadis*, around the Mediterranean in the summer. The *Vanadis* was not a yacht with sails but was steam-fired with a funnel and fully equipped with staff and *Vanadis* silver. I have inherited napkin rings and table silver with *Vanadis* engraved upon them. Ted is reputed to have had a mistress behind every haystack in the North of England during his hunting winters and embarked on his Mediterranean cruises during the summer where champagne was served for breakfast. This high life was to remain a background problem. My grandmother, Banny, and other members of my family somehow expected large inheritances. It never happened. Ted Whitwell may have lived in style off his sinecure, but the Friarage at Yarm was rented from the Meynell family. Basically there was no money; something which was going to catch up with the family later on.

Ted and Janet Whitwell had two sons and three daughters. I did not know the sons; but the three daughters were important in my life: Violet, Muriel and my grandmother Banny. Of the two sons, Cecil's existence I only discovered when I was about twelve or thirteen and becoming interested in the family genealogy. On my enquiring about him, my mother took me aside and said I should not ask about Cecil. Dropping her voice, she told me that he had fallen off his bicycle into a pile of flints, thus suffering from brain damage. I suspect that my mother was simply passing on to me a story which she had been told and which many other children must have heard to account for distressing relations.

Poor Cecil spent the rest of his life in a private nursing home costing the family some considerable sums of money. Photographs of Cecil in his sailor suit as a small child accompanied by nannies and references to him in Banny's childhood diaries do not ever indicate that he played a full part in family life even before whatever accident may have happened to him. He died in his nursing home in 1950 recognizing nobody.

The second son, Leatham Whitwell, 'Uncle Leatham', was also a shadowy figure who died before I was born, leaving somewhat

indifferent paintings of hunting which were often turned into
lampshades, an enormous painted mobile which hung over Banny's
kitchen table, and were elsewhere framed down passages and in spare
bedrooms. Those who knew Leatham had a great affection for him;
but I am not aware that he ever had a job in life except for
commissioning horses for use during the First World War.

When I was about ten I was introduced by my mother to 'Cobby',
the chief whip of the South and West Wilts whose hunting life had
apparently started with my great-uncle Leatham. Cobby was full of
his praises but told me that he was known as 'a gentleman among
grooms and a groom among gentlemen'. He related stories of trying
to smuggle him back into the Friarage in a drunken stupor without
the knowledge of his father. Leatham's one ambition was to hunt
hounds which his father, Ted Whitwell, stated emphatically was not
befitting a gentleman. Gentlemen could only be masters of hounds.
Leatham died of cirrhosis of the liver in 1935 at the age of sixty,
having had two wives and one son. I never knew the next generation.
The only knowledge I have of this son, another Ted Whitwell, is that
he locked up my mother's nanny in a cupboard with a mouse. He
died young and, although married, had no children. Thus terminated
four generations of Whitwells.

Cecil and Leatham I may not have known, but the three Whitwell
sisters I did. They were a formidable combination and were the only
generation on any grandparent side that featured in my life. The
eldest was Violet, regarded as the plain Jane of the family, and a
contrast to her sisters who were flattered into considering themselves
great beauties. In fact I would describe the youngest, Banny, my
grandmother as good-looking in her youth and distinguished in her
middle age. Sadly she put on much weight in her old age, but
nonetheless I found this delightfully warm and cuddly. The second
sister, Muriel, remained astonishingly striking until her death.

Violet had surprised the whole family by her sudden appearance
on the lawn at the Friarage turning somersaults and announcing her
engagement. Nobody had ever expected her to acquire a boyfriend
and certainly not a husband. Her younger sisters on the other hand
were much in demand. Violet's husband was to be Marston Buszard,
a QC, a widower and the best man at her parents' wedding. A year
after her marriage Violet gave birth to twin daughters.

Petite Aunt Violet with her thinning red hair, doubtless helped by the rinse bottle, was to live at 44 Ladbroke Grove in London. She detached herself from her Quaker background and became somewhat churchy; her fingers were smothered with rings, her drawing room was full of my great-grandmother's paintings and a much pampered Persian cat. The staff in the basement sent up food by trolley service; and when I became a teenager we sat at either end of a large dining room table convulsing in giggles at the expense of other members of the family. Unfortunately, her sense of humour was not extended to Christmas presents. Every year she sent me a half a crown book token (now worth 12½p). If I did not send a thank-you letter within a week, my mother would receive a letter enquiring as to whether or not Peter had received his present. Thank-you letters were expected by return; and presents remained somewhat impersonal.

The second sister Muriel was always to be whimsical and capricious. Four years older than my grandmother, the relationship between the two sisters was to remain close but seldom easy. This could also be said of my own relationship with my great-aunt. In Banny's childhood diary Muriel is frequently described as quarrelsome and disagreeable. All three sisters inherited the red hair of their Leatham grandfather. Banny was auburn and then somewhat mysteriously changed to blond during the course of my early childhood. Muriel retained her auburn hair until her death at the age of nearly ninety although there were a number of grey streaks. Presumably no assistance from the rinse bottle was required; but I never questioned her maid, 'Crabbie', who would dutifully comb out Her Ladyship's hair before working it into a bun.

Muriel was an imposing figure at six foot and a face that was beautiful rather than attractive with large eyes and high arched eyebrows. Everything was heavily powdered. At the age of thirty she married George Clerk, who was to become Ambassador in Turkey, Brussels and Paris. Banny always remained very fond of her brother-in-law; and George was my mother's godfather. It was a great sadness to my grandmother that her sister Muriel's marriage was not a success. I suppose the marriage must have been consummated; but there were no children. However Muriel, who was much prone to fantasy, claimed that she was once impregnated by a water nymph who subsequently changed his mind and took the child away. I declined to tell her that I thought nymphs were usually female and therefore incapable of impregnation. Whether her story indicates a miscarriage I do not know. I rather suspect it was her imagination or an attack of wind.

Trouble with Muriel's marriage came in Prague where George was First Minister, by which time she had acquired a considerable reputation as a faith healer; and an account of many of her cases has subsequently been published in France. Perhaps rather more whimsical was her belief in reincarnation; and in due course the British Embassy in Prague was subjected to various thumps and bumps. The entire Embassy was evacuated except for Muriel who was left to communicate with the ghost responsible. This ghost was apparently a Countess who had lived during the Thirty Years War and had been rescued by my great-aunt in one her previous incarnations. This phantom Countess had returned to give belated thanks; and thereafter the mysterious noises ceased. I do not know what the Czechs or poor George or the other British in the Embassy thought of this episode. It must surely have raised a few eyebrows.

Marriage matters came to a head when Muriel returned early one afternoon from riding in order to arrange a dinner party. She discovered George having an affair with his secretary; and a major scandal erupted. Since Muriel had lived on a different floor from George; and George had occupied rooms adjacent to his secretary with adjoining doors, it is perhaps surprising that Muriel seems to have been unaware of an affair which was discovered to have been in existence for a number of years. This effectively ended the marriage although the couple continued to keep up appearances during George's subsequent postings. The secretary was married at the time and had a son who subsequently inherited the husband's peerage title and took his seat in the House of Lords. In 1968 I witnessed various documents subsequent to Muriel's death which released capital to the Peer in question. George had established a trust to provide for Muriel during the rest of her life and then the capital passed to His Lordship. On George's death, the rest of his estate passed to the peer's younger brother.

As a result of these domestic problems, Muriel sought solace with the arts. She had inherited painting ability from her mother whose watercolours she particularly disliked. She turned instead to oils, painting whimsical clowns, flying carpets and grotesque buildings, peopled by weird twisted figures in fanciful landscapes. She had an exhibition in February 1937 in Paris entitled *Exposition Janet Clerk and quelques peintres Français* who included Bonnard, Braque, Chagall, Dufy, Matisse and Picasso. A later exhibition in the same year in London at the Lefevre Galleries entitled *Janet Clerk and her Friends*, included works by Bonnard, Chagall and Dufy. She seems to have been particularly close to Chagall, who gave her a number of paintings which she then passed to the Tate Gallery, but one she kept and it is reputed to have ended up in Banny's attic. I have subsequently been accused of burning it in a clear out. I have always hotly denied this!

Her association with French artists and her own whimsical character had its effect on the British Embassy in Paris. Sweet peas and roses were banished from the dining room table which was then strewn with ivy, more akin to a bistro. After dinner diplomats were made to play musical chairs while Muriel stood as an imposing figure above the pianist, tapping him on the shoulder whenever she wished the music to stop. I have little doubt, knowing my great aunt, that she ensured that her particular favourite or pet for the evening was victorious. I do not know whether such as Mussolini or Hitler were party to these antics. I do know that she considered Mussolini to be one of her admirers and that he gave her an antique clock. I seem to recall asking her about Hitler and that she said something to the effect that he was 'a rather tiresome and common little man'.

Muriel wrote plays which were recorded on the radio and published her own music. While her husband George was Ambassador in Turkey, she was responsible for producing *The Heart of Turandot*, which was the first time that Turkish women had been allowed to take part in serious acting; and it was a major step in their liberation. I have inherited an extensive scrapbook of international newspaper cuttings of this event. Needless to say Muriel played the principal part of Turandot herself. She was also to be a sculptress and to have her own exhibition at the Galerie de Berrie. It is a pity that most of her sculptured animals including many delightful fish, frogs and dinosaurs were subsequently lost, for which I must take much of the blame. On one of her whims she decided to sell much of the contents of her spacious flat in Lennox Gardens, London. I was at Cambridge at the time and did not bother to go to the sale, where they fetched ridiculously low prices. Most were bought by a dealer whom I subsequently tracked down in the Portobello Road, only to find that Muriel's pieces had been sent to Scandinavia. I only wish I had been more alert in the matter.

The third sister, Banny, found her life changed when in the summer of 1902 her father, Ted Whitwell, had moored the *Vanadis* off Gibraltar. Friends and family were aboard, apart from Ted's wife who was probably painting watercolours elsewhere. A lonely figure appeared on a bicycle; this was Arthur Patrick Bird Harrison who had bicycled from England to the south of Spain and was requesting an easier way home. He stayed on the yacht; and as Banny subsequently said, refused to leave the family on reaching England. Since the Yarm visitors' books show Arthur Harrison as a frequent guest, I cannot believe that he was not a fully welcomed visitor.

Arthur and my grandmother came from somewhat different backgrounds, which may explain the disaster of their subsequent marriage. Banny, albeit originally a Quaker, was thoroughly Edwardian in outlook. The Harrisons were not; they were Victorian. Arthur was the only son of General Sir Richard Harrison who had had a distinguished career in the nineteenth century Army, starting with the Crimean War and ending with the Boer War. The main controversy over Richard Harrison was his part in the Zulu War, where his arguably unclear orders to his ADC led to the death of the Prince Imperial of France. Although criticized in public, behind the scenes he remained much in favour and became a close friend of members of the Royal Family, including Arthur, Duke of Connaught, who was my grandfather's godfather, hence the name Arthur. This also explains why my grandfather was subsequently commissioned into the Duke of Connaught's Own, the Rifle Brigade. A further influence on my grandfather was another of Queen Victoria's sons, the Duke of Edinburgh, who was the Admiral stationed at Devonport when my great-grandfather was the General of the Western District. The children of both families were brought up with continuous comings and goings between them during their formative years. I have inherited a number of photographs of Christmas tableaux which they put on together; and subsequent god-parentage between the two families indicates a close bond. The bond resulted in Arthur being appointed ADC to the King of Serbia during the First World War. Possibly Arthur suffered from being the only son of a distinguished father; but for whatever reason he seems to have been a somewhat troubled person. Again for whatever reason Banny married him at Holy Trinity, Brompton in London in 1906.

Exactly where, why or when this marriage between my grandparents broke down I am not entirely certain. Two children were born, my uncle Richard Arthur Harrison and my mother Mary Muriel Daphne Harrison, to be known as Daphne, thus inviting my great-uncle Leatham Whitwell to comment that Daphne was an absurd name and one only given to hounds. Arthur and Banny eventually took Harthover in Hawley in Hampshire. Hawley House had originally belonged to Sir Richard Harrison until it was burnt down, after which he had moved to Ashton Manor in Devonshire. I was always told that the burning of Hawley was caused by a maid leaving a candle in the attic and that nothing was saved from the house except the grand piano which all the staff wasted time on bringing out of the drawing room. When I subsequently went to Wellington, I was told by Taffy, the house servant in my house or dormitory, that he could remember lines of buckets being passed up through the village in a vain effort to put out the fire. The idea that nothing was saved is an example of how families can exaggerate facts. The Harrison portraits were certainly in the house at the time; and they have subsequently come down to me. Apart from one missing early eighteenth century clergyman, who may have been hung in some obscure top passage, all survived.

Shortly before his marriage to my grandmother in 1906, Arthur had retired from the Army. He settled with his new wife and tried to find a job in London. Various partnerships were found; but the poor fellow clearly hated any civilian job; and there was no money. The Whitwells were living in grand style at Yarm; and Sir Richard Harrison, with an estate in Devonshire, was presumably living off the sizeable pay of a retired full general. His mother had been widowed at an early age; and although the Harrisons had been noticeably rich in the eighteenth century, their wealth had been dissipated by overbreeding; and they lost their commercial base by moving into the rather more fashionable Law, Church and Army.

Arthur's last hope of success was the turtle soup project. Somehow money was raised, and beaches in Queensland were duly purchased. Fertilized turtle eggs were laid down to make the family fortune. Unfortunately, each turtle hatchling disappeared into the ocean with a Harrison pound note on its back and never returned. My indefatigable grandmother rose above all these domestic problems. Harthover was extended so that it became a seven-bedroomed house with extensive stabling, a tennis court, orchards, rose gardens, herbaceous border and a field for the horses. My uncle Dick was sent to Harrow following his father Arthur and his grandfather, the general. This was a definite concession to the Harrisons because her own Quaker forebears had moved across to Eton. Banny hunted with the local pack of hounds, the Garth, and took her children stalking in Scotland. Arthur in the meantime does not appear to have shared his wife's interest in hunting. He delighted in trout fishing and immediately clashed with his wife who preferred going after salmon. Arthur in fact was an extremely good fisherman, and this disagreement with his wife suggests that the problem with the marriage was rather deeper than a difference of opinion over fishing. Like her sister, Muriel, my grandmother seems to have remained aloof from any sexual relationship even within marriage. Arthur on his visits to London in various unsuccessful jobs was to take recourse elsewhere.

In the meantime the First World War had broken out. Arthur Harrison was posted as Military Attaché to the British Embassy in Serbia and played a not inconsiderable part in mobilizing the Serbian War effort. Banny, my grandmother, was equally active on the home front, raising money for the Serbian cause and sending out supplies through the Red Cross, and was decorated with the Serbian Order of St Sava. Unfortunately patriotism did not bring my grandparents together. After a brief attempt at reconciliation, which resulted in the birth in 1919 of my aunt Barbara Anne, known as Bobby, they separated. Arthur in his excursions to London rescued a very pretty girl from a serious fire during which she lost a leg. Banny always maintained she was an East End music hall turn, and that was her politest description. In fact Ursula Hughes was a well-known actress and singer who built up a very considerable reputation and had her own show in the West End. She was thirty years younger than my grandfather; but they had a wonderful and happy life together. She died short of a hundred still teaching music in Cheltenham. They had cohabited together for some time before Banny would agree to a divorce. Banny was not prepared to lose her tickets for the Royal Enclosure at Ascot which banned divorcées. Subsequently she raised the question of pensions for Army Officers' widows and how she had been deprived of it. Rightly or wrongly I told her to shut up; and I and my first cousin Georgina started referring to my poor grandfather as her 'husband'. Banny had other expressions for him.

To put Arthur in perspective, he was a great sportsman, a first class shot and a dedicated fisherman. He was a hopeless businessman and socially ill at ease. On the one or two occasions that I was eventually taken to see him he was the epitome of a kindly old Colonel Blimp living in Cheltenham with his devoted second wife. Every birthday and Christmas he sent the usual two shillings and six pence postal order with a letter which was always signed 'your affectionate grandfather APB Harrison' with underneath, almost as a concession, 'Granpy'.

On the separation of my grandparents, Banny was left bringing up two small children and a baby at Harthover. The eldest, Dick, was a man of considerable charm and was to acquire a wide circle of friends. Unfortunately, he inherited his father's lack of business acumen. After Harrow he went to Clare College, Cambridge, where he accumulated gambling debts which were paid off by his Whitwell grandmother. Money problems remained with him throughout his life. He always expected to inherit, little realizing that both the Harrisons and the Whitwells had long since disposed of any capital assets and inclination to regenerate money on a sound financial base. Although Dick's Whitwell grandparents lived in considerable style, the house, the Friarage at Yarm, was only rented, and income came from Ted Whitwell's chairmanship of the Horden Collieries. His other grandparents owned Ashton Manor in Devon, an estate which included several farms. However, Sir Richard Harrison was not a particularly rich man and was largely dependent upon his pension. Matters had been made worse by a child having his foot blown off by a mine on one of the farms and Harrison finances were somewhat embarrassed by the subsequent court case and the resulting damages.

My mother and Dick would visit their grandparents at the Friarage for Christmas and Ashton for Easter. Dick was doubtless impressed by sizeable households with numerous staff, but failed to see that such

households were largely self-contained, being fed from home products. Both families shot and fished extensively. Game was therefore
plentiful, and fruit and vegetables came from the kitchen garden, the
fruit cages and orchards.

Dick's inability to grasp facts was manifested years later when he
explained to me that he was brought up to believe that a gentleman
never had to work. I recall pointing out to him that his uncles
included an Ambassador, a Queen's Counsel and a Barrister and that
his grandfather had been a successful General. I am afraid the point
was not taken. As the only son he was much spoilt by a doting mother
and the formidable Muriel. Photographs show him dressed up as
Cupid complete with wings and bow and arrows at the age of three or
four, posing for photographs. This was possibly not a good introduction to life and the subsequent social changes of the twentieth century.

He inherited an artistic ability from his maternal grandmother but
sadly lacked her imagination. He won the school prize for art at Harrow.
Much encouraged by his mother, Banny, and her sister Muriel, he
eventually settled down to painting game birds, out of which he
endeavoured to make some sort of a living. Never a great artist, his
pictures had an appeal to the hunting, shooting and fishing fraternity; and
by courtesy of the company 'Lady Clare', his trays, table mats and waste
paper baskets are still widely in use. I still frequently come across them.

I also remember only too clearly how he would telephone me to
say that he had had a very good Badminton horse trials or game fair,
selling original paintings or his 'Lady Clare' trays and table mats from
his tent. I would enquire as to the cost of the site, what he had paid
'Lady Clare' and the cost of the whisky and sherry which he offered
in generous quantities to potential clients. I always received an evasive
reply. I retained a great affection for Uncle Dick, sometimes tinged
with irritation. This was such that I once told him straight to his face
that he was the worst disaster that ever happened to the Harrison
family since the Black Death. Typically I was merely told to pour
myself another whisky and given a lecture on how it was the duty of
a nephew to support an ageing uncle.

To give credit to Dick, he was ADC to Bomber Harris during the
Second World War, when he was much liked and respected. I have
inherited a silver cigarette box given to Dick by Bomber Harris
confirming the latter's gratitude.

CHAPTER 2

Parents and my war effort

M Y MOTHER WAS BORN IN 1911 and baptized Mary Muriel
Daphne. She was known as Daphne which, as my great uncle
Leatham Whitwell had pointed out, was a name fit only for a hound.
She was three and a half years younger than her brother Dick.

My mother inherited a love of dogs and horses from her Whitwell
forebears and her ability to paint and draw from the Leathams. Unlike
her brother Dick, she had a highly imaginative mind and was in the
future to draw me wonderful dragons and humanized animals. We
always drew our own Christmas and birthday cards for close members
of the family; and it was a special treat to see how my mother drew
all the dogs carol singing or having pillow fights. If she was somewhat
awkward socially, she made up for this by being game for anything.

My mother was the smallest of the three children. She had
inherited her size from her Harrison grandmother, always known as
Little Granny, together with a sensitive nature sometimes bordering
on the highly strung. Her angular features also came from her father's
side. In her they were not unattractive; but in her son I am certain
they are far less successful. I always endeavour to avoid the camera
and seeing myself in a mirror. As a child and teenager, my mother
had the auburn hair of the Leathams but this darkened to mousy
brown as she grew older. My mousiness replaced my own reddish
hair at an earlier age. My mother's eyes were grey; mine are hazel.

She must have been a difficult child; and the separation of her
parents when she was eight greatly affected her. Originally she was
devoted to her father but was to be greatly upset by an incident
involving her younger sister Bobby who was then a baby. Somehow
the baby had fallen into an ornamental lily pond. My grandfather,
walking with my mother, discovered this, and merely took his
walking stick and hooked the baby out onto the path, telling my
mother to run and fetch Nanny, and continued his walk. My mother
was not impressed by my grandfather's distinct lack of sensitivity. As
the final separation of my grandparents was about to take place, it was

17

easy for Banny to take this incident and turn my mother against her father. Banny succeeded; and my mother was never to see or communicate with her father again until I was used as an excuse for reconciliation some thirty years afterwards.

My mother's notes say that she had lessons in French and music 'which were unbearable at three years old'. She then had lessons in the village with five or six others from six until thirteen when she was sent to Luckley School near Wokingham. She 'disliked this intensely except for games, sports, drawing and dancing – ninety-nine per cent in algebra – best at maths, geography and Old Testament – refused to have singing and music lessons'. Unlike the pond baby, my aunt Bobby, who eventually became head girl at Luckley, my mother detested school and once she was able to escape decided to try everything. I once asked her after dinner to scribble a few notes on her teenage and pre-marital life in the nineteen twenties and thirties. She wrote 'rode from the age of five or six – went up to ten or twelve miles to meets of the Aldershot Beagles, with garden boy as escort. Lost my nerve when run away at about fourteen years old and took to riding side-saddle. Then bought Beacontree at Ascot for twenty-five guineas to learn to ride astride on'. Beacontree not only restored my mother's confidence; but the two of them went on to win a number of point to points. She monopolized the ladies' race at the Berks and Bucks hunt meeting for several years. Apart from varied jobs in racing stables, she had lessons in jujitsu and in her own words 'can throw a man'. She learnt to fly gypsy moth aeroplanes and took part in various flying competitions. She inherited a gymnastic bounce and suppleness from her father who had been the Army's Inspector of Gymnasia. I was not to inherit these physical abilities. My mother's notes say that she 'trained at theatrical school and then specialized in Lift Tricks e.g. flip flaps, butterflies, back somersaults et cetera . . . Did cabaret and was the only solo in Grafton Galleries' and then went on until she turned down a solo engagement at a Buckingham Palace theatrical garden party as it clashed with Ascot races. She also notes that she took a job as a solo acrobatic-dancer at Woolwich but subsequently tore up the contract as the manager seldom paid and had raped a girl at Aldershot. Photographs of my mother as a teenager and in her twenties show her at ease in strangely contorted postures. She had the ability to turn her head backwards and twist her backbone so that her head popped out through ankles, knees or crotch. What my grandmother Banny thought of all these antics I do not know; but the relationship between mother and daughter was always close. My grandmother ensured that my mother was properly presented at Court. Giggling debutantes ganged-up together and somehow or other my mother and her then great friend, Patience Culme-Seymour, decided to leave their knickers in the Buckingham Palace aspidistra. Whether or not one or both of them were eventually presented to His Majesty in a knickerless condition, I do not know.

Thereafter there followed a succession of dogs, horses and boyfriends, interspersed with working in racing stables and running the local girl guides from Harthover, the converted gamekeeper's cottage where her mother, Banny, had remained after the separation from her husband. Inheriting shyness and social unease from her father, she made up for this with her drive and enterprise coming from the indefatigable and possibly somewhat bemused Banny. In 1931, when she was out hunting with the Garth, the horse in front of my mother refused at a fence. The rider asked her for a lead. She obliged with Beacontree and both horses went over. Seeing that the stranger was a good-looking man, she was happy to strike up a conversation. As there was a gap in the house party for a forthcoming ball, she decided that one good turn deserved another. Jack Gwynn-Jones therefore accepted her invitation to join the party and thence began an affair which resulted in marriage in 1934.

My father was an Officer in the Royal Artillery and was horse orientated, both racing and hunting. In 1930 he had inherited some forty thousand pounds from an uncle which was fully sufficient for a young subaltern to live an affluent life without much thought of the future. Something of a cynic and possibly even a poseur, he was a hit with the girls not least because of his good looks. He acquired a reputation of taking socialites to Quaglino's, one of London's fashionable nightspots. Thereafter a move towards seduction would take place; but having succeeded in divesting the girl, he would then simply say 'That is very nice, please get dressed . . .' and then make some excuse to go off to place a bet or have a drink elsewhere, leaving the girl somewhat humiliated. From what little I know of my father, this anecdote recalled by his son would highly amuse him. Good looks and sex appeal were to descend ultimately to my half-sister, Alexandra, who flirted not unsuccessfully with modelling and starring in films. My father was to have little or no influence in my life, other than providing me with a Welsh surname and what my mother described as 'a dustbin brain'.

During my life the possession of a Welsh surname has never presented me with any problem, with the exception of Welsh peers coming into the House of Lords years later, who attempted to no avail a few sentences of the Welsh language, and Peter Snow, the newscaster, who had a tendency to place a leek on my breakfast table at school and once made me learn and sing *Land of our Fathers* at a school singsong. Jack Gwynn-Jones had one considerable advantage. He charmed Banny. He ragged and teased her. Like her daughter, she was captivated by his looks and his wit; but, perhaps above all, she was taken by his ability with horses and his success at point to points. Abandoning hopes of a Northumberland baronet with whom my mother had been dallying, she was anxious to settle her somewhat wayward daughter. The affair with my father had gone on too long so she pressed for a conclusion, even bringing in his commanding officer. Being a cynic, my father protested that he did not believe in marriage let alone having children. He agreed to marriage on condition that he could have a divorce whenever he wished; clearly an unsatisfactory attitude, and one which he was later to regret. I am sure that my mother was the great love of his life; and he was devastated when the divorce eventually occurred. He was never a man to show any emotion, believing firmly in the British stiff upper lip; but on the rare occasions that I saw him up to his death, the affection and feeling he had for my mother was always apparent. In possibly the last conversation I ever had with him, he said 'She was one hell of a girl'.

The marriage took place on 11 January 1934. On 12 January it was splashed all over the national press. Even *The Daily Telegraph* had a photograph of my parents on the front page with my mother leaning over kissing one of the dogs, a Sealyham, held by a soldier servant, and my father standing centre in the background looking extremely happy. Behind the scenes, which had been orchestrated by Banny, matters were perhaps unusual. The bride's father was absent and would not have been asked. He must have been surprised to see his daughter, upon whom he once doted, splashed across the newspapers.

Perhaps more unusual was the absence of the bridegroom's mother, Edith Gwynn-Jones.

Edith Gwynn-Jones claimed that she was still mourning for her husband who had died five months previously. The fact that she never came to my christening six years later suggests that mourning was merely an excuse and that she was deeply jealous of my mother for replacing her in the affections of her precious boy. She remained a shadowy and somewhat sad person in my life. She had passed her good looks to my father with perhaps a certain vanity. When visiting her family in Warwickshire she would take a first class ticket from Brighton to Birmingham, but her niece told me that all the family were amused because she stood for the whole journey in the corridor as sitting down would crease her dress. Subsequently my mother and I would visit her in Hove during the war. I recall dropping crumbs from a cake on the floor; and there was a scene with a maid being summoned with dustpan and brush. It was a tradition inherited from Banny and continued by my mother that members of the family should all send their own personal hand-drawn and hand-painted Christmas cards. When I was four my parents separated; but I continued to send a card to my grandmother, Edith. It might have been a dog in a Christmas hat or even a picture of a pony with exaggerated knees, fetlocks and hooves. Whatever my effort, my grandmother sent my Christmas cards back to my mother. Thankfully I was never made aware that this happened. The final effort to contact my grandmother was eventually made by my stepfather who felt strongly that a grandmother should take an interest in her then only grandchild. When I was later at a prep school in Eastbourne, not far removed from Hove, he arranged for me to be taken over to see her. She agreed; I was taken over by a family friend only to find that my grandmother had changed her mind and was 'out'. The front door bell was rung in vain. I have no more memories of her, until Banny asked me one day whether I knew that my grandmother had died. She had seen it in the papers; and I am sorry to say that I was totally uninterested.

Following my parents' wedding, they settled down to six years of married life before I appeared; a situation which reflects my father's reluctance to breed. Eventually, my mother had other ideas; and I was born.

My first achievement in life was to win a competition as the prettiest baby in the local garden fete in Yorkshire. I suspect that this may have been nothing to do with my reddish hair and robin's egg nose but rather more with an orchestration by Nanny and Banny who had doubtless played a part in organizing the fete for the war effort. Shortly afterwards Banny had decided to give up Tanfield House and base us all at Harthover. In the meantime my father had come out of the army because of the dog and horse situation. He had been posted to Malaya; but my mother had objected because it would have meant leaving the dogs and horses. After many floods of tears he gave in and resigned his commission. Running a pub or training horses seemed to have been the alternative; but war broke out and he rejoined the army. It may be asked why an army officer's wife could not accept that her husband might be posted overseas and why the husband did not put his foot down very firmly.

My father was in the retreat to Dunkirk, playing hide and seek with a German officer through the trees. He shot and killed the German officer. I asked him what he thought about this; and he simply replied 'I was the better shot and if I had not killed him he would have killed me'. He came back to England and was responsible for placing our limited supply of anti-aircraft guns in choice positions throughout the country and gave several broadcasts on the wireless as to what he was doing. While this was happening I lost my Nanny. She had remained in Yorkshire while I was taken on the anti-aircraft round with my mother and father, being largely based in Manobier Castle in South Wales, where a bomb landed nearby, causing some consternation, throughout which I slept happily oblivious.

Family problems then took over with the illness of 'Auntie Mattie', my step-great-great-grandmother, the second wife of Edward Aldam Leatham.

On the death of Edward Aldam Leatham it was hoped to keep Misarden Park in Gloucestershire in the Leatham family and also to provide for 'Auntie Mattie' his second wife. Bagendon Manor in Gloucestershire was purchased for 'Auntie Mattie', where she continued to live for the rest of her life, with a particular interest in small black dexter cows. Death duties had to be paid to retain Misarden Park in the family. This involved selling an Italian Renaissance painting which Edward Aldam Leatham had acquired during a trip to Italy. Unfortunately it seems to have been uninsured when it was sent to the auction houses of New York. It sailed on the Titanic. Thus the means to pay the death duties went to the bottom of the north Atlantic. Misarden was therefore sold, but Auntie Mattie remained at Bagendon Manor; and my mother with her small child went to look after her in her last few months of her life. Meanwhile my father went on active service to India.

I do not know how far back a child's memory can go. However, I remember being much taken by a little old lady in black waving a walking stick at me. She was standing in front of a large stone house with French windows. I was at the far end of the lawn and beyond a little stream. I was crawling on my hands and knees examining with some considerable fascination a large number of small froglets. How I had arrived at the far side of the stream I do not know nor do I recall how I was rescued from the situation. Presumably the figure with the walking stick was my step-great-great-grandmother and the little frogs were one of my first introductions to wildlife. It was the late summer of 1941, and I was barely eighteen months old.

Years later I described the scene and my mother and uncle confirmed this description as being that of Bagendon, and thus my link with John Bright.

Soon afterwards my mother and I joined Banny at Harthover where I spent the next five years of my life. It was wartime, much of which I found enjoyable.

Blackbush Airport was barely three miles away; and as the war progressed I was allowed to watch the squadrons of bombers and fighters fly overhead on their way to Germany. This was usually out of the bathroom window when I had had my bath at six o'clock in the evening. I dimly recall my grandmother and mother counting them back in the morning, but I am afraid that any loss in the number meant little or nothing to me.

Tanks were a frequent sight, making their horrendous but somewhat exciting noise through the village; and then there were the air raids. The siren would sound at night; and my mother would come and collect me from my bedroom. We would go down to the cellar where there was a tin of Ovaltine tablets for me to suck. I remain mystified as to why I was fed Ovaltine tablets; but I rather enjoyed them. My mother and her sister Bobby with her baby

Georgina made up the four of us. Banny remained upstairs, much to the consternation of her two daughters. She sent her jewellery down to the cellar, but flatly refused to be dislodged from her bed by 'tiresome' Germans. We waited for doodlebugs to fall. These German missiles were supposed to whine overhead then cut out, and the silence gave us time to prepare for the worst. I remember listening in vain for this experience which never occurred, being totally oblivious of its potential effect.

The 'blackout' was in force. Every curtain of the house had an additional thick black curtain hung behind it which was drawn dutifully every evening. I well remember at the end of the war going around every room with Banny taking them down. Gas masks were also issued; possibly my mother and Banny were concerned that I might be alarmed. My gas mask had a Mickey Mouse face, complete with ears, and my mother and grandmother donned their gas masks in the drawing room as we played hide and seek, so that I was far from being frightened. I thoroughly enjoyed Mickey Mouse and much regretted that he subsequently disappeared; and I do not recall ever seeing him again.

Wartime rationing was in force. I remember my mother taking a brown ration book into various shops to buy me clothes. As far as I was concerned, I was more apprehensive about the sweet supply. However since most of the Leatham clan were sympathetic towards a small child, I did not go short. I had to compete with Banny who forever enjoyed chocolates, marzipan and crystallized fruits, which she consumed with great gusto between her Du Maurier cigarettes and Amontillado sherry.

Food was in plentiful supply. Dallimore the gardener carefully nurtured the vegetable garden, which grew everything from asparagus to the strongly flavoured globe artichoke which I particularly detested. The fruit cages and orchards were far from basic. Banny delighted in such exotica as loganberries, white currants, cherries and white raspberries, fighting an endless battle against birds and insects that attacked the apple trees and strawberry beds. Dallimore was forever rigging new netting over the strawberries and wrapping sticky anti-insect papers around apple and pear tree trunks. Fruit was bottled in Kilner jars; eggs were plentiful.

Hens in the front garden were immediately chased back. Many a lunchtime was interrupted by such a chase with a small boy leading the way. They were fed with scraps in the late afternoon when eggs were collected, and the hens were locked into their houses. This was always supervised by Banny with me in tow. With basket and secateurs and suitably garden hatted in white-brimmed straw with ribbon, she would clip roses on the way. Whatever was happening in the war, it was essential there were fresh flowers in the house every day. Roses were her particular delight, especially those with scent. I well remember sampling the smell of different roses and other flowers, a smell which now alas seems to have been lost in post-war gardening.

Banny with her First World War experience in raising money for the Red Cross in aid of Serbia went into action. Garden fêtes were her response to Hitler. A small grandson could be useful. I was therefore dressed up in a pair of brown corduroy leggings, a red frock coat and a velvet jockey cap. In this somewhat preposterous garb I was put into the green pony trap which was festooned with Red Cross tins and led around various fields and orchards by a particularly pretty girl whose name I have long since forgotten. My mother in the meantime was running a dog gymkhana. Being painfully shy, I did not appreciate being approached by numerous women in hats and flannel coats and skirts. The skirts I seem to remember hung at curious angles. I was bombarded by such questions as 'Dear little boy, what is your name?' and 'What is the name of your nice little pony?' The pony was a skittish Shetland called Nibbles which I renamed Diddles. I sat grumpily, being too shy to say anything until my patience eventually snapped. I had learnt a useful expression from Banny's gardener, Dallimore. I now used this to great effect. 'Bugger off!' I exclaimed. The crowd of women scattered like a flock of chickens. Better still, news of my behaviour must have reached the ears of my mother, because shortly afterwards I was taken off Red Cross duty, presumably given a lecture and allowed to spend the rest of the afternoon poking grass through the wire of cages and hutches containing rabbits, many of which were old friends. They belonged to Murphy, the caretaker of the village school, who kept his rabbits behind his house on the village green where I was a frequent visitor.

CHAPTER 3

Ponies, pets and Uncle Ted

THE SHETLAND NIBBLES, RENAMED by me Diddles, had arrived at the end of 1942 or the beginning of 1943, but was not my first experience with horses and ponies. I had long since been placed on my mother's hunter, Testuda, sitting in a leather bucket riding chair with an iron bar across the front to prevent me falling out. This chair had been brought from Spain by my Whitwell great-grandmother especially for use by children in the family; and I was duly led around the local woods clutching reins and the iron bar. However, I do not remember the incident when Testuda was made to stand on the tennis court with me on board so that my mother could walk some thirty feet away to take a photograph with an extendible Kodak camera in a wood and brass mount, somewhat different from today's photographic equipment. My Spanish chair slipped; and I was left dangling under the mare. Thankfully Testudo was good natured and remained still while my mother rushed to my rescue.

Interspersed with garden fêtes were horse shows; and I won my first cup at Arborfield Show in 1943 at the age of three.

Blackwater Railway Station was well used to the family with my grandmother frequently telephoning to say that she was catching a particular train. Presumably the train was meant to wait for her. As she was frequently late, I imagine there must have been a number of very disgruntled fellow passengers. However, I do not ever recall a train going without her. It was not therefore difficult to arrange for a horsebox to be attached. Diddles with her plaited mane and tail and her owner in his inevitable red frock coat were put on board. I did not have to do much at Arborfield Show except be led around the ring by my mother with numerous other children. My cup was not the result of any riding prowess or the good looks of Diddles; it was simply given to me as the youngest competitor in the show. I became something of a star at Arborfield because the following year at four and a half I won another cup. Not only was I still the youngest competitor in the same frock coat or its replacement, but my new pony Patball won the 12.2 show pony class; and we had our picture taken for the *Picture Post* with the caption: 'The Youngest Competitor at the Meeting. He is four and a half but in his red coat and jockey cap he is as comfortable and self-possessed as an MFH.' I was thus the youngest competitor for the second year in succession according to the *Picture Post*, but as I have learnt so often with the press over the years, the accuracy of the report is not to be trusted. If it had been correct, where was my second youngest competitor cup? Patball had his for being good looking and I had mine from the previous year. Both were treasured for forty years until removed by burglars.

Patball was a 12.2 chestnut New Forest three-year-old gelding. My mother had gone to the New Forest to find me a pony, which she proceeded to break in. She was not entirely successful, and for many years he remained unpredictable and wild. He was hardly a beginner's pony. Diddles disappeared. She was only on loan, although subsequently she reappeared for a brief spell when we went to Dorset in 1946 where she bolted with me through a gateway, which gave rise to her second and thankfully permanent disappearance aided by a horsebox. Patball on the other hand remained with me until 1952. We were to spend ten years together.

Why Patball was so named is a mystery. I was being bathed by my mother when she asked me what I would like to call my new pony. 'Patball' was my immediate reply. I have no idea why this name suddenly occurred to me or what could have inspired it. Naming or renaming members of the family whether human, equine or canine seems to have become a small boy's means of self assertion. Patball took up residence in the stables and in my grandmother's field from which he frequently sought to escape. I remember coming back from a walk with my great-great-uncle Ted Leatham to find a fair proportion of the village pulling and pushing at Patball who had stuck in the ditch while seeking to make an escape from the field. Worse still were his antics with the green pony trap. In 1943 the pony trap was frequently used for shopping expeditions, having the advantage of saving petrol, which was strictly rationed during wartime. This arrangement ceased abruptly one morning on the way back for lunch. Patball began playing up; and when we reached the turning towards Harthover, my mother turned in the other direction being determined to teach Patball a lesson and keep him under control. I remember being extremely cross, as for some reason, I particularly wished to go home. We turned in the other direction to go up a hill towards the village green. The pony became even more uncontrollable; and much to my annoyance I was told to get out and walk. The hill was steep and I was becoming sulky. Suddenly to my delight there was a commotion ahead with Patball kicking and bucking. The trap overturned. My mother spilled out onto the side of the road; and Patball galloped off into the distance with bits of cart left as large pieces of debris on the way. My mother's ill humour was not assisted by her small son. I am sorry to say I sat in the middle of the road and howled with laughter. That was the end of the trap; and the bicycle took over.

Patball was not allowed everything his own way. Panniers were attached to him, usually filled with a picnic. My mother's bicycle had a front basket into which her two small dogs, one white miniature poodle and one black, were placed. I sat in another basket at the back, receiving frequent admonitions about holding on to my mother's waist too tightly. In between bouts of nerves my attention was directed towards watching her legs freewheeling or peddling and studying her latest fashion in hats. No respectable woman in those days went out without a hat, and I particularly recall a bottle-green felt brimmed hat crowned with a mound of pink and white wool. Between peddling and Patball's pulling on the leading rein, this combination was effective in covering a number of miles, usually to the Officers Club at Minley where assorted small children would bathe in the lake. These were the days when bathing dresses for men and boys had short legs and covered the chest with straps over the shoulders. Inevitably my bathing dress was red. My red frock coat for riding presumably reflected the hunting field and red extended to my trousers and hence to my bathing dress. Made out of wool it always seemed to acquire moth holes, often in embarrassing places, for which there was little sympathy. Regardless of petrol rationing, my grandmother would drive in her old Wolseley, change in a bathing hut and join me in the lake. Patball in the meantime was tethered to a tree. This was not always successful. On one occasion my mother and I discovered that Patball had disappeared. So had the tree, which had been a somewhat frail birch sapling. We eventually found him, after particularly tedious searching, some distance away with tree still attached. Ponies were part of life; but sometimes they could be tiresome and alarming.

Until my great-great-uncle Ted Leatham came to stay, my knowledge of wildlife had been largely restricted to 'Auntie Mattie's' frogs and Murphy's rabbits. There had also been walks around the garden with Banny as she cut and pruned her roses and introduced me to the assorted bugs, birds and beasts that frequented an English garden before the intensive and intrusive use of insecticides. We often found such excitements as the stag beetle; and we were always looking out for bullfinches and nuthatches, Banny's two favourite birds: 'bullies' and 'nutties'. However, Uncle Ted's arrival added a new dimension to my life. He proved an infectious companion for a small boy. The old man with his walking stick, with his great-great-nephew, spent many hours walking in the woods, and while there or with me sitting by his bedside he would relate tales of smoking tigers out of their caves in China, encountering bear on a rocky shelf in the mountains of Canada and setting fire to the Nilgiris Hills in India after shooting gaur, the Indian bison. Such bear, tiger and particularly the Nilgiris hill gaur were to become familiar in years to come; but Ted sowed the seed.

Perhaps his favourite tale was of smaller game. When Ted was a child, the little owl had only recently arrived in England and was something of a rarity. At that time Ted Leatham skinned and mounted birds at his home in Gloucestershire; but his father, Edward Aldam Leatham, had issued a succinct order for the preservation of the owl; and any killing of the bird by guest or keeper ranked in his eyes as little short of a criminal offence. Unfortunately the bird was found in the bag at the end of a day's shoot. The keeper entered it as 'water rail'. Ted appropriated the bird and after skinning it received a request from the butler. Might he be allowed to eat for his supper the water rail which Ted had skinned? Ted agreed; and the butler, overstepping his province, placed the carcase of the owl onto a plate and the plate in the kitchen oven. When the cook inspected the oven and found the bird, she and the kitchen maid promptly ate it, being infuriated with the butler who had infringed her rights and privileges in her kitchen. The bones were decently rearranged on the plate; and the plate was replaced in the oven. The butler was furious and complained to a sympathetic footman. 'Those infernal women in the kitchen have eaten my water rail!' the butler is said to have exclaimed. Ted, who subsequently wrote about the issue, reports that the footman replied, 'Oh well, you've no call to make such a fuss about it seeing it wasn't a water rail at all but only an old owl as Ted poisoned.' The footman had seen both the owl in its original condition and also the arsenic which Ted had used for preserving the skin.

The butler was delighted and lost no time in returning to the kitchen and informing the cook and the kitchen maid that the delicacy of which they had been partaking was nothing more or less than a poisoned owl. There then followed shrieking and beyond all doubt instant recourse to mustard and water, ipecacuanha, and similar restoratives. As a result, late that night the mistress of the house, my great-great-grandmother, was called out of bed to cure the disorders of internal economy, the result not so much of the feast of an owl but on 'the over-imbibing of the plurality of emetics'.

Unperturbed by this childhood incident, Ted continued to mount birds and animals. Some of his rarer species such as the Ichang tufted deer and the yellow-throated goral, both from the Himalayas, were presented to the Natural History Museum. The rest were eventually divided between the MCC and the Natural History Society at Eton. The MCC trophies were lost in a bombing raid during the war. The collection at Eton was disbanded in 1996, the reason given was the need to raise funds to modernize the Natural History Society's facilities. The sale gave rise to a number of articles, editorials and letters in the national press. One such letter came from my own pen, as I pointed out that gifts of collections to museums and the like were intended to provide a permanent home and should not be sold off at a later date. This would discourage others from making similar bequests in the future. Sir Anthony Acland, the Provost of Eton, persuaded me to keep quiet and in return sent me one of Ted's trophies. This was the head of a black buck shot near Delhi and which now hangs on a wall of one of my rooms in the College of Arms, suitably adorned with a medallion on orange ribbon with which I was subsequently to be presented at a dinner held in New York. It has been somewhat presumptuously described as the first heraldic Oscar.

Filled with enthusiasm for wildlife as a result of Ted's tales, my mother took me to London in 1943 to visit the Zoo. We passed the grimy buildings of the Clapham area with their thousands of chimney pots spewing forth plumes of black smoke, while overhead floated huge barrage balloons to deter the German bombs. I remember being appalled by the Clapham suburbs, which are now very fashionable and expensive! We stayed at the United Hunts Club; and I was introduced to the London Underground and London taxis; but most exciting of all was the Zoo itself, especially the feeding of the sea lions and the hippo which surfaced from its murky pool to give a huge yawn in my direction.

I returned home determined to have my own pet animal. Horses and dogs were domestic and not quite the same. The pet came shortly afterwards. He was a wonderful woolly bear caterpillar, a garden tiger. He was found near the stables and thereafter spent the rest of his caterpillar life in a jam jar munching dock leaves. Although unsexed, to me he was male and named Jimmy. He went shopping, sharing the front basket of my mother's bicycle with her two poodle dogs and was carried by me everywhere on walks. Undeterred by these adventures, he continued to munch until he spun himself into a cocoon under the lid of his jam jar. The day came when he hatched into a beautiful tiger moth, cream upper wings and red under wings, all liberally covered with large brown spots. My mother placed a stick for him to crawl out and dry his wings. I was allowed to stay up late and eventually watch him fly off out of the open window and into the night with a touch of sadness at the loss of my friend.

In addition to garden fêtes, horseshows and visiting relations, there were children's parties. I was naturally a shy and introspective child in red trousers and white shirt, particularly disliking boisterous and noisy parties. These usually started with games such as ring-a-ring-o-roses or hunt the thimble. I made myself scarce, and after a search I was often to be found under the table. What I was doing was pretending to be a bear, but being shy I never admitted to this. My mother became increasingly concerned. Party games were followed by tea where her small son again proved difficult. I dreaded heavy currany and fruity birthday cakes and could not eat them. This was doubtless caused by nerves. Somewhat naturally this drew attention to me, increasing my shyness and causing further embarrassment to my mother. Tea was usually followed by a Punch and Judy show, a conjuror, marionettes or a ventriloquist and doll. The conjuror had great appeal, although I dreaded being picked on to act as his assistant. Punch and Judy held a certain fascination. Although Punch was a frightening rascal, he was small enough to present no great threat. This was not true of the ventriloquist's dolls which I found especially frightening. In fact I was terrified of any human form with funny clothes and funny antics. I was to remain deeply apprehensive about Father Christmas, whilst Mr Hare at Easter, being an animal, was fully acceptable. My Aunt Bobby had a hare costume; and one Easter during lunch I saw Mr Hare's head with its long ears poking over the yew hedge. This proved a great excitement. This excitement was of course much enhanced by being released into the garden after lunch to find 'Mr Hare's Nests' set in garden nooks and crannies and containing Easter eggs and other Easter goodies.

Circuses were to prove a problem. The performing animals were a great source of enjoyment, but surviving the clown acts was difficult. In consequence, my mother always arranged for us to have seats at the back of the circus tent.

Faced with these difficulties, my mother decided I needed a governess. I had other ideas. Her efforts culminated in the arrival of a buxom blonde, wearing a turquoise coat and skirt. I watched her from the dining-room window coming up the front path. I decided that this intrusion into my life was not to be tolerated. I simply refused to communicate and in spite of all her well-intended efforts, the would-be governess made no headway against my silence. To my great relief she departed, never to return.

In spite of her efforts, my mother remained concerned about her child and his apparent lack of communication. My fantasy world of animals brought matters to a head. She came to wake me up one morning to discover me lying amidst a pile of large round pebbles which somehow I had smuggled into my bed. On enquiring what I thought I was doing, my mother was greeted by my usual ploy of silence. Perhaps I realized that she might not understand that I was pretending to be a chicken and that the pebbles were my eggs. I was taken off to a child psychiatrist who informed my mother that there was no cause for concern. I was simply a child with an independent mind.

I am sure this episode was something of an over-reaction on my mother's part. Although I may not have enjoyed the company of other children, I had a great rapport with Banny, chattering away as I followed her around the garden as she cut roses or collected eggs from the chickens. Early in the morning I would often wait outside her bedroom, listening for her to wake up and switch on her electric kettle for early morning tea. The noise of the kettle was my cue for knocking on the door and going in to snuggle up with her in bed while I played with small lead models of Beatrix Potter animals which she kept on the mantelpiece. The wireless would be switched on while she listened to wartime bulletins. In the afternoon I would frequently join her for her afternoon nap in a hammock which was slung between fruit trees in the orchard.

Not only did I establish a close relationship with Banny, my uncle Ted Leatham and Murphy with his rabbits, there were also Mrs Woolley and Mrs Webb, both of whom worked for Banny at Harthover. As a special treat, I was sometimes allowed to go and stay with them. Mrs Woolley's husband had been the Commandant's servant at Sandhurst, where he and his wife had a cottage full of Landseer prints and an intriguing collection of brass objects. Mr Woolley grew pumpkins in his garden, which were a great delight, and took me looking for toadstools through the Sandhurst woods. Mrs Webb had an infectious sense of humour and a somewhat irascible husband. Mr Webb was subsequently found dead, smouldering on his garden bonfire. I regret to say that nobody seemed to be particularly sorry.

Perhaps my mother realized that all was not lost and took over where the governesses had failed. Mornings were spent in the sitting room where I learnt my alphabet, rudimentary reading with *The Good Dog Rover* and other beginners' books. She also taught me elementary arithmetic. More exciting was cutting out and pasting various paper models, especially a Christmas crib and a three-dimensional see-through version of the Pied Piper of Hamelin. I was also made to draw, pencil and crayon. My mother was particularly good at fanciful dragons while I struggled with lions, Mickey Mouse, butterflies and a dreadful brown wallflower. This plant was growing in the front garden. During my efforts to reproduce the wallflower on paper, I was subjected to an attack of diarrhoea the colour of which bore close resemblance to my flower subject. I have heartily disliked wallflowers ever since.

These learning sessions were something of a relief from the nursery which was now occupied by the baby, Bobby's first child, Georgina, who had been born in May 1943. Georgina was too often released from the playpen and wreaked havoc among the bricks, Noah's ark and other toys left over from the Victorian era, which I had painstakingly built up or, in the case of the Noah's ark, had carefully arranged the crudely carved wooden animals in pairs. I was eventually able to retaliate by putting her into the garden swing or large wicker rocking chairs and by pushing and shoving her into the air was able to gain some measure of control over the situation.

CHAPTER 4

Kindergarten years

IN THE SUMMER OF 1943 my mother considered that I was sufficiently prepared to attend a kindergarten in Camberley. It must have been in the summer because I well remember waiting for my mother to bring me home, when my attention was caught by swarming ants at the base of the tree outside the school. I also remember that school began with prayers and a hymn. As it was summer, I could not understand why we had to sing *The Holly and the Ivy* which I considered belonged more appropriately to Christmas. I also remember that the head girl was a pretty brunette, but there was no way that I could do other than admire her from a distance. I was put into the junior class under the mistress Suzette Richards to arrange alphabetical bricks in their correct order. I did not know that some ten years later I was to be the youngest usher at Suzette's wedding. I also do not remember making any friends except for two sisters who shared my interest in keeping caterpillars. Whether we went from school to home by bus, pony trap or car I cannot remember; but in those days small children moving around on their own was regarded by all parents as safe.

Christmas 1943 was to change my life. Aunt Muriel was coming to stay. My first recollection of her was passing through the hall to see this imposing figure standing at the top of the stairs. I was duly beckoned, and when I reached her I was informed that it was a nephew's duty to escort his aunt down the stairs. She ushered me to her left-hand side and rested my hand over her forearm. Halfway down the stairs Muriel bent down and put her right hand inside her quilted coat and onto her silk dicky which covered her chest.

'What would you do if I told you I had a snake in here?' she enquired.

I do not remember the exact course of the subsequent conversation, except that by the time we had reached the bottom of the stairs I had been lectured on how to suck out poison from a snakebite. It was with some relief that I was able to abandon her to the other grown-ups when we reached the drawing room, where a magnificent Christmas tree had been erected, fully covered with dust sheets so that I should not see it until it was unveiled before Christmas tea.

When Christmas day arrived, I was taken into the drawing room where the tree had been fully uncovered. It was before the days of Christmas lights and so was lit spectacularly with real candles and adorned with animals which my mother had drawn and cut out from sparkling silver cardboard. In addition there were a number of glass balls and baubles. After this excitement I was taken back into the dining room, little expecting what horror I would find. The lights had all been turned off, and the room was lit by the candles on the Christmas cake. Beyond the Christmas cake was my high chair and sitting in it was a ghastly apparition. This had been made by Muriel and was my Christmas present. It was a large grinning clown in beautifully worked silver-threaded clothes and a black matador's hat and a ghastly paste white face with a huge embroidered grin beyond the flickering candlelight. This immediately activated my great fear of any jokey human animation whether puppets, marionettes or ventriloquists' dolls. Muriel's well-intended horror was too much; and it was removed for at least four years when it reappeared from some hidden drawer to reside for a few more years on a window seat before again disappearing.

Muriel in the meantime went back to London; but typically her departure was not uneventful. A damaged blackbird was spotted in the shrubbery, possibly the victim of a cat attack. Dallimore, the gardener, gave chase; and the wretched bird with much exposed pink flesh was caught and put into a cardboard box for Muriel to take back to London where she planned to exercise her faith healing abilities. I never enquired of the outcome.

Muriel's visit had succeeded in instilling in me an even greater fear of clowns which I did not finally overcome until about the age of eight. It was therefore to be a problem when the circus came to nearby Aldershot. I was determined to go for the sake of the performing animals and persuaded my mother to take me. We arrived to queue for tickets for the afternoon performance. Unfortunately the last ticket was sold to the people immediately in front of us. I considered this nonsense and dived into the tent exclaiming there were still plenty of seats. I was retrieved; and my mother agreed that we should come back for the evening performance even though this would be after my bedtime. My ambition was achieved; and we duly bicycled back to the circus in the evening. We took our seats; and I watched with somewhat sadistic pleasure a buxom and scantily clad girl performing tricks with a python. This particularly intrigued me as my mother had a singular dislike of snakes. In the interval we went out to see the cages; and I was able to press my nose up against the python's glass case and thoroughly enjoyed seeing the lions and other creatures in their cages.

The second half of the performance was to be the problem. So far I had somehow survived the clowns. However, clowns apart, I had another phobia and that was the dentist; periodic visits to the dentist at Camberley, the grinding drills and elevating chairs filled me with dread. It was a recipe for disaster when a clown entered the circus ring with his head swathed in bandages complaining of toothache. Another clown took an outsize pair of pincers and extracted a long nine-inch pink tooth from his swathed colleague. I remember nothing more of this horror; but I am told that I became totally hysterical and had to be taken out. My memory returns when I vaguely recall myself sitting in a corner in the bar in the Officers Club at Aldershot. My mother, understandably, had decided she needed a stiff drink.

Standing at the bar was a man in military uniform. This was one Gavin Young. Somewhat typical of him, he had run out of money and was unable to pay for his drinks. He struck up a conversation with my mother and presumably this conversation soon touched on horses. He borrowed money from my mother to pay for the drinks, and thus began their relationship. My mother subsequently told me that when Gavin met her some few days later to repay his debt, he also announced that he was going to marry her. She explained that she was already married, but that did not deter him. He became a frequent visitor to Harthover. Banny was not amused; but her small grandson was. I thought he was great. Ultimately he did indeed become my stepfather and a great influence on my life.

A man of very considerable charm, Gavin captivated me with a collection of small cuddly toys which he brought out during meals, pretending that they shared my food and performed various tricks. He was also a wonderful relator of ad lib children's stories. It was not

long before he ceased to be Colonel Young and became 'Cousins'.
The domestic drama unfolding was over the head of a small boy. My
father, maintaining a cynical view of marriage, had at least pretended
that a man could have the occasional affair. A wife could not.
Whether or not he had put his views into practice, I do not know;
but my mother always had it in for what she called his 'Irish
bookmaker's tart'. Perhaps unwisely she wrote to my father while he
was serving in India and informed him that she was having an affair.
Had she not done so, I suspect the whole matter would have blown
over; and my life would have taken a different course.

My father somehow obtained leave and came home. I remember
being informed of his arrival; and early in the morning I armed myself
with half a dozen Beatrix Potter books and made my way to my
parents' bathroom in a state of some apprehension. There I saw a man
dressed in a dark red silk dressing gown with a black paisley pattern,
shaving with a cut-throat razor. He turned as I entered and without any
sign of affection merely said 'Hello small boy'. I fled. It was not a very
endearing reunification between father and son. My father stayed for a
day or two during which my parents and I took a car to Maidenhead
and went boating on the Thames. It must have been during the
summer because the fruit cages at Harthover had provided us with
fresh currants which ended up in the river during a confrontation with
swans. For all I know, this may have been my fault, staging a minor
panic at over-inquisitive birds. My father left Harthover and went
straight to a solicitor in Camberley where he applied for a divorce.
Banny attempted to follow him in an effort to rescue the situation. She
failed; and my father effectively disappeared from my life.

Like my father, Gavin Young had been a regular Army Officer. He
had served in the First World War with the Inniskillings; and in 1922
had transferred to the Welsh Guards where he was Regimental
Adjutant from 1931 to 1934. Gavin's career in the Welsh Guards
must have added a certain colour to the Regiment. He was an
excellent mixer, moving at ease from Field Marshal to Guardsman.
Where there was any party he was guaranteed to bring it to life, not
least by his extraordinary gifts on the piano or on the dance floor. He
was highly articulate but his power of argument with cutting
facetiousness was not always well received. I remember him standing
up at a hunt committee meeting and calling a distinguished General,

Dick McCreery, 'an old woman' and then wondering why Dick did not speak to him the following day when they encountered each other in the streets of Sherborne, Dorset. Dick McCreery subsequently confided in me that Gavin was difficult and if I was ever in trouble, I could come to him for help. This was not the only time that people were to offer me friendly lifelines. I never took them up, as I always considered that the relationship between Gavin and myself was a personal affair and one to be resolved between us. In this we were invariably successful.

When I meet people who knew him I do not know whether they will turn round to me and say 'He was one hell of a guy' or whether they will say little, seeking to be polite but clearly attempting to mask a hidden animosity. For my part I would be delighted to meet him again; we would fall on each other's shoulders, I would tell him that he was difficult and sometimes bloody awful. 'I remain one of your greatest fans, so go and buy us a couple of whiskies – I suppose you haven't got any money!'

I was never a games player, being totally unable to co-ordinate stick, foot or hand with any form of ball. Gavin however represented the Army at most forms of sport, excelling particularly at swimming, cricket and rugby football. In the Welsh Guards he captained their side for five years, taking them to the top of the Army cup. He subsequently captained the Army and as such was able to break the long run of the Royal Navy's victories at Twickenham. He was a reserve international cap; but never quite made it to the top. He had left the Welsh Guards in 1938, after some fit of pique. Thereafter he rejoined the Army at the beginning of the war, commanding Battalions of the Devons, Gloucesters and RAF Regiment, seemingly abandoning the latter to rejoin his old Regiment, the Welsh Guards, when they relieved Brussels.

He returned to England and in 1946 bought Spring House in the village of Long Burton, some two miles south of Sherborne in Dorset. Gavin and my mother were still unmarried, so for appearances' sake my mother took up residence in the nearby bungalow which was occupied by Gavin's soldier servant, John Ware, and his wife Verna and their son David. I followed shortly afterwards; and as was usual, my grandmother rang up the station to notify them of the need to catch the train from Farnborough to Dorset. I was put in the charge of the guard and duly arrived at Sherborne to be greeted by my mother and Gavin, who brought me to my new home on a late summery morning. I was greeted by the dogs and saw Patball and Testuda in the stables. My newly decorated room had all my favourite toys and Beatrix Potter books. As a special thought, a brass cat and fiddle doorknocker had been attached to my bedroom door.

My mother and Gavin were married in January 1947 and spent their honeymoon in the Scilly Isles. I had helped Gavin pack his suitcase in his dressing room; and I had announced that when he returned I would be able to call him 'Daddy' and not 'Cousins'. This was fully accepted before once again I was placed in the guard's van on the train between Sherborne and Farnborough. Whilst my mother and new stepfather explored the Scilly Isles, Banny, who had taken up skiing at the age of fifty, had decided that she should take her grandson skiing at Zermatt. This went no further than my passport photograph being taken in a strange corduroy jerkin. My mother put her foot down firmly. Patball was not to be kept in the stables eating his head off. Ponies took precedence over skiing; and in consequence skiing has never been part of my life. My parents returned from their honeymoon, and I was sent back to Spring House where I attended a kindergarten in Sherborne. Both the Scilly Isles and the kindergarten were to end in disaster.

For several years thereafter we would visit the Scilly Isles, staying at the Tregarthens Hotel in St Mary's, having stopped off at Bude on the way. Gavin had been brought up at Stratton near Bude and always regarded that area of North Cornwall as his real home. Bude had been the scene of one of the two occasions that his touchy temper had ever turned to violence. He was friends with two sisters, the Thomases, one of whom was to marry the Duke of Somerset and the other Rex Harrison, the actor largely remembered for his part in *My Fair Lady*. Gavin disliked Harrison intensely; and after a row punched him. Rex, so I am told, sailed over a sofa and was knocked out cold. The only other occasion that Gavin resorted to violence was when he threw a fist at a Dorset haulier outside the Rose & Crown pub in Long Burton. There were no repercussions other than that the haulier's horseboxes were never again used by us.

Two days in Bude, where Gavin would play cricket for the Devon Dumplings, dive off dangerous rocky points into the sea in his black woollen bathing dress, covering not only his bottom but also his top with woollen straps, introduce my mother and myself to the chilly sport of surfing, and then we would sail from Penzance on the *Scillonia* to the Scillies. There we would take a tourist motor boat and visit each day another island. I was made to collect and press wild flowers and sketch island scenes, into which I usually placed seals sitting on a rock or diving into the sea. Out of these motorboats we always took the *Zedora* captained by one John Clare Jenkins. Being the slowest of the motorboats, it was the least used by tourists, who in those days were not very numerous. We normally had the *Zedora* to ourselves. John Clare and Gavin took to each other; and in consequence I had many happy early mornings with John Clare and the *Zedora*'s mate visiting tide-exposed rocks for hoicking crabs and conger eel hunting. The two of them then attacked conger eels with poles topped with a vicious serrated spear. I was made to perch on the top of the rock and told to keep my feet out of the way as the lurking conger eel might bite one of them off. Gavin's interest in the Scilly Isles led to him buying the *Zedora*. This was to be a money-making project. With hindsight it was not a good idea, as the *Zedora*, being the slowest of all the motor boats, was hardly likely to attract tourist attention, as the principal purpose of using such a boat was to move from one island to the other as fast as possible. It never made any money and came to a sad end when John Clare Jenkins and the mate took the *Zedora* out fishing near the Wolf Lighthouse. A storm blew up and poor John Clare, the mate and the *Zedora* went to the bottom of the Atlantic. Mary Wilson, the wife of Prime Minister Harold Wilson, recently reminded me that this happened on the first day of her honeymoon in the Scillies and all the islanders were plunged into gloom. Gavin, my mother and I never returned to the Scilly Islands.

The second financial project involved my kindergarten. I spent one term in a small Sherborne kindergarten with some thirty children and promptly decided that I was in love with a girl called Diana Golledge. Gavin believed that kindergartens offered another financial opportunity. He bought a large property, Newell House. The intake of this new school immediately rose by two or three times that of my first school. The Woolleys were persuaded to come down from Sandhurst to act as caretakers; and my old Camberley mistress, Suzette Richards, was also enticed down to Sherborne to teach. This last I accepted with some apprehension as I knew from time to time I would be 'put into the corner'. This was an effective punishment whereby a small child was taken out and placed in the corner of the schoolroom facing the wall in disgrace. On the other hand there was a system of coloured stars whereby good work was rewarded; and I particularly remember being thrilled by a gold star being applied to my drawing of a tropical forest, complete with monkeys and parrots. There were school plays; and my first appearance on the stage was as a playing card, painting rose bushes in a scene from *Alice in Wonderland*.

Newell House had wonderful cellars to explore which were supposedly out of bounds. I went through a mock marriage with Diana Golledge which was a great excitement; but the divorce took place the next day which filled me with great depression and incomprehension. In spite of my mother's divorce and remarriage, I did not fully understand how divorce could occur. My mother presented the prizes on the school sports day; and although uncoordinated with bat and ball I had proved to be quite a good runner, sack racer and jumper; and I had to go up and receive various awards; and I do not know who was more embarrassed, my mother or myself.

The problem with this seemingly thriving enterprise lay with the headmistress. For some reason beyond me, a row broke out and Gavin stupidly wrote to her saying that she was 'not right in the head'. She sued and won the case. In consequence he lost a great deal of money. It is distressing to think today how much the Newell House property would be worth. As far as I know, it is still a fashionable school with large grounds in the heart of desirable Sherborne.

I was removed from Newell House; but before my education could be furthered, I was taken by Gavin, screaming, into Sherborne Hospital early one morning wrapped up in a blanket in the back of his car. My appendix had blown up, and I was operated on immediately. The problem was compounded by an attack of measles. The result was that Sherborne Hospital was unable to provide me with a private ward, and I was sent home, where I remained bedridden in a darkened room for six to eight weeks. I was not even allowed out of bed but was subjected to a routine of night lights, bells, water flasks for peeing and Gavin sitting by my bedside telling children's stories or reading *The Wind in the Willows*. By Christmas normality had returned, and Gavin took me back to the Sherborne Hospital with presents for the other children in the ward and where he doubtless carved the Christmas turkey and flirted with the nurses. This established a tradition, much to my mother's exasperation. Year after year Gavin would visit the hospital on Christmas Day, disrupting our own family Christmas arrangements.

After my recovery, my education was placed in the hands of Mrs Picton who lived in Sherborne, had taught at Newell House, but had resigned in support of my stepfather. I was to remain under her tuition until I went to my prep school in the summer term of 1948 at the age of eight.

Life at Spring House meant horses and everything allied to the horse world, to the extent of Gavin's organization of inter-hunt swimming competitions at the Sherborne School swimming pool and inter-hunt cricket matches. Thankfully my participation in these latter events was confined to being a spectator. This was not true of the Spring House stables where I had an uneasy relationship with my chestnut Patball. With Patball I progressed to cantering, but dreaded the end of the morning's ride when my mother would arrange a small pole or a bit of brush in what was known as 'the bottom field'. This was jumping time. However low the pole or brush, Patball would leap like a stag; and all too often I would fall off. On more than one occasion this was into a cowpat. My floods of tears received little sympathy from my parents; my mother merely informed me that it was necessary to fall off twenty times before I could ride properly. I must have reached that twenty before I began to master the technique. It was also necessary to learn stable management. Patball was good natured; but I was not. Gavin would come into the stable and carry out an inspection with military precision. On one occasion my temper snapped. I hurled the stable shovel at him and once again used my favourite expression 'bugger off'. I stomped across the yard, went upstairs and locked myself in the lavatory, refusing to come out. My mother fetched a ladder and, after reasoning with me through the lavatory window, peace was restored, and I escaped subdued but unpunished.

Gavin in the meantime was largely preoccupied with his own horses as he endeavoured to find a compatible hunter. Horses came and went with considerable rapidity, Smokey Moses who curiously was fed on Guinness and eggs, the friendly Hurry Push, Double Brandy and an unmanageable bay named Trinket which kept me much amused with its attempts to knock Gavin out of the saddle. Eventually Gavin settled for one John Brown, with whom he seemed to establish a reasonable working relationship.

My mother's mare Testuda who had come from Harthover did not survive long. I was taken on foot to a meet of the Blackmore Vale in November 1946. Hounds were in a covert when a solitary and lonely figure was seen walking across the field towards us. It was my mother; and Testuda had dropped dead from a heart attack. I was kept away and did not meet my mother until the following morning at breakfast. Searching among my possessions, I found a curious wooden pug dog with felt tongue and ears. I presented this to my mother saying that I was sorry to hear about Testuda and hoped that she would accept my pug dog as a replacement. My poor mother was overcome by her small boy's gesture and left the dining room in floods of tears. Testuda was replaced by Brandy, a bay cob, who soon acquired the stable name of Hippo. She was to win a number of show prizes and proved an admirable hunter. I was to hunt her myself in years to come.

One of Hippo's first public appearances was at Dorchester Agricultural Show where she won first prize. Aged seven, I tagged along on Patball. Being somewhat alarmed at the size of the ring and the crowds, I insisted on my mother taking me in on the leading rein. I was placed in the collecting ring, satisfied with her assurance that she would soon join me. Deliberately she failed to appear; and I was left on my own and managed a canter and even a gallop before being awarded third prize. This proved a problem, as I had to keep the third prize card under my knee and a yellow rosette in my mouth while I performed the lap of honour. I was unable to use my legs or make my usual clicking noises to induce Patball into a canter. Together we performed the lap of honour at a sedate trot to the loudspeaker announcement, 'Will the little boy in the bowler hat please hurry up as the hounds are waiting to come in.' This was particularly alarming as Patball was thoroughly unreliable with hounds and had a tendency to rear up on his hind legs whenever they came near. He also had a tendency to clamp down his tail, a fact noted by a horse judge who came to stay. The judge recommended that in future a stick of ginger should be implanted up his arse or some similar irritant. I was sufficiently attached to my pony to plead that he should be spared this indignity. I cannot therefore report as to whether or not any such application would have been successful.

Testuda left a foal, Miss Kitty Fisher, named after the celebrated eighteenth century courtesan. She was put into training; and I was therefore taken to various race meetings. She never managed better than third. To my enquiries as to why we never won a race, I never received a satisfactory reply. She eventually broke down, was put out to grass and drowned herself in the nearby Butterwick Brook.

In following my mother's career as a racehorse owner, I once enquired what made a good racehorse. My mother replied, 'Look for a good sloping shoulder'. I interpreted this in my own way; and would thereafter watch carefully as every horse entered the paddock, working out which horse had an elbow that reached the furthest back over the girth. With hindsight I suppose I was finding the horse with the longest stride. This system proved remarkably successful, and I landed winner after winner. On one occasion I went with Banny and Dick to Sandown Races and to their surprise picked five winners. I only missed the sixth because there were two or three horses that, using my system, I was unable to distinguish which had the best elbow movement. I eventually picked the one whose colours, emerald green with red spots, appealed to me. It only came in third.

My skill at picking winners reached something of a zenith at Newton Abbot where I was standing in the paddock with my mother and Nancy Sweet-Escott. Nancy had trained Miss Kitty Fisher and she had a horse in the sizeable field called Aladdin Clover. Both Nancy and my mother were agreed that Aladdin Clover was much the best looking animal and should be unbeatable. Someone suggested that small Peter was rather good at picking winners, so my opinion was asked. According to my system of elbow and girth, there was one animal that was outstanding. I pointed it out. Everyone was extremely rude, and my choice was dismissed as not having a chance. On the first time round I was delighted to find that my horse was some three lengths in the lead; Aladdin Clover was lying about sixth. On the second time round my horse passed the winning post some twelve lengths or more ahead of the field with Aladdin Clover putting in a somewhat dismal performance. Unfortunately, as the years went by, watching horses come into the paddock was invariably disrupted by chattering friends, making concentration difficult if not impossible. I do not know whether my system merely produced fluke results or whether there is something in it. I have to say that I have tried it once or twice since without great success.

My mother's somewhat unsuccessful career as a racehorse owner with Miss Kitty Fisher stimulated another family project. This was plastic horseshoes. The idea was that plastic horseshoes could be applied by an enterprising owner using a rapid adhesive. It was never really practical, not least because horses would move at an inopportune moment. Nonetheless, plastic horseshoes did feature on the racecourse and in the hunting field. I believe there were similar attempts made in America; but the idea never came to anything, and the old system of shoeing with metal shoes, nails and the blacksmith still prevails.

When not involved with horses, I was sent out into the fields to look for wild flowers and to catch butterflies with my butterfly net and killing jar. Only the good or unusual specimens were kept; the others on close inspection were rejected, allowed to revive and had a lucky escape. These were the years before insecticides and intensive weedkiller, when the hedgerows and fields were alive with wildlife. My interest in butterflies was greatly enhanced by my kindergarten friend Robert Goodden. In spite of our rivalry over Diana Golledge, we struck up a good friendship; and his knowledge of butterflies for a six or seven-year old was remarkable. Robert is a good example of someone following a childhood interest and turning it into a successful career. He went on to run Worldwide Butterflies and is one of the world's leading authorities on lepidoptery.

If Robert was set on butterflies, I was more interested in becoming a zoo keeper. Banny had given me a model zoo to which I added over the years until it covered the whole floor of one of the Spring House spare room. I was given four volumes of *Hutchinson's Animals of All Countries*, which I read and studied repeatedly, and began drawing up lists of monkeys and snakes. This listing was perhaps not far removed from my later interest in genealogy and the drawing up of pedigrees.

Further lists were compiled of King Arthur's Knights which far exceeded the Knights to be found on the Round Tables at Tintagel and Winchester. Knights of the Round Table were a fascination which was further stimulated by Gavin reading me their tales and even inventing some of his own.

It may have been King Arthur who introduced me to heraldry. For whatever reason David Ware and I took up fretwork in the old dairy in the Spring House yard; and I cut out a large fretwork shield and hung it on the door to keep out intruders. The shield showed a quarterly achievement, the quarters being crayoned with a hunting cap, a fox's mask, horseshoes and crossed hunting whips. There was also an inescutcheon or central shield on which I had worked my cypher. Further stimulus was provided by the Royal Standard which I found in a box with other assorted flags in the dairy. This flag was clearly intended for a Royal car. How it arrived in our possession, I do not know. However it was tied to the handlebars of my bicycle, fluttering as I journeyed through the country lanes to Marsh Court, the home of my friend Sarah Fox-Pitt. I was operating a delivery service of the *Beano* and *Dandy*, comics which we shared and which I obtained from Lou Pearce. Lou was the husband of the postmistress and our daily help. Nobody queried the use of the Royal Standard in this way; but I doubt whether the Lord Chamberlain's office would have approved. In return for the delivery service, the Fox-Pitts gave me at a children's party the *Nursery History of England*. I have never yet encountered any other child's history book so well illustrated or so succinct in relating all the romantic and traditional stories. History became a great interest; and by the time I reached my prep school I had a good working knowledge of the subject.

A further shift towards heraldry was provided by Robert Buxton, father to my two childhood friends Lavinia and Lettice. I would ride Patball to stay with the Buxtons at Galhampton Manor near Wincanton. This was a considerable journey for a small boy. It involved riding through Sherborne, crossing the Dorset/Somerset border and on through several villages until I reached the A303, the main road to the west. I then rode along this road before turning left to Galhampton. It is extraordinary now to think that Alyson Buxton did not ring my mother to say I had arrived safely, nor did my mother ring Alyson.

Robert Buxton was never one to allow children to be idle. There were always projects to be done. I seem to recall that a psalm or

prayer was set to be learnt over the weekend with recitation on
Sunday. Not even his wife was spared; but church might be avoided
with Alyson remarking 'I exonerate you'. One project was to be in
the library, where copies of *Burke's Peerage* or *Burke's Landed Gentry*
were removed from a shelf, and we children were made to draw or
paint heraldry. I remember executing a very passable ram's head; and
Robert Buxton thereafter claimed that he was responsible for my
eventual arrival at the College of Arms. Certainly he helped to give
me an inceptive knowledge of heraldry.

If butterflies and collecting birds' eggs was not practical during the
winter, there were always the rabbits. They thrived in the bramble
bushes in an old quarry beyond the garden back wall. I had been
given a bow and six arrows with which I was not very efficient. In
firing the arrows down the backyard, I succeeded in hitting Jeremiah,
our black stable cat, and firing another arrow into a loose box, much
to the consternation of Hippo. I was removed to the back wall and
told to aim at rabbits instead. My efforts proved fruitless; and I
therefore recruited our dogs. These consisted of a pack of three or
four miniature white poodles, close shorn by my mother, game little
animals with a real farmyard nature. Armed with Gavin's hunting
horn and taking my pack, I would draw the bramble bushes in the
morning and again in the evening. My efforts on the horn may not
have been successful, but they were certainly noisy. They must have
disturbed the rest of the village, but nobody dared complain. Very
occasionally we caught a rabbit; but generally speaking they fled
across the fields only to return to the bramble bushes shortly
afterwards to be chased again the following morning or evening.

I am undoubtedly biased when it comes to hunting. If the hunting
of rabbits with the poodles was so cruel, I cannot help asking why
those rabbits did not move a few fields further away. They never did;
and I conclude that any distress I caused must have been minimal.
Those who oppose hunting might perhaps be advised to study hunted
animals in the wild and watch their reactions.

In 1947 I set off on Patball for my first Pony Club rally at
Sherborne Park. Towards me came a small seven-year-old girl with
pigtails riding her grey pony Playmate. This was Pat Young who had
come to meet me and to unlock the park gates. She was to replace
Diana Golledge in my affections; and at Pony Club dances and

children's parties I tried to engineer most of my dances with her. The Pony Club proved a great meeting place for children, many of whom had parents like my own who were ex-Army and had retired to hunt with the Blackmore Vale. A hard core of some thirty children was established and there followed endless children's parties. As time went on this social life extended to cover neighbouring packs of hounds. Many of these parties were dances with a liberal sprinkling of Scottish reels, the Eightsome Reel and the Dashing White Sergeant being particular favourites. A weak cider cup or claret cup was served and the music was provided by a small band. When the band was given a break, Gavin would often take over on the piano, strumming out popular tunes. Other parties were given by those whose houses were unsuitable for dancing and often took the form of a paper chase, sometimes on foot and sometimes with our ponies. Spring House having stone floors, low ceilings and small rooms, was not suitable for dancing. My mother therefore revived her wartime idea of a dog gymkhana, which followed a paper chase in the afternoon preceded by tea. A motley collection of dogs were then taken into the field and went through bending races, obstacle races, sack races and the like. My own chosen dog was our old fat Susan. She was a round headed barrel-like poodle with a deep gruff voice. I once took her to a comic dog show where she won the dog with the shortest legs, beating even the dachshunds. Short though her legs may have been, she gave plenty of rabbits a good run. At that same dog show she entered the begging competition. As far as I know, she had never been made to beg before. I sat her up holding a biscuit and told her to stay. Minutes passed. We stared at each other and she remained firmly in a begging position, defeating all others. To the best of my knowledge, she never begged again.

CHAPTER 5

Prep school years

THESE HAPPY DAYS AT Spring House were soon to be interrupted. They were now to be confined to school holidays, while I was sent to spend term time at St Andrew's Preparatory School, Eastbourne, starting in the summer of 1948. It was to be a miserable experience. My trunk, packed with my animal books, paint palettes, a cricket bat and my butterfly collection went separately. I was dressed in a dark blue long-trousered suit and provided with a school cap sent down from London by Messrs Gorringes. My mother broke down in tears, and Gavin took me to London. After a lunch of jugged hare at the Trocadero in Piccadilly, I was put on the school train at Victoria Station. I was placed in a compartment where Gavin detailed another small boy to look after me. The journey down had its problems, as I discovered I was the only boy in the school with long trousers except for the very senior. My suit was blue; everyone else wore grey. Far worse, Messrs Gorringes had provided me with the wrong cap. Far from having the general school cap in bilious colours of green, pink and maroon stripes, I had been given the cap worn by those with their school cricket colours, dark blue with some white motif on the crown. It was not a good start.

That night I found myself in a dormitory with three others, two of them new boys like myself. Both of them wept bitterly during the night. I think I was too stunned to join them in their tears. I merely lay awake and had my first experience of the ghastly iron beds which squeaked and creaked every time I moved. These were to become all too familiar over the years. St Andrew's had made its name in a bygone age when games and good south coast sea air were considered necessities for small boys. I did not appreciate either.

St Andrew's had been chosen by my mother as my great aunt Violet's two sons had been there. Gavin approved of the choice as the school had had a good reputation and he was particularly taken by its games-playing prowess. One of the masters had, I believe, played cricket for England.

The early morning regime was nothing less than barbarous. By a series of bells, boys descended in order of seniority down to the washroom where we each had our own basin. Baths, I seem to recall, took place only twice a week in the evening with much orange carbolic soap. After the morning washing we went to matron or nurse to show both sides of our hands, our ears and our teeth. Thereafter we were released into the plunge bath or small swimming pool where we stripped and were not allowed out until after our heads had gone under. To the best of my knowledge, the water was seldom changed and attracted a somewhat unpleasant scum. I suspect that most small boys, having just risen from bed, urinated in the water. In consequence a number of poor children suffered from ear and throat infections. Happily the school doctor came to the rescue and banned this early morning horror. As a result the doctor became to me something of a hero, even though he was somewhat prone to administering penicillin injections for every boil or sore throat. He was a tubby little man who wore an intriguing collection of fob seals from his black waistcoat. This was Dr John Bodkin Adams who subsequently acquired notoriety for his treatment of elderly East-bourne widows. His trial for murder and subsequent acquittal proved something of a national sensation.

Ablutions were followed by dressing and physical exercise outside on the asphalt. This was bearable; but the subsequent breakfast was not. It began with porridge which had been ladled out during our asphalt activities. It was therefore invariably cold and came in several forms. On some days it was like cold semolina with a gelatinous top layer. On others it was thick and full of uncooked lumps. It was several terms of retching before I was able to explain to my mother the porridge problem; and I received a doctor's prescription which allowed me to apply my porridge with a thick layer of glucose. This was not ideal but it certainly helped. Matron was not impressed.

The headmaster was possibly more concerned with public relations and somewhat out of touch with what actually happened within the school itself. Visits by Princess Margaret and other dignitaries were all very well, but the behaviour of staff and the lack of supervision over boys did not seem to concern him. The school received its own coat of arms; and it is one of the very few preparatory schools to have done so. For a future Garter King of Arms, I am afraid I did not really understand what all the fuss was about, as the new flag, consisting of the St Andrew's cross surmounted by the torch of youth, was raised above the school building.

In the meantime masters were not averse to a touch of sadism. I well remember some of the weaponry. One master had an inflexible stick known as the Iron Cross, another threatened with Conker while a third had a white strip of plastic topped with something like a hard cork. Yet another would rap small boys over the head with his knuckles or take the hair above the ear and painfully twist it. Lack of supervision of the boys was perhaps less serious. Nonetheless, there was always a measure of bullying; and on my first day I was taken by some wretched child up into the gym where he tested me with mathematics on the blackboard. When I gave a wrong answer, I was thwacked with a ruler.

My inability with bat and ball invoked some teasing in a school which excelled at all types of games. However in spite of bouts of gloom and depression, I always seemed to have a fair circle of friends. I even wrote to my parents threatening to run away, but my threat was ignored.

Lack of games-playing prowess was redressed by other means. Shortly after my arrival, the craze of snail racing took hold. I had pre-empted this by finding snails and painting my initials in some orange metallic paint on their shells. I was therefore able to hand out my snails and thus gain a measure of respect and popularity. Some of this was lost when my locker was inspected to reveal my butterfly setting boards. Unfortunately, one or two of my butterflies had survived the anaesthetic of the killing jar, had come round and were heaving on their pins and under their strips of setting paper. The resulting outcry spelt the end of my butterfly collecting.

Academically I was believed to be backward. This was probably the result of my inherent shyness with schoolteachers, the setback I had had with my serious appendix illness and my subsequent tuition with Mrs Picton. However, thanks to the *Nursery History of England* I proved a star at history and became fascinated by the series of pedigrees of Kings of England found in the school textbooks. These were just as exciting as my animal lists, and I set about sticking together sheets of paper and compiling a continuous pedigree from King Egbert down to the present day. My interest in genealogy had begun.

PETER LLEWELLYN GWYNN-JONES
GENEALOGIST
MCMXCV

1. *The Coati Crest in the design for the Stall Plate in Westminster Abbey. The Stall Plate is for the Genealogist of the Order of the Bath and the Shield of Arms shows Gwynn-Jones quartered with Harrison.*

2. *Edward Robson Whitwell, 'Ted', the most influential great-grandparent. His parenting style influenced his daughter and grand daughter and hence shaped my own upbringing.*

3. The three Whitwell girls: Violet seated with cat, Muriel with cockatoo, and Gladys, 'Banny', standing rear. The German governess, Fraulein Ker, is shown with a pigeon.

4. Muriel Clerk (née Whitwell) in her production of The Heart of Turandot
performed in Istanbul in 1931. Known as Muriel to her parents and siblings, she used Janet when signing her paintings, Helena when making exotic dolls and the like, and insisted that the younger generation of the family called her Zandra.

5. My mother and my grandmother, 'Banny'.

6. My father.

CONGRATULATIONS from the bride's dog after the marriage at Hawley (Hants) of Mr. J. L. Gwynn Jones, Royal Artillery, and Miss M. M. Daphne Harrison.

7. *My parents' marriage, 12 January 1934, attracted coverage in local and national newspapers including The Daily Telegraph.*

8. With my mother in 1942.

At the end of the term I had worked myself up to the top of the bottom form. I had only seen my parents briefly at half term when Gavin had excelled himself in a match between the fathers and the school eleven; whereby I had become something of a short-time hero. I was despatched home on the train to be met by a weeping mother who told me that I had done extremely well. Apparently I was no longer considered a backward child; and Banny was able to tell my mother firmly, 'I told you so'.

As a result of my school achievements, I was at last able to persuade my parents to allow me to have a pet. They returned from two nights out in London and introduced me to Hamlet and Ophelia the following morning. They had been bought at Harrods for a guinea each and were golden hamsters. At that time, hamsters were virtually unknown; and I at once embarked on a hamster breeding project. Hamlet was housed in a birdcage in a draughty through passage. This was probably not wise, as thereafter he always seemed to have a cold in his head and was extremely bad tempered. Ophelia fared better, living in an old tea chest. She survived for the best part of three years and became delightfully tame. At an opportune moment she was introduced into Hamlet's birdcage for mating. When ready to return to her own tea chest, she would drive Hamlet out of his little wooden house; and he would be found hanging on to the top of his bird cage chattering with fear. Ophelia in the meantime would have filled her pouches with Hamlet's store and back in her tea chest she shortly afterwards produced sixteen offspring.

This was lucrative business. A telephone call to a pet shop in Bournemouth promised me ten shillings and six pence for each of my hamster babies. Eight pounds and eight shillings was a considerable amount of money for a small boy in 1948. Unfortunately, I soon learned that business was not that easy. My parents insisted that I paid the petrol down to Bournemouth and for their drinks in a hotel after my sale had been clinched. I was allowed an interesting cocktail of minimal alcohol content called 'pussyfoot'. I was also made to invest in sunflower plants to provide sunflower seeds for hamster food. Worse was to follow as Ophelia's litters shrank in size and she eventually settled for only four or six at a time. The price for hamsters also dropped and ten and six soon became three shillings or less. The hamster market was becoming flooded. The last of my hamsters,

Miranda, eventually died some three years later. I found her dead in her cage when I went to say goodbye on the morning I was returning back to the dreaded St Andrew's. She could not have chosen a worse time to bring my hamster episode to an end; the departure from my mother was more tearful than usual.

Apart from porridge, the other horror I associate with St Andrew's was the cold. Being especially useless at soccer, I was usually placed as a back on the winning side. This meant standing for a good hour or more in a thin vest watching the large clock on the school wall move slowly round. In those days winters seemed to be much harder than they are today; and when the ground was too hard to play, we were sent up on to the top of the white cliffs leading to Beachy Head. The wind was perishing. Sometimes the cold was such that it was not unknown to slip into a bed with another boy in order to keep warm. There was nothing sexual about this; it was simply a means of combating the cold. Perhaps I felt the cold more than most; and I received little sympathy from my family. Banny in particular seemed impervious, and on one occasion she came to visit me to share our birthday on 12 March. As a special treat she announced we would bathe in the sea. I managed to go in for a few seconds while she proceeded to swim to a breakwater and back. Thankfully this only happened once; and her visits tended to be in the summer when a much better treat was strawberries and cream on the South Downs.

After five years of St Andrew's it was time to leave. Money at home had become an intense problem. The idea of Eton had been abandoned, and Wellington offered a cheaper alternative. I was not sorry to leave St Andrew's, where the headmaster said goodbye to me and wished me well at Sherborne School. Since I had taken and failed the scholarship to Wellington but been successful in Common Entrance, I found it somewhat extraordinary that he seemed to have no idea where one of his boys was to further his education.

With an enormous sense of relief I left St Andrew's for ever. I was taken down to Eastbourne Railway Station by the Classics Master, John Page. John was a young graduate from Cambridge with a particularly pretty wife. They had purchased one of our farm poodle puppies which was suffering from diarrhoea. The results were only too apparent on the back seat of the car as I was driven to the station. Apart from giving me a basic knowledge of Latin and Greek, John was responsible for moulding my signature. He wrote his own with a huge flourish, exaggerating the initial 'P'. Like other small boys seeking to ape their elders and betters for whom they had respect, I adopted this flourish, and in my subsequent career at the College of Arms, it has found its way onto many Letters Patent granting Armorial Bearings and other official documents. Using a dip pen and liquid ink with such a flourish is fraught with difficulties. The ink can easily splatter or fail to run. It is his legacy to the College of Arms and frequently calls him to mind. I have not endeavoured to modify my signature nor my form of block lettering when filling in forms, much to the consternation of such as American immigration authorities. I continue to write a capital 'E' as if it were a Greek epsilon. This too is a legacy of Classics classes at St Andrew's and is combined with other capital letters based on the flourishes of long forgotten palaeography found in Victorian copybooks which we were forced to reproduce for prep between tea and bed.

CHAPTER 6

Wellington College

T HE SUMMER HOLIDAYS OF 1953 were halcyon days. St Andrew's could be forgotten; and I was able to share much of my time with a very remarkable companion. This was my pony Fly. Fly, or Firefly to give her her full name, had replaced Patball a year earlier. Childhood friends included Jenny and Charlie Bullen. The Bullens dominated the pony world, and three of them went on to represent Britain in the Olympic games, Jenny in dressage and Michael and Jane in three-day eventing. Their mother Anne had found me a fourteen-two hands pony which had belonged to one of her girl grooms. With a few tears I had said goodbye to Patball. After ten years of his life the old fellow showed little affection. I went to see him a year later in the lines of the Pony Club camp. I am afraid he treated me like a complete stranger. I might never have existed in his life.

Fly was a different character. I have heard it said that horses have preferences for people but are incapable of affection. Fly was an exception to this. She had arrived at Spring House and the change of ownership and the strange place affected her greatly. It took her a long time to settle down, not before she had rushed out of the stable, lashing out and killing my mother's favourite poodle that was lying in the yard. She eventually settled, and her first public appearance was at Mere Show in the summer of 1952. All my friends were intrigued by my new pony. She excelled herself by winning the fourteen-two show pony class. Good looking though she may have been, I do not see that she was top show pony material. Her worst feature was the length of her back, a fault which my mother and I seemingly overcame by placing the saddle as far back as possible. Between us we did well. Fly by showing off her looks, and I by winning the competition for the best rider. Fly shortly afterwards saw me through my pony club B test. Whatever my failings on the playing fields at St Andrew's had been, I felt I was making up for this by my achievements in the horse world. It was not generally thought that anyone could be expected to achieve the B test at the age of twelve. However, I arrived in front of the Inspector, Doreen Whitehead, a formidable figure sitting on a shooting stick. I doffed my bowler hat and said, 'Good morning Mrs Whitehead', whereupon, rather startled by my greeting, she promptly fell backwards off her shooting stick. She was kind enough afterwards to say to my parents that I 'rode like a bomb'.

I hunted Fly with the Blackmore Vale during the Christmas holidays of 1952; and it was then that I jumped some rails onto a sunken road. Fly did not fall or come down, but unfortunately jarred her feet badly, from which she was never to recover. There followed several occasions when Fly was taken up to the Veterinary Research Station at Bristol for operations on her feet. When I had returned for the school holidays she had always been excited to see me, whinnying, pawing at her stable door until I went to see her with the inevitable apple. After her operations she was always distressed and I would spend many hours with her to extent of spending a night in the stable. This was not a very comfortable experience but deeply rewarding to be with an animal who would move around and nuzzle you from time to ensure that you too were there as a friend and companion. We both lay in the straw, as I used her shoulder as a pillow.

Fly's last days were spent with me grazing in the orchards at Spring House during the summer holidays before I went to Wellington. She had to miss out on four or five days when I went to the pony club camp where both my parents were instructors. I was lent a vicious pony, one Tikka, which had a habit of plunging whenever it was confronted with a fence. This was the first in a series of ponies and horses which I was lent during the Fly tragedy and its aftermath. I returned from the pony club camp; and Fly and I would saunter out into the orchards, where I would lie on her back reading a book. Her long back now proved an advantage; and I would prop my book on her hindquarters, facing her tail, while she munched grass at the other end of operations. Sometimes it would become uncomfortable; and I would resort to lying on the ground. This evoked one of the most rewarding experiences I have encountered with animals. She would graze and move off for some ten or twenty yards. From my knowledge of horses, most of them would then go on grazing as far as the grass allowed. Fly did not. She would come back and nuzzle me as if to say, 'Hey, get up. What are you doing? I need you with me. Let's go together and move.' Not until I had done so would she carry on grazing. I was then to go to Wellington; and I never saw her again. I have never afterwards found any other horse or pony that defies the assertion that horses have only preferences and no affection.

In September 1953 I arrived with my parents at Wellington with some apprehension; but, in spite of the imposing Victorian building, I was soon made to feel at home in an atmosphere totally different from St Andrew's. My new housemaster, or tutor to give the correct Wellingtonian nomenclature, Philip Letts and his wife Heather, greeted my parents in their flat attached to my dormitory, the Anglesey, named after Wellington's cavalry commander at the battle of Waterloo.

Gavin, unlike his stepson, was totally undaunted by the situation and had breezed into my tutor's flat to have tea and biscuits and for us all to meet the other parents of the five new members of the dormitory. I already knew Richard Caldecott and his mother Cecilia. They were old pony club friends from Dorset. Gavin, however, also seemed to know Randal Stewart's mother and he was, as ever in such circumstances, in good form. Philip Letts must have been totally bemused when the last parent arrived to be confronted with Gavin shouting across the room, 'Bonzo you old bugger, what the hell are you doing here?' Much better from my point of view was that 'Bonzo's' son, Peter Rogerson, had arrived at Wellington with a supply of silk moth and hawk moth chrysallises. Richard Caldecott had come with Dorset and pony club background; but he also had an interest in wildlife. Some school holidays previously he and I and his brother Gerald had been poking our noses through a hole in a rotten old tree containing a crèche of two tawny owl chicks. Wildlife, therefore, was definitely on the agenda.

Wellington has a flurry of memories. Outsiders tend to see public schools as places which were full of fagging, beating, homosexuality and much indoctrination in Latin and Greek, offset by encourage-ment on the cricket pitch or rugger field, the product being either a Field Marshal or a hippy drop-out on some distant oriental beach being nurtured with rum punches by a dusky maiden. Wellington has produced Field Marshals and drop-out hippies; but most of us have forged our own lives between these two extremes.

Most of the houses at Wellington were known as dormitories. This is somewhat misleading. Each boy had his own separate room or cubicle leading onto a broad central passage which served as a general socializing area and scene of dormitory or house communal activity. Each cubicle was furnished with the bare essentials of a mat, bed, chest of drawers, a widow seat with a long cushion known as a 'hard arse', a cupboard above the bed affectionately termed a 'birdcage', and a chair. Thereafter the occupant could add additional furniture such as a desk and cover the walls or partitions with material or pictures. I seem to recall having a rather splendid paisley shawl belonging to my great-grandmother. Unlike St Andrew's, the cold was overcome by an efficient system of heating through the 'fug pipes'.

Among the boys was Richard Caldecott's elder brother Gerald, one of the Pony Club gang from home, and Peter Snow, later to become the well-known television presenter, who like me had suffered five years at St Andrew's. Both were helpful in making me feel at home. A fag teacher Stu Stranack was designated to look after me and ensure that I passed the fags' exam. Fagging was considered essential for the running of the dormitory. Prefects charged with particular duties often found it necessary to communicate with other houses or dormitories. This was before the days of the mobile phone and required the sending of a messenger or fag who was obtained by the prefect shouting 'Fag'. The last boy to appear on the scene was given the job, unless he had good reason to the contrary. Other fags were designated specific tasks, such as the time fag, who would yell out the minutes and seconds before we had to be out of the dormitory in time for breakfast in the central dining hall.

Prefects also had their own personal fags whose duties were relatively light. I seem to recall being the personal fag of Bruce Tulloh who became an Olympic athlete. Bruce would insist that all runs, whether across country or on tarmac roads, were undertaken with bare feet. He was also a biologist who kept locusts in his room. I complained that cleaning out locusts was beyond the normal duties of a fag. Either I gave notice or I was sacked. I do not remember exactly how the matter ended except that there was no subsequent ill feeling on either side. Thereafter I worked out my fagging career as a 'brew fag', washing up the prefects' coffee cups and the occasional saucepan.

On the academic front, I found work light and easy. Although I had failed the scholarship for Wellington, I found that once there I was able to compete with the scholars and in my third term I managed to beat them all and came out top of the form. My mother was summoned to see Harry House, the Headmaster, and I was awarded a scholarship, which reduced my fees to £40 a term. In view of the ongoing financial problems at home, this must have proved a great relief and compared very favourably with £120 a term, the fees at St Andrew's during my last year. I had vindicated my mother's choice of Wellington over Eton.

The relative ease of work provided much spare time which was largely given over to natural history, an interest which I shared with three others of my own term, Richard Caldecott, Peter Rogerson and Randal Stewart. As members of the Natural History Society, we took a brief oral exam which allowed us to become select members of the Field Club and entitled us to bicycles. As junior members of the school, our use of bicycles was to be confined to the pursuit of natural history. Unfortunately, my bicycle was discovered by a school prefect outside Grubbies, the school shop, where I was refreshing myself with a Pepsi Cola and one of the excellent Grubbies' ice creams. I was duly interrogated by the school prefect; and my excuse, that I was studying the weevils in the school biscuits, proved unacceptable. I might have been beaten for breaking school rules and compounding the offence with cheek. However, I managed to escape; but my bicycle was impounded for a few weeks. It was removed from the bicycle sheds and deposited in one of the underground air raid shelters left over from the war.

In visiting my impounded bicycle, the Anglesey Natural History Group continued its wildlife recreation. This took the form of a somewhat disgusting competition involving mosquitoes. The air raid shelters abounded with these insects, and the competition involved baring one's arm and encouraging a mosquito to alight and feed. Once a mosquito's proboscis has penetrated the skin, a capillary action takes place; and the mosquito cannot control the flood of blood into its body unless it withdraws its proboscis. Prevention of such withdrawal can be caused by stretching the skin. The unfortunate mosquito is then left in place, drawing in blood until eventually it blows up, keels over and dies. The first of us to blow up his mosquito was the winner.

Rather more serious was our collecting, leading up to the natural history exhibition which we mounted for speech day weekend in the summer term of 1954. My cubicle gradually filled up with tanks of lizards, frogs, toads, two species of newts, slow worms, sticklebacks and a grass snake. During the exhibition there were even water spiders and damsel flies. Philip Letts expressed the hope that I would not seek to supplement matters with an adder. Adders did eventually feature, but I believe they came from the school's biological sixth. The nearest I came to an adder was three of us finding and stoning one to death. I placed it in a jar with the intention of curing the skin. On my return to the Anglesey bathroom, I ran a basin of hot water with the intention of cleaning up the corpse before gutting it. I tipped the adder into the hot water whereupon there was violent thrashing for several minutes. It must have been dead, and this was merely the contracting of muscles. Nonetheless it was an alarming experience; and I have always thereafter remained apprehensive of snakes. I have subsequently encountered a number in the wild, and I have never fully overcome my innate distrust of them.

The speech day exhibition of 1954 was a moderate success. It was marred by the death of two young squirrels which we had taken from a drey. Richard Caldecott had tried to rear them. I remember an electric light bulb placed inside a tin can wrapped up in a sock over which the squirrels were laid in an endeavour to resuscitate them. This was to no avail, and one of our star turns did not therefore make an appearance at the exhibition. Neither did the sparrows. Two nestlings had been reared with success and had become very tame. They were free range in the natural history room, which was essentially a classroom beneath the Anglesey. The evening before the exhibition opened, there was a school concert. I was sitting with my parents when two sparrows fluttered over the orchestra and in something of a panic went to a high window. Some saboteur had been active; and I remember plaintively saying to my parents, 'Those are our sparrows'. At that point someone managed to open the window, and they were released. Not surprisingly we never met up with them again.

I am not certain that my parents were impressed by the efforts of my group to lay on this exhibition. Gavin was on top form, charming everyone. When roll call took place that evening Gwynn-Jones was mysteriously absent. Six people were relaxing in the headmaster's house, the headmaster and his wife, Field Marshal Sir Claude Auchinleck, my parents and myself! I expect Philips Letts was somewhat mystified by this. I recall being given a mild rocket for not informing him of my whereabouts; but I am not entirely certain how I was supposed to have done this.

Wellington had originally been founded as a school for Army Officers and not surprisingly many of the boys had an Army background and followed in their father's footsteps to Sandhurst. I was destined for the Welsh Guards. However, in my first few terms at Wellington I observed that all those of a non-academic bent tended to leave early to join the Army. During my first school holiday Gavin and I were sitting in the drawing room at Spring House. He lowered his newspaper and enquired whether I thought the Army would suit me. I probably made one of the most tactless remarks possible. I replied to the effect that Sandhurst was a dustbin for all who could do nothing else in life, a remark I have long since regretted. However, it did not help relations between stepfather and stepson, and something resembling a cold war broke out.

Inevitably at Wellington the Combined Cadet Force was a major factor in life. However, before joining it we had two or three terms in the Scouts known as the 'Tweenies'. When not learning about knots, first aid and making twist (flour and water wrapped around a stick and cooked over a camp fire), we spent our time burrowing tunnels and caves in the sandy soil of the birch and coniferous Wellington woods. Natural history also played a part as we searched successfully for nightjars and the nests of wood ants.

Occasionally we went on parade, which was to prove a disaster for my scouting career. Being on parade necessitated executing the Boy Scout salute. The right hand was raised with three fingers erect and the little finger bent down to be touched by the thumb. I found this impossible. The third finger on my right hand would not go into the upright position nor would my little finger bend sufficiently to touch my thumb without sustaining a twitch. I can only attribute this malfunction to riding and pulling ponies. Whatever the cause, it did not impress the Scoutmaster who considered that I was putting this on as I stood with my ridiculous effort at the Boy Scout salute. I was therefore informed that I was the worst Scout he had ever seen and was rather relieved when shortly afterwards my time came to leave the Tweenies and join the Combined Cadet Force.

This was to provide me with an opportunity to compete with the games players in the Anglesey and to get my own back on Gavin. I was eventually to become Head of the Corps as RSM of the CCF, barking orders at some six hundred boys on the Battalion Parade Ground and organizing field days against Sandhurst cadets. I am not certain whether this really impressed Gavin or my housemaster Philip Letts. The latter remained mystified and commented 'well, we have never had one of those (meaning the RSM) in the Anglesey before.'

Being essentially a non-games player in a games-playing house, I was let off lightly. There was the occasional game of rugger, which I spent in the back row of the scrum with my friend Nicholas Tyacke. Nicholas and I spent most of the dreaded one and a half hours passing cynical comments about the game and its players. In the summer I pretended to be an athlete. This generally meant jogging around the track once or twice before escaping to spend the rest of the afternoon on other more rewarding pursuits such as compiling a pedigree for some project or newting in the Wellington ponds.

In fact, I was not that unathletic and was able to put in a pretty good one-hundred-yard or even eight-hundred-yard sprint. Philip Letts, an avid cricketer, took little notice of the athletics. However he came down to find me representing the Anglesey at running and passed the comment, 'I don't believe it'. He was also surprised when I represented the athletes against the cricketers. Having spent hours in cricket nets at St Andrew's, let alone being taken by Gavin to the nets at Sherborne for tuition at an even earlier age, I am able to take an impressive stance at the wicket and execute an elegant stroke. It is the connection which is the problem; but on the one occasion at Wellington when I was made to play cricket, I managed to score a handful of runs, much to everyone's surprise.

These minor achievements on the track or at the wicket were not sufficient. Philips Letts was to summon me four terms before I left Wellington. I went into his study where he was inevitably puffing on his pipe. He looked at me quizzically and announced that with me on the games front he had been a failure. Apparently everybody in the Anglesey was good at some sort of game. He had been informed

that I had a good seat on a horse, but added that this was no use at
Wellington. To make up for this, I was therefore to become games
prefect. I would like to say that I protested, but the truth was that I
meekly accepted. Thankfully this chore was not as onerous as it
sounds. The Anglesey was by any standards for any house at any
public school at any time quite exceptional. When I became head of
the Anglesey at the end of 1958 it had five members of the rugger
fifteen, including the scrum half and the hooker. Among the school
officers it had the captain of cricket, the captain of shooting, the
captain of racquets and the captain of fencing.

There had, I believe, in the previous term, been five members of
the cricket eleven. I recently had a happy encounter with one of my
fellow prefects whom I thought was captain of boxing during my last
term. He told me that this followed on after I had left. One of my
fellow prefects also became captain of hockey. Since each of these
captainships was occupied by a different person, this domination by
a single house was an astonishing achievement. We were one house
or dormitory out of fourteen.

My job as games prefect was to report on Anglesey's prowess at
weekly dormitory prayers and to organize 'the remainder' into
enterprising activity. Inevitably there were some, like myself, who
were not gifted on the sports field. It was the games prefect's job to
ensure that they were sufficiently occupied and taking required
exercise. My simple ploy was to stick a notice up on the board saying
'Remainder, Dormitory Run'. This was a half an hour jog around a
favourite route; but Philip Letts had other ideas. 'Enterprise' and
'initiative' were his two core words as I went to see him after lunch
on my daily visits. 'I think we should have a hitch-hiking competition,' he announced one Friday. 'Sir?' I queried. He then announced
his grand scheme of sending everybody in the Anglesey on a hitch-
hiking competition. They would leave the house and go as far as they
could and bring back evidence of their furthest point. Hitch-hiking
in the 1950s was relatively safe, schoolboys are not. Setting I thought
a good example, I made it to Salisbury and back to find that tea in
the dining hall was conspicuous by the almost total absence of anyone
at the Anglesey table. Most were living it up having tea in the Ritz
or enjoying the doubtful entertainments on offer in Soho. We never
again had a hitch-hiking competition. Philip Letts remained a great

friend and long afterwards, as we walked across Offa's Dike reminiscing, he admitted it had been one of his greatest mistakes as a housemaster.

On my arrival as a new boy in the Anglesey I was greeted by Peter Snow, 'Not you again!' Peter could well have taken it out on me, because I recall school breaks at St Andrew's where I and one Brian Fuller had gone on Snow baits. This involved pursuing Snow with a pair of extendable pincers which Fuller had acquired. Their target was Snow's backside as he was chased across the St Andrew's playing fields. 'Let's go for Snow!' we would shout as the school bell announced the beginning of the school break. In consequence I was slightly apprehensive when I encountered Peter Snow on my arrival in the Anglesey. I need not have worried; he has since claimed to have forgotten the Snow baits. Nonetheless he got his own back in a different way.

Peter was not a games player. Like me he had been through the strictures of St Andrew's and had arrived in the games-playing house at Wellington. He had found another niche in public speaking and drama. My arrival and our re-acquaintance led to him picking me out to read a lesson at the school carol service which took place at the end of my first term. The Anglesey's pews were by the main door, underneath the headmaster's stall. I was suffering from a sore throat, and my lesson included the phrase 'I will multiply thy seed as the stars of the heaven and as the sand which is upon the sea shore'. This tongue twister was a somewhat alarming experience as I was left standing while six or seven hundred people in the congregation sat down. I am told I was fully audible and correct intonation ensured that 'the sand which is upon the sea shore' was not delivered as 'the sandwiches upon the sea shore'. It was this one occasion which enabled me to conquer my innate nerves and gave me a measure of confidence to speak thereafter on many public occasions.

Life at Wellington with my natural history bicycle allowed me considerable freedom of which one had been deprived at St Andrew's. In consequence I was able to keep in touch with my family, bicycling over to see my grandmother, Banny, at Harthover and to meet up with my parents who would be staying there for a horse or regimental event. The bicycle would also take me over to see my godmother at Bracknell and more particularly my grand-mother's cousin, Helen Woodbridge, who lived near Ascot and held grand tea parties for Etonians. I had to confess that I was always rather pleased when I arrived in a tweed suit to be surrounded by Etonians in their morning coats only to be promptly put at the head of the table as we were waited upon by her maid with a veritable feast. I shall never forget Helen's glass bowl centrepieces with floating orchids and the quizzical looks of Etonians as I was given the most important place at the table. It has to be said that young teenage boys can be appalling snobs; and there was a great difference between morning coats and a tweed suit. However I was family; and therefore Wellington firmly trumped Eton on these occasions. Helen was the daughter of the pretty Maria Jane, the sister of Ted Whitwell.

O Levels came at the age of fifteen. Two weeks before the exams I had risen at some early hour, not to revise, but to inspect the state of tadpole metamorphosis in progress in one of the school ponds. I had also hoped to see a local girl who was the subject of my adolescent fantasy, a village girl who had a habit of sitting on White Bridge between two of the ponds.

I never made it out of the Anglesey, because I yawned, slipped on my mat and pushed my arm through the window. I sustained a particularly nasty cut which involved a multitude of stitches and being confined to the school sanatorium with a plaster cast. There was considerable concern that I might lose the use of two fingers in my left hand. This never happened; but I had to take my O Levels from the sanatorium and have a minder as I negotiated such obstacles as the chemical practical, pouring bilious liquids in and out of test tubes via pipettes and other laboratory apparatus.

During the subsequent school holiday my mother totally ignored my injury; and with plaster cast I continued to jump fences one-handed on borrowed ponies. Eventually the Bullens once again came to the rescue and gave me the registered Storm III, otherwise known as Goofa. She was a fourteen-two hand grey mare of curious temperament, a mouth like iron and no great beauty. She had run away with Colonel Jack Bullen at a trot out hunting; and that was the end of Bullen patience. Several of the Bullen children had had mixed experiences with her in the show jumping ring. She had bolted with Jenny Bullen at Dorchester Show. Her nickname was well deserved. I paid the Bullens a nominal five pounds, and I suspect they were pleased to see the last of her.

Goofa had serious mental problems. In the field she was vicious and circled her victim in ever decreasing circles, lashing out with her hind legs. Catching her involved standing still, as she charged towards me then started the inevitable anti-clockwise circling with ears back and hind legs seeking to hit their target. The answer lay in cutting her off, and I only had to rush forward and touch her head as she circled. She stopped immediately, her ears went forward and she would follow meekly down the field, through the paddock and into the stable without even the necessity of a halter. In the stable no pony could have been more docile, and my small cousins were able to slide off her back and play around her hindquarters without fear. This was not always the case with men; and Gavin was certainly made unwelcome in her stable.

Goofa had been bought as a show jumper and had come from Ireland; and I suspect had been ill-treated. Anne Bullen was certain that she had acquired her circling habits at Wembley where she had performed a cabaret of plaiting the maypole in a musical ride at the Horse of the Year Show. Goofa could certainly jump; but her show-jumping career was marred by her temperament and innate fear of human beings, particularly men.

On occasions where there were spread-out fences in a large arena with few spectators she was capable of winning and did so; but major agricultural shows with stands and spectators banked up against the ringside proved too much for her. She would simply stop dead at the last moment, usually at the second or third fence, and we had to beat an ignominious retreat, made even more ignominious by the fact that her abrupt stop only too often meant that I had landed on the ground. She excelled across country where spectators were less in evidence. Being unsound in the wind, we dosed her with aconite powder the night before any event. Nowadays I suppose this would constitute a performance-enhancing drug and would be banned. It did however enable us to achieve success in the horse world; and there were two occasions where I was particularly proud of her.

In the summer of 1956, when I was sixteen, Goofa was put into the trailer with its canvas top rolled back. This was not so that she could admire the view but rather to ensure that fresh air went into her lungs and kept her wind in order. We were off to the Cotley Hunter Trials in Devon. Open hunter trials in Dorset and Somerset were banned to children and ponies, the reason being that adults had somewhat unsportingly objected to being beaten by their juniors.

The course of the Cotley Open Hunter Trials incorporated much of the Cotley Hunt's point-to-point course consisting of sizeable banks. Large timber fences had also been added to what was a good galloping course. I had trained surreptitiously over the fences of the Sherborne one-day event course with my mother and stop watch, and I knew enough about large and difficult obstacles; but banks were another matter. I need not have feared. Goofa sprang over the banks and gave the last of her energy. I remember my mother giving me strict instructions to remove her from public sight as her gasping for breath and heaving flanks would attract the attention of the Royal Society for the Prevention of Cruelty to Animals.

We won these open hunter trials. I was then approached to ask whether I would give a repeat performance to show how it could be done, as the British Olympic team were training at Porlock and had taken part only to be beaten by a teenage boy on a fourteen-two pony. This was not a problem, as I was to take part in the pair competition later that afternoon with Charlotte Ingram on Romany. In fact, Charlotte was only twelve at the time and Romany was another top-class sporting pony, not gifted with good looks but game for anything. Charlotte and I set off against the adults; and we won the competition. Hopefully the trainees for the Olympic team learnt something from us. I came home with my winnings of sixteen pounds and silver cups. Goofa had excelled herself.

Her second major achievement was in the pony club inter-branch competition. Each pony club sent four representatives for a one-day event consisting of dressage, cross country and show jumping. Many of the competitors were already experienced at a national level, at Badminton and Burleigh. I had been kept out of the Blackmore Vale team the previous year thanks to Goofa's objection to enclosed arenas and massed spectators at the Castle Cary show. The following year I was allowed to represent the Blackmore Vale as something of a wild card. The night before we had gone up to the Cotswolds and inspected the cross country course. It was certainly stiff; some parents complained, and consequently one or two minor modifications were made.

Goofa's dressage was as usual moderate. We did the best we could and came in at about forty out of some eighty children. The cross country phase began. It was a disaster. Whole pony club teams were being eliminated. I suspect that only about fifty per cent of the competitors were able to get round the course. I set off with Goofa, negotiating a small fly fence and galloping her as fast as I could in order to sort out her nerves. The second fence was a large stone wall, capped with a broad piece of timber leading into a dark wood. I suspect that many horses and ponies objected not to the size of the fence but to jumping from light into dark. It was touch and go. I timed her correctly and yelled like a fury. She sailed over and we were home. The rest of the course was no problem. We were the only competitor to complete the course with no faults. It took us up from our fortieth position into number one or two.

Unfortunately, the inevitable happened with the show jumping. Goofa saw spectators through the poles that she was about to negotiate and stopped dead at the last moment. The Blackmore Vale survived the competition, coming in third. In spite of our one refusal, Goofa and I also came in third on the individual basis and might have won the 'individual boy' had not numbers one and two also been boys. The idea that girls dominate pony clubs is not strictly true. On this occasion boys were in the ascendancy; and the two that defeated me, Jeremy Beale and Jeremy Smith-Bingham, went on to pursue distinguished careers in the equestrian world. Goofa, when she was put down some three years later, received a glowing obituary in the *Horse and Hound*.

This was to be the summit of my competitive equestrian career. Thereafter I spent a last season hunting Goofa with the Blackmore Vale; and our last experience together was jumping a fence at the end of the day into a ploughed field. Hidden in the plough was a strand of twisted wire which caught her front feet. I threw myself off and landed in the plough to look across to her lying on her back waving all four feet in the air. We were both unharmed; but it was the last fence we ever jumped together.

At this stage, aged seventeen, it was time to quit riding which had been such a time-consuming part of my life; but the severance from the horse could never be complete. Gavin was building show jumping courses throughout the West of England where I helped pace and measure. He was also judging hunters. My mother was a British Show Pony panel judge. I remained a stopgap and on several occasions was roped in as a spare judge for twelve-two and fourteen-two ponies. I confess to knowing little about judging a good dog or horse, and this was something of a farce. If my mother was judging, I was told to shut up. However, my own views, which I still managed to express, were based largely on good looks. They generally agreed with those of my mother who then got to work on such as splints and spavins and other physical defects of the animals which I had considered worthy of consideration. What I wonder would she think of some of the animals I was to ride forty years later in India or South America?

After taking O Levels, I chose maths, physics and chemistry as my A level subjects. Physics and chemistry were not generally taught at prep schools; and I had only encountered these subjects for the first time at the age of fourteen at Wellington. The novelty element doubtless played its part in my choice. This may not have been wise. I managed to achieve eighty-nine per cent in chemistry A level and won the school chemistry prize, being presented with the *Oxford Dictionary of Quotations* and Bernard Berenson's *The Italian Painters of the Renaissance* by The Duke of Gloucester on speech day. Neither work seems to reflect a scientific bent; but they were my choice. I won this chemistry prize by measuring the thickness of the skins of various types of bubble and in manufacturing various amino dyes of psychedelic orange and blue. The dyes coloured various handkerchiefs and succeeded in removing layers of skin from my hands. After A level, I fear, I began to lose interest in science, which did not help achieve a place at Oxford or Cambridge.

Time spent on chemical practicals was replaced after A level by producing a dormitory play, *The Strong are Lonely* by Fritz Hochwaelder. It was a serious play set in South America in 1767 and told of the dissolution of the Jesuit state. Apart from the obvious advantage of having an all-male cast of twenty boys, it was rather more serious than the usual Agatha Christie or light hearted comedy so popular as public school productions. The principal part was played by Nicholas Tyacke. Our friendship had survived his assaults on my remaining wildlife. He had chosen to chuck flowers and sulphur over our adjoining cubicle wall or worse still pour milk over my stickleback fish which turned them a curious pale luminescent blue. Nicholas was an excellent Father Provincial in the play where I acted as his opponent, the Spanish deputy.

I was helped in the production by the wife of my chemistry master, Isabel Waddington. Isabel was in the theatrical world, was young, attractive and enthusiastic about my production. She was to help with many of the rehearsals. Our friendship almost put an end to the whole project at its very inception. I was not then a prefect. It was in the summer of 1956 when for reasons that I cannot now recall, the head of the Anglesey decided that I needed to be put in my place. It was Peter Snow again! Beyond the school grounds there was a long and tedious stretch of road known as Wellingtonia Avenue. It was bordered by Wellingtonias or Californian redwoods and led up to Finchamstead Ridges where there was a sundial. Peter had given me a sheet of paper which he had initialled. I was supposed to run to the sundial, take a rubbing of it and then run back again within a set time, something in the region of three quarters of an hour. On my return run down the avenue, Isabel passed by in her blue van. She spotted me, stopped the van, and I was given a lift. She dropped me discreetly by the Picton dormitory; and I then jogged back happily into the Anglesey. Unfortunately, Peter Snow had set off on his bicycle to see how I was proceeding; there was no sign of Gwynn-Jones on Wellingtonia Avenue. I had to confess to my misbehaviour. To my surprise, I was not beaten, possibly it was thought this might compromise Isabel's position or perhaps it was merely considered that I had shown a measure of enterprise and initiative. Most people were amused by the incident, and I was merely given a ticking off. I am delighted to say that Isabel and I continued preparing for *The Strong are Lonely* for school presentation. This eventually took place at the beginning of 1958; and letters and reviews suggest it was a great success. Unfortunately, its success was such that news of the Anglesey's *The Strong are Lonely* circulated at Cambridge University; and this, as it later transpired, was to prove something of a disaster.

After three terms as a dormitory prefect, I became head of the dormitory or house and a school prefect in the Michaelmas term of 1958. During that term I took a scholarship in science to Clare College Cambridge, hoping to follow in the footsteps of my uncle, Dick Harrison, who had been there in the nineteen twenties. My enthusiasm for science had waned after A and S levels, and the following year showed a distinct decline in scientific ability. I began to feel even more depressed at my first meal at Clare when I went to take the scholarship exam. It was dinner; and I found myself surrounded by intense scientists sporting mainly bogus heraldry on their school blazers, with the top pockets sprouting slide rules, pencils and rulers. I left the dining hall to be greeted outside by a rotund and jovial fellow, 'I see you are the only other person wearing a tweed suit,' he said, 'I think we need a drink.' This was Anthony Bowring who was then at Ampleforth.

Anthony and I took the scholarship exams together until I fluffed the physical practical. I was supposed to do something with ball bearings and a glass beaker full of treacle. Everyone else's ball bearings dropped smoothly downwards through their treacle. Somehow mine succeeded in going upwards on tiresome bubbles which had appeared through overheating. I had let fly with a canister of liquid oxygen to cool down my experiment; and this had caused some degree of chaos and consternation in the Cavendish Laboratory. A glance sideways showed that Anthony's graph was moving in a different direction from mine. He went on to take the chemical practical; but I was barred from further experiments.

I also interviewed badly. Doctor Northam, the tutor of admissions, had an interest in Scandinavian playwrights. He had heard of my production of *The Strong are Lonely* and asked whether I would produce plays at Cambridge and started testing me on Ibsen and Chekhov. Unfortunately I had no particular view on either of these playwrights. Being a scientist, it is hardly surprising that Ibsen and Chekhov had played no part in my education. I failed my scholarship and have detested Chekhov ever since. In spite of these setbacks, Anthony Bowring has remained a close friend ever since. He was accepted by Clare to read law.

Apart from this tiresome attempt at a scholarship, my last term at Wellington was crammed with school and dormitory duties, which included running the Corps and being prefect in charge of bicycles. My last field day in the Corps was something of a disaster. The opponents sabotaged the walkie-talkies before the scheduled start of hostilities. This lack of communication meant that I was kidnapped by Sandhurst Cadets and spent most of the day in their custody. Nevertheless that same term I barked orders at the School Corps consisting of some six hundred boys and led them in a respectable march past Field Marshal Sir Gerald Templar. Walking in solitary state in front of six hundred boys whilst doing an eyes right and keeping a straight line certainly requires concentration.

As head of the dormitory and as a school prefect I had to administer the occasional beating, sometimes at the specific request of Graham Stainforth, the forbidding headmaster, or Philip Letts, my tutor. There has been much written in recent years about corporal punishment at school. As one who beat and was beaten, I have always remained sceptical as to the suggested psychological effects of this punishment. It was my experience that administering the cane was nearly as unpleasant as receiving it. Not being a good games player, my aim was frequently erratic. I recall the first beating that I gave in the Anglesey which took place in the bathroom after 'lights out'. My first stroke of six clipped the unfortunate victim around the ears. He rose to his feet and rather endearingly said 'Do you mind', before returning to the bent-over posture. Long after leaving Wellington, I have met several who received the cane from my erratic aim. Only one was remotely huffy; and I am convinced that this is simply because he felt the punishment was unfair.

CHAPTER 7

The gap year and a half

I LEFT WELLINGTON AT THE end of 1958, aged 18, without a university place. I was now in the outside world and brought down with a bump. Gavin had two friends who were directors of Unilever. I went to London to work as a filing clerk in Unilever House near Blackfriars. My salary was in the region of seven or eight pounds a week, with four or five pounds a week paid for a bedsitting room in Courtfield Gardens near Earls Court until I moved into 49/51 Onslow Gardens, a hostel for debutantes and suitable young men. It was owned by friends from the West Country. I recall ringing up the landlady who enquired whether I had been to Eton or Harrow. When I replied that I had only been to Wellington, there was an ominous pause. I was subsequently interviewed by this formidable matron and explained that I knew the owners. Presumably on that basis and, in spite of not being an Old Etonian, I was allowed to take up residence. The rent swallowed up most of my meagre salary, so I had little chance of much in the way of a social life. My mother's telephone calls, suggesting that I come down to Dorset for the weekend, met with my bleat that I could not afford it. The family finances were as usual in a mess and she was seeking, not without success, to earn a few pence mending china. Although I had given up riding, weekends were inevitably spent building show jumping courses with Gavin, and acting as announcer at varied shows and gymkhanas.

Life in Unilever House proved deeply depressing. As a filing clerk, I was responsible for collating commodity orders, invoices and other paper forms which were deposited on my desk to ensure the safe conveyance of Unilever products to East African ports. Slipped in among the Unilever products were crates of booze destined for African heads of state. Unfortunately my collation of paperwork led to whisky erroneously going to Lagos in Nigeria when it was properly destined for Accra in Ghana. The relevant head of state was not exactly pleased. I sat in an open plan room with some fifty other clerks and was plunged into increasing depression.

To the rescue came Philip Letts, who was determined that I should go to Oxford or Cambridge. Many housemasters at public schools doubtless consider their duty discharged once a boy has left school. Philip was not one of these; and it was through him that I went for an interview with Alan Carr, one of the tutors of admission at Trinity College, Cambridge. The recommendation of Philip, *The Strong are Lonely* and my A level marks saw me in. I was accepted by Trinity and ironically the same day received a letter of rejection from Bristol University. During my interview with Alan Carr, I made it clear that I did not wish to read science at Cambridge but would prefer to read history. He suggested that switching from science to the arts might be difficult. I volunteered that I would take history A level in the year before going up to Cambridge. This I was to do; but when I eventually arrived at Trinity nobody expressed any interest in my past academic career.

The second lifeline during my Unilever experience was my great aunt Muriel. I was a frequent visitor to her flat in Lennox Gardens. Dining became somewhat difficult. Her maid, Crabbie, would telephone to say that Her Ladyship did not consider eating necessary. All cutlery had been sold; but Crabbie would try and give me a surreptitious meal in the kitchen. Muriel was clearly becoming increasingly whimsical in her old age. She did not seem to lose weight, so presumably she was nibbling biscuits and other sources of sustenance late at night. I asked Crabbie whether there were crumbs in Her Ladyship's bed, but never received an affirmative answer. Perhaps she was kept going by her consumption of port and Cinzano.

This was Muriel's Pekinese period. Ming was a pleasant enough dog, but inconveniently died in the middle of Ascot week. Muriel rang Banny; and Dick was given instructions to meet the train from Waterloo down to Camberley which was bearing Ming's casket, and to ensure that it was buried under a cherry tree. Not only did this disrupt my grandmother's Ascot party, but the cherry tree at the back of the tennis court was subsequently sold as a building site to finance future Ascot parties, so poor Ming is now somewhere long forgotten under suburbia. If Ming was tolerable, Typhoo was not. This Pekinese was paraded around Lennox Gardens and Cadogan Square in a harness in between being dusted down with talcum powder and scent and being fed little pieces of chocolate from silver boxes. Typhoo strongly objected to this pampered treatment and acquired a tendency to snap and bite at the first opportunity. The result was that putting him into his harness was frequently abandoned half-way through, so that the unfortunate Typhoo was dragged around Cadogan Square with a leg caught up in his harness somewhere across his flank. As Muriel, with her striking looks, was herself heavily hatted with something more suitable for a Cossack regiment and with full length coats made either of fur or, worse still, pleated damask with flowing sleeves terminating in bells, we must have presented an interesting sight to the inhabitants of London SW1. It was typical of Muriel that one morning I was sent out to retrieve a book on dinosaurs that she had lent to a friend. I rang the friend's front door bell; and the result was that I had breakfast on my own with Claire Bloom, the internationally acclaimed actress.

My father meanwhile had played no part in my life since he and my mother divorced. His second marriage had been announced in the papers; and when I was seven he apparently sought to lay claim to me. It was only in 1980, after my mother's death, that I discovered letters from his solicitor demanding custody. Gavin, always the brilliant letter writer, had seen off this assault on my life with him and my mother in Dorset. There was then a ten-year silence from my father until he wrote to me at Christmas in 1956, saying he would like to know what I was doing and wished to see me. Gavin again rose to the occasion and arranged for a meeting at some hunter trials. Gavin's charm carried everyone through an awkward situation; and I well remember at the end of the day he turned to my mother, placing his arm about her waist, and saying, 'I think you should take both your husbands for a drink'. My father accepted the invitation and was encouraged by Gavin to envelope my mother from the other side, and off the three of them walked to some convivial tent, while I was left to put Goofa into the horse trailer. She and I were not on good terms as we had performed badly and been eliminated. Unlike Gavin, Goofa had not risen to the occasion.

Subsequently I met my father once or twice, theatred with him in London and endured a weekend visit to Wellington where he flatly refused to meet my tutor Philip Letts. Philip was furious; and I had to draw on great reserves of tact to cover up parental behaviour.

I had learnt that I had a half-sister, Alexandra, but shortly after the reunion with my father, he, my stepmother and Alexandra emigrated to South Africa. Muriel was intrigued that I had a half-sister whom I had never met and rescued me from my Unilever experience by presenting me with a cheque to cover my fare for sailing to Cape Town on the *Windsor Castle*. Apart from a week staying with friends of Gavin in Belgium as a legacy of the Relief of Brussels by the Welsh Guards, I had never been abroad. The *Windsor Castle*'s stop in Madeira introduced me to flowering jacaranda, bougainvillea and hibiscus. I became aware that the world had something more to offer than the mists and mud of the Blackmore Vale in Dorset.

I arrived in Cape Town to watch the sun rise over Table Mountain. It was Alexandra's tenth birthday. The Gwynn-Jones lifestyle was based on Parel Valley, the exclusive area of Somerset West which then considered itself the epitome of South African social life. This revolved around endless cocktail parties, racing at Kenilworth and hunting with the Cape drag. I drank my share of gins and tonics and rode my father's somewhat second-rate horse, Cavalier, with Alexandra on her pony, Henry, across the backdrop of the Hottentot Holland Mountains. Alexandra had been totally unaware of the existence of a half-brother until the evening before my arrival. So there was much chattering as we explored the Cape countryside on our horses.

South Africa was in the grip of apartheid. I recall taking McKenzie, one of my father's servants, down to the local sawmill to collect sawdust for the horses' bedding. Being white, I was not allowed to hold the sacks to allow McKenzie to shovel in the sawdust. I overruled these objections and between us we put bags into the boot of the car and then filled up the back seats. With the car loaded, I told McKenzie to get into the front seat next door to me as I drove home. This created a further problem. McKenzie told 'Master' that he would be arrested if he were seen sitting in the front seat next door to a white man, and the solution could only be resolved by his walking home. I am afraid I insisted that he get in. He did so, but crouched down on the floor to avoid being spotted and was clearly distressed by the situation.

Parel Valley was not police territory unless they were summoned by whites, when there was a rapid response. I doubt whether any infringement of apartheid between McKenzie and myself would have taken my father more than a rand or two to keep McKenzie out of trouble. I subsequently learnt that McKenzie fell foul of the South African authorities and became a member of some terrorist group. I recall he made wooden cages, to keep wild or domestic birds, and had a number of mistresses who caused problems in the Gwynn-Jones servants' quarters with their agitated rivalry which gave rise to much shrieking and yelling at night. My father would descend with a hunting whip and all would be resolved. I had some insight into McKenzie's life. I would like to think of him as a friend. If indeed he did become a terrorist I can feel some sympathy for him, and suspect that his terrorism went little further than organizing and taking part in demonstrations.

It is perhaps difficult to realize today the pettiness of apartheid as it existed in 1959. Seats in all public places were designated '*blankes*' or '*nie blankes*'. At suburban railway stations in the Cape peninsular paper stalls would consist of a single counter behind which one person served, I seem to recall they were usually white. Customers buying a newspaper from the stall were required to stand to take into account a metal bar which projected horizontally for several feet before descending vertically to the ground. It was necessary for a customer to stand on one side or another of the bar, depending on his or her colour, to purchase the same newspaper from the same vendor. All too often I was the only customer. The Nationalist government had also drawn up a list of proscribed books, which included *Black Beauty*, presumably failing to recognize that the offending title referred to a horse. This caused much hilarity at Somerset West cocktail parties.

I returned to England, without having the opportunity to see any African wildlife, in order to become a prep school master. I had chosen to do this for three terms. It provided a faintly academic background with school holidays, which was to enable me to coach myself in A level history, thus fulfilling my promise to my tutor of admissions at Trinity. Self tuition in A level drew heavily upon the *Encyclopaedia Britannica* for information, on mediaeval German emperors and the French Capet and Valois royal dynasties, together with sundry mediaeval Popes. This somewhat improbable exercise was to prove rewarding; and I was to sit for my A level as an external candidate at St Lawrence School, Ramsgate, and passed.

Gabbitas and Thring, an agent in the West End, provided the name of the prep school St Peter's Court. I met the headmaster, Charlie

Ridgeway, and his mother at a pub in Devon; and I was duly employed. I then purchased my first car. She cost me £35 and was an old Vauxhall complete with curtains, running board and a satisfactory growl to her engine. Her consumption of oil exceeded her appetite for petrol, and her braking system required a certain measure of pumping before becoming effective. Even so I soon learnt that the brakes, when in operation, somehow had a tendency to swerve to the right. She was to serve me well until the MOT test was introduced. My Vauxhall was then a disaster, not least because the floorboards were found to be so worm ridden that I might have descended onto the highway at any moment. My mother engineered a sale for £5 or so to Richard Caldecott who wanted to use her as a henhouse.

Before her humiliating demise, Vauxhall and I drove from Dorset to Kent and arrived at St Peter's Court, where I was to be form master of the fourth form for three terms. We swept in through leafy gates leading to rambling red brick Victoriana beyond which stretched extensive playing fields. Victoriana was complete when I was greeted by an appropriately clad maid, the exceedingly pretty Barbara, who showed me to the master's lodge and my room. Here I met the caretaker, Hamlyn, and his wife. Poor Hamlyn suffered from goitre which was to prove an endless source of amusement to the boys, who joked that he kept his money in his disfigurement. Hamlyn was to knock on my door every morning, bringing in a ewer of hot water which he placed on a washstand, leaving it for me to pour the water into a china basin to wash and shave. He would then dutifully return to remove the results of my ablutions.

The school was dominated by Mrs Ridgeway, the widow of the original headmaster whose son, known to the boys as 'Mr Charlie', had taken his place. The school rested on its reputation built up in the early twentieth century, when it numbered members of the Royal Family among its schoolboys. At least four members of the staff were well over seventy, so it was perhaps not surprising that the school had failed to move with the times. Nonetheless in comparison to my experience of St Andrews, the boys at St Peter's Court had a much easier and more comfortable life.

I was introduced to my form after chapel and breakfast on the first morning. Some ten boys stared apprehensively at me, and I stared apprehensively at them. I was determined to have the upper hand. I was eventually to know them all well and was somewhat surprised to discover that they were, without exception, likeable. Discipline never seemed to be a real problem; and only on very rare occasions did I have to resort to banging the top of my desk or flinging a piece of chalk. I taught them all Latin, English, history and geography. I seem to recall teaching another class mathematics but refusing to have anything to do with French. It was also a condition of my employment that I did not teach games, using the excuse that I needed the games–playing hours to tutor myself for my A level. On the rare occasion that I was invited to wield a cricket bat, I agreed to stand at the crease while a small boy hurled a cricket ball in my direction. I took a monumental swipe, and by sheer fluke the ball sailed above the field and over the hedge into the grounds of the neighbouring school. All the boys were aghast at my prowess, and on that I left the crease. I was not prepared to ruin my fluke by completely missing any further deliveries. I let my cricketing reputation rest on that single stroke.

Enjoyment of life at St Peter's Court was much enhanced by Pauline Shearburn who had joined the staff with me, teaching the junior form. Pauline and I would frequently repair to the local pub where, I am afraid, we enjoyed many a joke at the expense of the school and its staff, before the formal staff dinner where members, who had known each other for decades, continued to address each other by their surnames until the meal ended with smoking Turkish cigarettes taken from suitably engraved silver cigarette boxes. Sometimes Pauline and I would request an evening off, which always seemed to cause some surprise, particularly if we chose to go to a cinema, which seems to have been considered highly improper. I particularly remember an excursion to Margate to see *Gigi* on a foggy evening. Making out a dim line of street lights ahead, I proceeded towards them. There was a monumental bang, shortly followed by another, and much shuddering from my Vauxhall. I had inadvertently crossed over a roundabout, ploughing my way through rows of civic flowers.

Life at St Peter's Court was not restricted to chapel, eating with the boys and taking classes. There were periods of being the duty master when boys were out of class. This meant dealing with anything from one poor child having an epileptic fit, to others requesting the reading of barely legible letters from relatives, and pursuing two boys who had run away. I caught up with the latter some half a mile away from the school and grabbed them both by the scruff of their necks to frogmarch them back. Their arms flayed in all directions with both yelling their heads off. I am not certain what the passing traffic made of this episode.

There was also the tedious problem of the lavatory. Schools of Victorian inclination seemed to have an obsession with bowel movement. St Peter's Court was no exception; and there was an elaborate system of pegs on a board which the duty master had to move to the appropriate place to show into which cubicle a boy had gone and then move again when the boy had reported that he had 'been' or 'not been'. If 'not been' then there were further places for the pegs to show that a visit to Matron had been made. My general impression was that boys usually said 'been' whether or not this was true. I had no intention of checking on this point by making any inspection.

Undoubtedly the most difficult aspect of school life was the school walk, which took place on Sundays. The St Peter's Court boys wore tweed knickerbocker suits and a tweed cap. The knickerbocker breeches and stockings did not always meet, and buckles were left undone. It was not easy to make legs presentable. Just as difficult was to ensure that the school kept together under the control of a single master. I soon discovered that boys formed themselves into two groups. The first was in a hurry to make the journey home as soon as possible. The second group, equally disliking the walk, proved bolshie and dawdled along at a snail's pace. The result was that the school spread out and control could easily be lost.

Knickerbocker suits were not the only somewhat ridiculous relic from the past. There was also the bathing dress. Boys used the school swimming pool in regulation woollen bathing dresses with short legs and a top half which covered their chests and were strapped over the shoulders. Bathing trunks or shorts were considered most indecent, as I discovered on the rare occasion that I donned my own and went out of hours into the swimming pool. I was spotted by a maid who reported me to Mrs Ridgeway; and I was given a sound ticking off.

On leaving St Peter's Court at the end of the summer term of 1959, I was invited to the Highlands of Scotland in order to tutor Hugh Gray-Cheape for his entrance exam to Eton. The Gray-Cheapes had taken a lodge at Lochindorb, south of Inverness. The loch meant fishing. Gavin had not had the patience to be a fisherman; and my mother considered lochs and rivers better suited for taking the dogs for a walk. Family fishing rods had therefore been abandoned and been stacked in a corner in what was known as the dairy at Spring House, where they were consistently reduced in number by being cut into sections for staking delphiniums, lupins and hollyhocks. However, I was able to rescue a serviceable split cane rod and another greenheart. I was also able to take possession of a sizeable collection of inherited fishing flies in their boxes and an assortment of tackle. Along with my rods I went to visit our friend Harry Elliott, a retired major from the Irish Guards. Harry had been one of the heroes of Colditz Castle, his part being played by Lionel Jeffries in the film *The Colditz Story*. He taught me to cast, aiming at his pocket handkerchief laid out on his back lawn.

With rods and tackle I was to arrive at some diminutive Highland station to be met by Hugh's elder brother, Hamish Gray-Cheape. Hamish was to become a good friend; and years later I was to enlist him as an Usher for the annual Service of the Order of the Garter.

My tuition of Hugh paid off, and he subsequently passed into Eton. Harry Elliott's tuition was also rewarding. Hugh's mother walked me to an upland loch; and from a boat I caught my first fish.

'Give him the butt!' she exclaimed, and I played my fish. It was a delight I have never forgotten. Thereafter I spent many happy hours rowing myself on Lochindorb itself and landing fish and learning my flies, the blue Zulu and bloody butcher being particularly effective.

On my journey back south I was bidden by Banny to stay with her and Dick at North Berwick where Dick was painting landscapes for his game birds. Banny insisted that I was to play golf with her. In her late seventies she played a good game, even if I had to spend much time retrieving her divots as she thrashed the ball with gusto. I am afraid I have to relate that her grandson was no match for her. Her behaviour was as usual bordering on the outrageous. I recall returning to the hotel; and the two of us went into the hotel lounge where assorted guests were watching Harold Wilson on the television. He was then speaking for the Opposition. Banny crossed the room and immediately switched off the television, exclaiming, 'I do not see how any of you can watch that perfectly dreadful man.' There was a stunned silence. Nobody dared say anything.

CHAPTER 8

Cambridge

IN THE EARLY AUTUMN OF 1960, I was back at Spring House, packing for Cambridge. Trunks and bicycle were loaded into the car; and my mother drove me to Cambridge by way of Iver in Buckingham-shire, where we stayed with Banny's cousin, Elise Solly-Flood. Elise and her daughter Noreen were members of what I have always thought of as the 'chicken part' of the family. Banny had given Elise one of her 'Rhodeys' or Rhode Island Reds. This remarkable bird became extremely tame and took its position at the dining room table, perched on the back of a chair and being fed with scraps. It was known, somewhat unimaginatively, as 'Mrs Hen'. This affinity with chickens extended to another cousin on the Leatham side, Kitsy Harberton, born a Leatham and married to an Irish peer. I used to visit Kitsy in her London house in Thurloe Square where she kept chickens and a chicken incubator on the top floor. The incubator was inherited on her death by her son, Robert Pomeroy, and taken to his house in Nunney, Wiltshire. Unfortunately the incubator exploded; and the house was badly burnt.

Arriving at Cambridge, I took up residence at Jubilee House in a street some five minutes from Magdalen Bridge on the far side of the river from most of the colleges. In spite of its grand name, Jubilee House was a modest semi-detached Victorian house owned by Mrs Ankin, my landlady, whose surname I am sure must have lost an 'H' somewhere through the generations.

I had received a County major scholarship from Dorset. As few from Dorset entered universities, funds seemed to have been plentiful; and my scholarship was extremely generous. I was given an additional allowance for books. As this was supposed to cover the purchase of at least three or four hardback books a week, I was able to put it to good use. I did not see the necessity of book purchasing since everything was already available in the University or Seeley Libraries, the latter being exclusively historical. I am afraid to say that my book allowance found its way into my account with the Victoria Wine

Company; and my friends and I were able to consume considerable quantities of drink at the expense of the Dorset ratepayers. Although the County Council notified me that my accounts might be audited, this threat never materialized. As perhaps a rather feeble excuse, being able to enjoy life and socialize with friends and acquaintances hopefully enhanced my education. I like to think that the ratepayers' money was not entirely wasted.

Reading history at Cambridge could be intimidating. Over-enthusiastic dons provided endless lists of lectures that should be attended and lists of books that should be read. For anyone taking these lists seriously, life must have been unbearable. I soon learnt to ignore them. In my first week I rode my bicycle to Mill Lane to attend lectures on English economic and constitutional history and mediaeval European history. It occurred to me that all lecturers had written a book covering the entire course of their lectures and that this could be digested in one afternoon. I soon abandoned the lectures after I had swept right on my bicycle into Mill Lane, shedding all my papers on the way in the face of oncoming traffic. This embarrassment also led me to dispense with the bicycle, which I left against a wall in the hope that it would be stolen or removed. It was; and it would be twenty years before I ever bicycled again.

As far as the list of books was concerned, an analysis of past examination papers was necessary. This revealed that some thirty questions were set on each subject, but only four required answers. It was therefore not necessary to cover the entire syllabus. In ancient history, for example, there was invariably a question on Augustus and another on Diocletian or Constantine. Covering these three Em-perors was sufficient to ensure two questions could be answered. All emperors in between could be forgotten. I used the process of writing essays for my Tutors each week, topping them up with one or two extra topics which I found of particular interest. I would return to Spring House for the vacation and learn my essays almost by heart so that the material was readily at hand in my mind during the exam when it could be adjusted accordingly. I even used this method with my special subject, American Expansionism and Sectionalism in the Nineteenth Century, where I declined to attend the lectures given by the don setting the paper and avoided reading the set books, choosing instead the short cut of digesting contemporary American newspapers. My method paid off; and I acquired a respectable 2:1 in both part one and part two of the history tripos.

In between visiting directors of studies and tutors, which was always on a one to one basis, new undergraduates spent their first few weeks forming friendships. Trinity was awash with Old Etonians, who therefore continued friendships which had formed at school. I recall having dinner in my last week at Cambridge at the Pitt Club with one Old Etonian who confessed to me that I was the only person not from his old school whom he had got to know during his whole time at Cambridge. I made the comment that life could exist outside the Etonian circle.

Trinity was too big to be other than cliquey; and these cliques formed early in the first term, and then tended to stick together. There always seemed to be some who remained outsiders and spent their undergraduate days as loners. My own particular clique in Trinity was Norfolk orientated, even though out of the four of us, Corbett Macadam, was an old Etonian. My Quaker forebears were responsible for my joining this clique. I had stood in alphabetical order among the other historians to be introduced turn to our new Director of Studies. Next to me was David Gurney; and I enquired of him whether he was related to Elizabeth Fry, the Quaker philanthropist. Elizabeth Fry was born Elizabeth Gurney; and Gurneys had married Leathams and were similarly connected with a number of my North Country Quaker ancestors. When David acknowledged Elizabeth Fry, I mentioned that we must be related. I was invited back to his rooms which were in Trinity itself and thereby I formed a friendship which was later to extend to his parents and three sisters. I like to think today that I am still an honorary member of the Gurney family; and I am hugely indebted to their friendship which has now spread across five generations.

David Gurney, Corbett Macadam and Roderick Wathen all came from Norfolk. Roderick also had Quaker connections and sported the signet ring and waistcoat of Thomas Fowell Buxton who has appeared with Elizabeth Fry on the five-pound note issued at the beginning of the twenty-first century.

Norfolk meant shooting. At the age of twelve or thereabouts my mother had decided that, being brought up in the country, shooting was an essential part of my education. I had been given a four-ten folding poacher's gun. Gavin disliked shooting; I suspect this was a legacy from the First World War. So my initial tuition was given by his soldier servant John Ware. After I had nearly blown off my foot crossing a bank with John and my loaded gun, I was released on the local rabbit population. Although I shot a number, I did not like breaking the hind legs and watching them crawl, unrecoverable, into a burrow. I also had to gut and skin my own rabbits, which were then hung in the larder for consumption by our poodles. I was irritated by too frequently missing my target, distressed by the broken legs and disliked the process of skinning and gutting, so I abandoned it. My Cambridge association with Norfolk reintroduced me to the sport; and I cleaned up a twelve-bore gun which lurked, like the fishing rods, in the dairy at Spring House.

My days of rough shooting in Norfolk ended on two high notes. I was placed in a line of guns on the home beat at Bolwick Hall, the home of Roderick Wathen. The pheasants did not seem to be prolific, and on this last beat anything was game. A wood pigeon emerged from the far end of the cover from where I was standing as the last gun. The bird flapped and undulated past the guns, who fired to no avail. Eventually it arrived at my end of the line, when there was a shout, 'Jones, your turn!' I fired. The unfortunate bird dropped like a stone.

This particular prowess or fluke was repeated on the last occasion that I fired my twelve-bore. I was staying with the Gurneys when Dick Gurney, David's father, announced that we would all go duck flighting. It was a freezing cold February evening; and I made my way to the gun room to collect a pair of waders. On arrival at the Gurney pond, Dick Gurney placed decoys in between blowing whistles to keep Gurney dogs under control. 'Jones, get out,' I was instructed, as he indicated that I should move towards the pond's centre. This meant breaking the ice and crouching low amongst the reeds. I broke the ice only to find that the Gurney waders leaked, so that for twenty minutes I crouched with icy water up to my knees. It was so cold that my bottom had not in fact broken the thick ice but was resting in chilly state on top of it. I was far from convincing myself that this was an enjoyable sport, when the birds flew in. Once again a shout went up, 'Jones, fire!' I muttered something about 'I am not prepared to kill your dog'. One duck was within a few feet of my gun and was blasted away, I let fly with the second barrel and somehow despatched another bird. This prowess raised a measure of Gurney acclaim; but all I could whimper was 'Please get me out of here'. My legs were then totally numb; and I had experienced the discomfort which numb and cold limbs induce when subjected to extreme cold and then return to life. It was not until I had been helped back to the car and fortified by a whisky or two that I recovered from the painful experience.

I have subsequently declined all invitations to shoot and have restricted my shooting excursions to sitting in wet butts, watching people swearing and cursing, as grouse do or do not take the right direction, and observing how partridges in Lincolnshire have recently learnt that they can walk through the line of guns quite safely. I am convinced that partridges are beginning to learn that staying on the ground and strutting perkily through the line of guns is their best way of survival. I am not opposed to shooting; but I happen to believe that it is a crueller sport than either fishing or hunting.

My life at Cambridge was probably typical of many undergraduates at the time: a jumble of recollection of the non academic. There were days with the Trinity foot beagles, equipped with flask and shooting stick standing on the infrequent hills of the Cambridgeshire fens, hoping that the hounds would move in circles. There were evenings with Anthony Bowring at Clare and a Clare clique with plenty of port over vingt-et-un or poker. There were evenings with Corbett Macadam watching many of the great Continental films of the nineteen sixties at the Arts Cinema, before returning to his 'digs' to loll on his black bear rug with yet another glass of port, listening as he expounded on some intriguing historical theory in an atmosphere of dim lights and the background music of the 1812 Overture. There was punting on the Cam with champagne bottles towed behind to keep them cool before they were drunk at Grantchester. There was Mary Gurney, David's sister, who was at Kirby Lodge, a girls' finishing school, and who was able to introduce a feminine element into what would have otherwise been a masculine society.

Our Norfolk clique frequently dined in Trinity wearing our obligatory gowns. Trinity seemed to have had an inexplicable obsession with braised celery. However, this indifferent fare and the tedium of wending my way back across Magdalen Bridge to Jubilee

House was alleviated by the courtesy of Messrs Cadbury, who conveniently installed a chocolate vending machine on my route home. One evening, still feeling peckish and needing a supplement to the braised celery, I dug into my pocket and found a piece of loose change. It was, I believe, an Indian anna. I duly inserted it into the chocolate machine and to my delight a bar of chocolate popped out. To my even greater delight and surprise, the coin popped out as well. Thereafter this coin became one of my prized possessions. Every evening I would insert a coin into the chocolate machine, and every evening the coin duly returned to its owner, bringing with it a bar of chocolate. Alas and eventually there was an evening when the chocolate machine disappeared; Cadburys had clearly realized that something was amiss.

Such was the indifference of the food at Trinity, that some of us decided to stage a revolution. Masterminded by one who was later to become High Sheriff of Hampshire, we decided to remove the temporary kitchens of Trinity to Trinity Street. As Trinity was endlessly redecorating its kitchens, temporary kitchen arrangements had been installed in a portacabin in Great Court. It was this portacabin which we conveyed across Great Court, where it became lodged in the gateway. The police appeared from nowhere; and we all scattered. I fled down Cambridge Backs, the gardens behind the colleges through which the River Cam runs. I was with my friend Anthony Hulbert, who suddenly froze and took up a strange posture. The police approached him and enquired 'Sir, what do you think you are doing?' to which he replied, 'Officer I am pretending to be a tree.' There is a limit to which one can support one's friends, so I continued on my flight. I took refuge in Clare. Somehow 'the tree' also got away with it; but I believe the future High Sheriff of Hampshire spent a night in jail.

Anthony Bowring had acquired a copy of *Boutell's Heraldry*, which I consumed, thereby renewing my acquaintance with coats of arms. Perhaps more important was my continuing interest in pedigrees. The University Library provided much information on my Harrison ancestors; and I spent many hours piecing together Harrison genealogy of the fifteenth and sixteenth centuries and gleaning information about distant forebears. I have always considered geneal-ogy to be comparable to detective work: but its excitement is not restricted to a simple pedigree of names. There is always the possibility of being able to obtain information on the character of an individual.

I recall how much I must have bored my friends, as I read them letters which I had discovered written by Richard Harrison who was Vicar of Poulton-le-Fylde in Lancashire in the late seventeenth century. Richard was something of a hypochondriac, endlessly complaining about his eyesight and apoplectic fits. He was much vexed by money problems, having being left to manage his cousin's estate. The cousin was a collector of taxes in Bristol and continuously failed to send money to maintain his mother, who was always 'lyke to dye'. The correspondence between the two cousins continued at length on the problems surrounding a water mill at Freckleton in Lancashire. My forebears began to come alive and could provide material for a historical novel.

I was less successful on my father's side. I had written to my father enquiring about his two grandfathers. He merely replied that he knew little about either of them. Almost inevitably, he claimed that our paternal ancestry was South Welsh squirearchy descended from Llewellyn, the antagonist of Edward I. This was why I had the second Christian name of Llewellyn. However a little knowledge of Welsh history and genealogy would have revealed that Llewellyn had no male-line descendants; and his stronghold in North Wales was not likely to have produced any squirearchy in the south of the principality. However, my father did volunteer that his paternal grandfather was something of an inventor and had been in the Royal Engineers. His maternal grandfather, whose name I subsequently discovered was William Edward Page, was according to my father a reprehensible character who threw 'the coffee pot' at his wife. He had a 'certain way with women'; and the wife was a French aristocrat whose family had fled France during the French Revolution. This garbled account is typical of the facts and fantasies which I have invariably encountered in my subsequent career at the College of Arms.

William Edward Page, my father's maternal grandfather, came from an iron-founding family in Birmingham. He certainly abandoned his wife and family who were totally ignored in his will; the main bulk of his estate went to various women, the principal beneficiary being a skinbroker's daughter. His wife, far from being of French aristocratic origin, was the daughter of a Norfolk farmer named Henry Bates whose wife's surname was Boutell and probably of the same family as the Boutell of *Boutell's Heraldry*. Although it sounds a French name, I am not aware that anything has been proved to show that the Boutells were of French origin, let alone of aristocratic descent.

Despairing of my descent from Prince Llewellyn, I started on original genealogical research, beginning with my grandfather who had been a successful surgeon. I extracted his birth certificate and found that he was born in 1868, being the son of John Jones, a quartermaster in the Royal Engineers. Further genealogical research revealed that John was the son of a stonemason near Bridgend in South Wales. This was not likely to reveal a line of South Welsh gentry. However, my father was correct in stating that his grandfather was something of an inventor. The iron-bound gabion which played a major part in the siege of Delhi during the Indian Mutiny was his invention. It was a metal basket readily constructed from strips of metal which clipped together and could be filled with rocks or earth for fortification purposes. Bridges, tents and other items of military equipment also sprang from his inventiveness. He was eventually commissioned and retired as a Major with an obituary appearing in *The Times* on his death in 1898. His uncle, Jenkin Jones, had a similarly successful career in the Royal Engineers. Having originally been a coal miner, he is cited in Connolly's *Histories of the Royal Sappers and Miners* as 'the best sapper and miner and pontooner that ever served in the Corps – perhaps the best in Europe'. Jenkin also rose through the ranks and retired as a Captain. These two forebears were clearly men of ability and demonstrate the mobility of British society, which has always been one of the great strengths of this country from the middle ages onwards. At the College of Arms, with the latter's involvement with genealogy, it is a fact which I encounter frequently.

Life at Cambridge also meant vacations. Short vacations were spent digesting essays written during the terms. The long vacations provided other opportunities. There were two such vacations before I left as a graduate. The first of these allowed for seventy-eight days touring Europe with Anthony Bowring and Christopher Wood, the latter subsequently to run the successful Christopher Wood Art Galleries. We set off in Anthony's red mini for Istanbul, packing the vehicle with sleeping bags and camp beds. Anthony and Christopher were modernized; but my camping equipment was another product of the dairy at Spring House. It dated from the First World War equipment; and I suspect may have been even earlier. The frame of my camp bed in particular consisted of a concertina of wood and iron; and gave rise to surprise and comment from my two fellow travellers, as the poor mini was weighed down with our luggage. Arguably my military legacy took up more than its fair share.

This was to be an educative tour of Europe. Apart from my fortnight with the Goods, Gavin's Belgian friends who lived near Antwerp, I had never been to continental Europe. It was time to catch up on such as the Rhine, the Alps, the Dalmatian Coast, the classical sites of Greece and the cultural centres of Italy and France. All of this ground was to be covered by the redoubtable mini, which took us to our furthest point in Istanbul, where we pitched tent in a Muslim cemetery. It was 1961, and many of the roads, particularly in Yugoslavia and parts of Greece, were unmade. Bouncing over a rough surface in the low-slung mini was not ideal and was to cause Anthony much agitation as the bottom of the car made contact with yet another protruding rock or boulder.

We were travelling in the days before mass tourism. This, together with inexperience, meant that I, at least, continued to wear suede shoes, thick cavalry twill trousers and tattersall check shirts in spite of continental heat in mid-August. Christopher, being less conservative, sported a pair of blue shorts with turn-ups, which gave rise to a few quizzical comments from Anthony and myself. Ludicrous as it may now seem, I never considered the possibility of wearing lightweight trousers. As the years have gone by, I have long since taken to lightweight clothes in the tropics and more practical shoes. However, I have never worn shorts or short-sleeved shirts. Apart from an innate dislike of appearing to be a typical tourist, I am particularly prone to sunburn. In addition, to cover arms and legs in the tropics is an essential precaution against nibbling insects.

Far from being typical tourists, dark suits were also packed somewhere in the mini, to be brought out on suitable occasions. Such was an evening at the Hilton Hotel in Istanbul. I recall having to pay for the drinks, which came to a little over one pound, two gins and tonics and a Campari and soda. Nowadays the Hilton is no doubt full of shorts and tee-shirts; but in 1962 travellers from England certainly thought that dark suits were more appropriate.

We camped where we could. Only in communist Yugoslavia and Bulgaria were we compelled to use camping sites. At dusk we would seek an appropriate place, even it meant a rubbish dump in Turin. Finding a site was not always easy as roads were invariably bordered by ditches; but somehow or other we found a place where the ditch could be negotiated and made our way into an olive grove or onto a patch of suitable hillside. As the budget became more limited, we were reduced to cooking our own spaghetti bolognaise over a primus stove. Anthony was allowed a few pence to search for the bolognaise in a local shop, but on a few occasions I seem to recall that we ate the spaghetti unadorned, without the contents of any small tin of a meaty nature.

Spaghetti bolognaise was supplemented by fruit. I have to confess that some of the fruit was taken by us from local vineyards or orchards. On one occasion we awoke in a vineyard near Brindisi to find ourselves looking down the wrong end of a shotgun. At the other end was an angry gamekeeper whose employer was about to conduct a shoot. Not only were we camping on one of his beats without invitation, but it was clear that we had helped ourselves to a few bunches of his landlord's grapes. Happily a smattering of English and Italian on both sides led to a brief discussion on shooting in England and Italy which convinced the gamekeeper that we were reasonably respectable. We were allowed to pack up and depart in a hurry. Figs were another supplement; but unfortunately Anthony's sudden disappearance and subsequent triumphal reappearance with twenty or so figs was to prove a minor disaster. I do not know whether Anthony and Christopher washed their figs; but I consumed mine unwashed and with relish. Thereafter I sustained a stomach upset. Years afterwards I was unable to walk past a fig tree without having a feeling of nausea. Presumably my ill-gotten figs had been sprayed with some insecticide.

Arrest near Brindisi was avoided; but a greater difficulty had arisen earlier on the Bulgarian Turkish border. At some stage I must have acquired a bug in the bladder which gave me an irresistible urge to pee at frequent intervals. Had I but known it, a visit to the chemist would have resolved this in no time. However, this minor ailment was to cause a problem in communist Europe.

On entering Yugoslavia we had each been asked to fill in a form. Being before the time of mass tourism, this form did not have any English translation; and inadvertently all three of us signed the form saying that we had a car; thus the Yugoslav authorities accepted that there were three undergraduates each with his own individual car, a situation which took some time to resolve when we crossed from Yugoslavia into Bulgaria. The Yugoslav authorities initially accused us of illegally selling two cars during our journey through their country. Eventually this was resolved; and we were released into Bulgaria. On nearing the Bulgarian Turkish border and being conscious that more bureaucratic nonsenses might arise, I asked for the car to be stopped so that I might go and have a pee. I do not recall whether Christopher or Anthony was driving, but whoever it was, with some exasperation, he stopped the car, and I disappeared into the bushes. My disappearance was necessary because the car was immediately surrounded by a gaggle of Bulgarian children.

I reappeared, and we drove on. Two hundred yards further, and we were flagged down by a couple of Bulgarian soldiers who seemed to speak English. In spite of a cheerful conversation, when we arrived at the border a posse of armed guards emerged; and we were marched off into a building to be interrogated by a toad-like individual in a green uniform with, I seem to recall, a splash of gold on his shoulders and down his front. He was flanked by two other similar individuals. Happily there was a Turkish interpreter at hand who, in English, explained to us that we were in trouble. The reason for this was that the two soldiers had reported our taking illicit photographs of peasant children with the intention of taking these back to the United Kingdom to use them as anti-communist propaganda. My explanation of stopping to have a pee was not immediately acceptable. Somewhat meekly I tried to explain that having a pee was a somewhat different human activity than taking a photograph and would they like to have a demonstration. There was then talk of taking us back under arrest to Sofia. Anthony saved the day by requesting the British Consulate on the telephone. This caused much deliberation; and after a while we were released and allowed into

Turkey. Unfortunately Christopher's innocent films of such as harmless Bulgarian churches were confiscated, and I retained my bladder problem, which was only to be resolved by an eventual visit to Everett the chemist in Sherborne who administered a simple pill.

With unmade roads, cavalry twill trousers, and ablutions aided by the car mirror with water collected from any local garage in our plastic containers, we survived and travelled on with the red mini visiting any starred site listed in *Michelin Guides*. Such survival was threatened when we gave a lift to a pleasant Swede over the mountains near Kalamata in Greece. I was driving. Our hitchhiker was squeezed in over the gear stick so there was little room for three of us in the front of a small mini. Unfortunately, I drove over the mountains with the handbrake on. The brakes, nor surprisingly, collapsed; and after a patch job in Kalamata, Anthony was thereafter pumping brake fluid and tinkering under the bonnet at regular intervals in order to keep us on the road through the rest of Greece, Italy and France.

Christopher left us to join his parents at Cannes, while Anthony and I went off to camp on a mountainside in Provençe. A thunderstorm broke out and, being exposed on a steep slope, our tenting abilities were put under severe strain. Anthony was the first to abandon the tent and make for the car. I remained holding the last tent pole; and somehow my wartime camp bed and sleeping blanket remained unscathed. Anthony's bedding equipment was strewn down the mountainside; and at the eventual end of our trip in the Bois de Boulogne in Paris he was still shivering in wet bedding. A final misfortune came on the Champs Elysées. Anthony was driving, and there was a sudden crack. The whole car lilted over to the right. The chassis had snapped. Somehow a garage managed some welding; and we were able to visit the French tombs at St Denis before reaching Le Touquet Airport. We flew back to England where the mini was despatched to a scrapyard. A flag should have been raised to her memory and a monument erected to commemorate her doughty efforts.

During my trip with Christopher and Anthony, I had seen much of Europe; and there was one place I wished to revisit. This was Arcadia in Greece. I had been entranced by its countryside where I could visualize satyrs and nymphs chasing each other. I saw this as the classic landscape which features in so much Western European art. Accordingly, on my second long vacation, off I set to explore this landscape.

I had acquired a student's pass and went on a students' train from Victoria Station in London to Athens. The journey across the Channel was unremarkable, but at the far side we boarded a new train to take us to our Athens destination. I considered myself to be an innocent and independent traveller on a train, albeit with a student's pass, and was not expecting to be ordered about by officious German students dressed in red coats and over-full of their own importance. I am not sorry to say that I flatly refused to take any orders from these individuals, which had the interesting result of my being asked to join them on several occasions in their own privately commandeered compartment for drinks and even a meal. Away from their officiousness, they were not unpleasant.

Internal train matters became more interesting as the outside scenery became less. We entered Yugoslavia, where food was not provided; and tiresome Yugoslavian officials stomped down the corridors and threatened to throw any baggage left there out of the windows if it was not immediately removed. The red-coated German students came into their element and marched up and down the platforms of all stations at which we stopped. Many students, without food or water, were anxious to make purchases at railway station stalls. This was strictly forbidden, and the redcoats had everyone under control except myself. I simply refused to accept this nonsense and, knowing that each stop was anything from five to twenty minutes, I was able to alleviate much of the distress on the train by conveying water, biscuits, chocolate and even watermelons back to grateful students. The redcoats never once objected. Their excuse to me was that students disembarking from the train at a station would be left behind when the train moved on. It was therefore their job to see that nobody disembarked. I found this most unconvincing and such regimentation a little disturbing.

On arrival in Athens and escaping from the German redcoats, I took a taxi to my hotel in the old part of Athens, experiencing taxi driving somewhat different from the sedate progress of taxi drivers through the streets of London and more akin to what I have since experienced in India. I remember a night of suffocating heat; but there were still no lightweight trousers! The following morning I toured the major sights of Athens, bumping into several friends and acquaintances. In fact, Athens in August proved to be more social than London's Knightsbridge or Cheap Street in Sherborne.

Towards the end of the day I was outside the Royal Palace when an apparently friendly Greek approached me, and we engaged in a cheerful conversation until arriving at the Parthenon at dusk. The typical friendliness of Greeks, which always involves much touching, suddenly became rather more than simple friendliness. I became aware that my Greek companion had homosexual tendencies; and a measure of aggressiveness came to the fore. Nowadays I believe the Parthenon and the Acropolis is out of bounds for tourists and may only be viewed from a distance. This was not the case when I arrived at its furthest pillars with my tiresome companion. As his intentions became even clearer as we reached the furthest pillar, I decided to beat a hasty retreat. There followed a ridiculous hide and seek around the Parthenon pillars until I was eventually able to escape and flee down into the Plakka where I dived into a restaurant for some retsina.

The following morning I took a boat from the Athens port of Piraeus for Monemvasia on the easternmost prong of the Peloponnese. Monemvasia had been the Gibraltar of the Eastern Mediterranean and was, I believe, the origin of Malmsey wine. East Mediterranean history had left it as an old half-deserted town with a crumbling castle on a hill and a more modern township over the causeway to the mainland. I disembarked, together with sundry peasants and their livestock, to be greeted by Tassos, the village policeman. I was looking for a room; and thanks to Tassos, I was given accommodation above a taverna in the old part of town. Village fishermen who had occupied my room were banished to the balcony outside; and on subsequent mornings I would wake up to see these fishermen tiptoeing quietly from their balcony across my room with their boots in their hands in order to avoid waking up their taverna guest.

Tassos proved a great friend, as did the village plasterer with his shock of red hair invariably covered with white plastering dust. The plasterer had a most infectious wit which was usually directed against his wife and marital problems. In return for my board and lodging at the taverna, I opted to make myself useful. I allowed myself to be enlisted as a goatherd. Accordingly, I took my goats up to the ruined fort above the village where they seemed to munch away quite happily on the surrounding bushes.

Lying in the sun in idyllic Grecian surroundings and reading a book, I fell asleep. When I awoke the goats were far from idyllic; and my herd had split. Half I was able to drive back to the village; but the others crossed a valley and made their way up a distant mountain. They had to be retrieved by Tassos and my other friends. My career as a goatherd came to an end; and instead I was put on fish duty. This meant putting out nets early in the morning and retrieving the catch in the evening; I recall little about this except sitting in a boat and being kept far away from any serious work.

Tassos, the village plasterer, and the local priest were as delightful as only Greeks can be. Their word 'xenos' is the same for stranger and guest. I recall going to their houses and dancing in a totally masculine society, holding handkerchiefs between our hands as we danced traditional Greek dances. I wish I could say that my childhood dances of Scottish reels were an asset here. There may be some similarity between Greek dances and those of Scotland; but I floundered badly. Nonetheless, the Greeks, being Greeks, made me feel fully at home.

I left Monemvasia in a car race; I was with the engineer of Niarchos, the Greek shipping magnate. The other car was occupied by my friend the local Orthodox priest. The chase over bumpy unmade roads was won by us. I waved the Orthodox priest goodbye, and Niarchos' engineer and I then spent a day or two travelling the Peloponnese until we parted company. My recollection of our travels together was that he had a mistress in every Greek village and would offer me her charms. Unfortunately, his taste in women did certainly not agree with my own. His women were distinctly crinkly and rumpled.

When I eventually arrived in Arcadia, I found it disappointing. Landscape is all very well; but looking at views has its limitations. A few wild cyclamens and a tortoise were all I mustered of interest on walking through idyllic landscape. Walking through Greece also had other problems. Being relatively close in time to the last World War, there was the German question. I had negotiated visiting a monastery where the village had suffered greatly from German occupation. This

I had done with a guide who was able to vouch for my nationality; but at another village I went on my own. The inhabitants had yelled at me 'Germania'. My Greek being nonexistent I decided to move on rapidly; but not before stones were thrown at me; and I had to beat a very hasty retreat. Thankfully Grecian aim was not up to Olympic standard, Olympia being nearby; and the rocks and stones landed to the left and right and behind me.

I sought a measure of relaxation in Sparta and its surrounds. I was ambling through an olive grove when there was a disturbed movement above me. I looked up and a green snake dropped onto my shoulder. I stood rigid as it crossed my shoulder, slid down my body and dropped off before disappearing into the base bowl of the olive tree. I walked on. Two minutes later I lit up a cigarette and sat beneath another olive tree, shaking like a leaf. I have since encountered much wildlife in many parts of the world, but that particular experience with a Grecian snake was perhaps the most alarming.

Back to Cambridge, where undergraduate life continued with a finale in the Pitt Club with a white tie dinner for the University Drag and the Trinity College Beagles. Henry Scrope, Master of the Trinity College Beagles, excelled himself. Festooned with lavatory paper, the port dripping down his white waistcoat, he cavorted on the top of a disabled if not broken table. I recall somebody attempting to set light to the lavatory paper. Late at night I went back to Trinity with Henry for another nightcap in my rooms. An hour or so later, I attempted to see Henry over the Trinity spikes in order to return to his own college of Selwyn. Trinity was locked; it was after hours and climbing in and out was a severe disciplinary measure. Henry was dressed in his green hunt tail-coat and would insist on blowing his hunting horn from the top of the spikes in the early hours of the morning. The College porters were most indulgent as they knew us both well. Eventually we coaxed him over to the far side; and thereafter he went off to become a monk. Not surprisingly, it was discovered that he was not monk material. Ultimately he became a barrister. Perhaps unbeknown to Henry, he played an important part in my life. I was subsequently to meet him in London where we discussed genealogy, and it was on his suggestion that I joined the College of Arms.

CHAPTER 9

Fish, snow and debutantes

L ONG BEFORE TAKING THE ADVICE of Henry Scrope and joining the College of Arms, I had the tiresome experience of finding a job on coming down from Cambridge. I had little or no idea what I should do. I had no professional qualification and I was convinced, after my Unilever experience, that I did not wish to chance my luck in any more open-plan offices. I returned to Spring House with excursions to London for various interviews. I was offered a job at a pittance as sub-editor of *The Field*.

I went to see Brian Johnston of cricketing fame, with the idea of finding a niche at the BBC. Brian was very pleasant and spent our interview discussing saffron cakes which Gavin's mother had made him as a child, and other family nonsenses and reminiscences. Our meeting was not particularly constructive. He asked me how many books I had written and what my television experiences were. This, as an undergraduate with no experience, was not helpful.

I also had recourse to Peter Snow, who was then broadcasting for ITV. I spent a happy day with Peter and was present when he gave out a news bulletin on Chi Chi and An An, the two giant pandas who had been brought together in London Zoo in order to mate. Sitting in the studio where Peter gave out the non-results of panda love life, our eyes met and he found it somewhat difficult to restrain his amusement as he announced the next item of rather more serious news. We repaired to a pub, where I recall that he was approached by other customers who accosted him with 'You are Peter Snow'. Peter merely brushed them off by saying that he had often been erroneously mistaken for Peter Snow's double. So much for being a celebrity.

Back at Spring House, Gavin was becoming more concerned about the depletion of the whisky decanter and the thought of providing for an unemployed stepson. Eventually, I decided to return to Cambridge and tackle the University Appointments Board. This yielded nothing except a few jobs with import and export companies and insurance. I decided that it would be better to be based in London rather than in Dorset; London was more likely to yield something in the future. I took up the Cambridge University Appointments Board's suggestion of a job with the Sentinel Life Assurance Company based over London's Holborn Station. I was interviewed by one Colonel Freddie Shrimpton, who was sporting an MCC tie; perhaps because I recognized his tie I was employed.

I was to spend three years with the Sentinel, arriving each morning with my Locks bowler hat and rolled umbrella. Thereafter the day was spent frolicking with secretaries, firing paper clips at plastic coffee cups, interspersed with turning the handle of my desk calculator. I was allocated a handful of insurance brokers; and business appeared to have been brought in by whether or not I proved to be convivial at an extended and well-imbibed lunch.

After three years in the employ of Sentinel, a small and now deceased company, I remained mystified as to whether life assurance policies were ever honoured or annuities paid. Nor do I understand why any worthwhile broker should ever have accepted one of our policies when our rates were no better or worse than rather more long established and better-known companies. Unfortunately, it was a murky area. Although I believe the Sentinel and its employees were honest, some of its broker clients were seemingly not. Subsequently I understand that a number of them came to untimely ends which included jail and suicide.

One in particular was an entertaining ex-jackaroo who then operated out of Notting Hill Gate. He provided me with a number of policies; but unfortunately I subsequently discovered that he was enticing immigrants to use his own private banking company. Loans from his bank would then be forthcoming to purchase a house with a life assurance policy from the Sentinel as security. It transpired that the bank was his own private account; and he left the country having spent its credit at the expense of his clients. I understand that he was subsequently picked up by Interpol in the Far East on his way back to Australia.

My experience with the Sentinel taught me that the financial world had a measure of charlatans and con men and that long lunches are not necessary for honest business. As a general principle, I have declined most lunch invitations in my subsequent career at the

College of Arms. Apart from anything else, it prevents one from putting in a constructive afternoon of work thereafter. On the positive side, the Sentinel taught me how to keep accounts, run a filing system and control a business. This at least was to prove invaluable.

On joining the Sentinel, I once more went into bedsitting-land. I took a room in Evelyn Gardens in South Kensington, covering the walls with Janet Whitwell's watercolours, supplemented by some of my Whitwell great-grandfather's sporting prints and pictures and further inherited Leatham pieces of blue and white porcelain and ivories which Banny released from Harthover on a plea from her grandson. This was to be base camp for twelve years.

During the nineteen sixties, the debutante season continued to flourish. Although girls were no longer presented at Court, parents continued to send them to finishing schools and secretarial colleges, and gave them dances in London or in the country. Nowadays girls tend to go to university and embark on gap years. Parents have little control and seem frequently to wring their hands in despair. It was very different in the nineteen sixties. When I was at Evelyn Gardens, the front door bell would sometimes ring and I would open the door to find a formidable matron who had come to assure herself that I was a suitable person to take her daughter out to dinner. A supply of sherry, gin and whisky, suitably decanted, usually won the day; and I proved to be acceptable.

Mary Gurney 'did the season' and her mother Betty came up to London for debs' mothers' breakfasts and tea parties to meet other debs' mums and to ensure that dances and dates did not clash. On finding that all debs' mums were supposed to have a London address as well as a country seat, Betty designated my bedsitting room as her substitute for a grand establishment in Mayfair or Belgravia.

Country house parties with their accompanying debutantes' dances were in contrast to the dances of my pony club childhood. The latter were perhaps more akin to the days of Jane Austin where the dances were often set pieces like Sir Roger de Coverley, the petronella, lancers and the barn dance interspersed with waltzes and various Scottish reels. Social etiquette dictated that partners were frequently changed. On the other hand, debutantes' dances were largely jiving or smooching in the nightclub; and partners were seldom changed.

Music had become electrified; and the noise was such that conversation was seldom possible. Unfortunately I find this tiresome trend has continued to this day.

Debutantes' dances also involved the use of a car. Hitherto parents had been responsible for depositing and retrieving their children. However, we were on our own once the driving test had been passed; and it was, of course, before any drinking and driving legislation had been passed.

I recall my first evening excursion after my driving test. My mother had allowed me to borrow her car on condition that I returned straight home and did not deviate. The dance was near Yeovil, and I am afraid I ignored my mother's instructions and took my friend Diana Boileau back to her home at Rampisham Manor, which involved considerable deviation through Dorset lanes. I overshot a turning and promptly backed into a ditch in the small hours of the morning. By chance there happened to be some hessian sacks in the boot; and I jammed these under the rear wheel and eventually extracted the car before taking the proper turning home.

I had not proceeded more than two or three hundred yards when what appeared to be a cowpat in the middle of the road began to disintegrate. I came to a halt and observed that the cowpat was in fact a mother hedgehog with her brood. The baby hedgehogs, disliking the lights of the car, took refuge behind the front wheels. I discovered that picking them up one by one and putting them on the verge was to no avail. They promptly ran back to join the rest beneath the car. In consequence I had to take each one through a gate to deposit it far out in a field and race back to retrieve the remainder before all those deposited beat me to it.

I was able to sponge down my somewhat muddy dinner jacket when I returned to Spring House, but forgot about the sacks which were in the boot of the car. My mother expressed surprise as to the sacks' muddy appearance; but I avoided ever having to give any explanation.

Another car incident occurred after a dance in Norfolk, probably the West Norfolk Hunt Ball, as it was a cold and frosty winter's night, and debutantes' balls were invariably summer affairs with floodlit houses and sundry garden adventures. I was staying with the Macadams at East Runton Hall and Corbett was driving. We were taking a girl to her home when the car skidded on the ice. We arrived on top of a bank. My caustic comment to Corbett that he had nearly killed us was dismissed with the assurance that we were lucky to be alive as he had avoided a telegraph pole by inches. In the freezing cold and in our tailcoats, we frogmarched the girl back to her home some three miles away, then telephoned East Runton Hall, and Corbett's father came out in the small hours of the morning with a tractor and pickaxes. We subsequently discovered that the accident rate on Norfolk roads that night had been very considerable.

Perhaps the most embarrassing car experience involved a dance somewhere in Berkshire or Hampshire. I had been invited to join a house party; and at the dinner before the dance my hostess had requested that I should drive the daughter there in their car. Later that night, I retrieved the daughter from her smooching in the nightclub at about four in the morning; and we drove home. Perhaps leaving it rather late, she suddenly said 'Turn right here'. I turned right and the car lodged on its side on the garden wall. My driving not being of expert quality made matters worse; and I was unable to extricate the situation.

The more I endeavoured to dislodge the car, the more damage ensued. I spent the next three hours in bed trying to assure myself that in years to come I would be able to relate this story without the dread and trepidation I felt in those small hours before my hostess came in bearing a tray of early morning tea. I had to confess that her car was on the garden wall. My offer to pay damages was ignored; but the rest of the weekend was a trifle strained, and I was relieved to return to London and despatch a letter of apology. Years later I related this story at a dinner party and the girl further down the table perked up and said 'Yes, I was the girl involved'. Happily the affair ended on a good laugh.

Debutantes' dances were lavish affairs. Although I was certainly no debs' delight, some of the evenings were memorable. I also was able to make a handful of good friends, including one of the aforementioned formidable matrons, Rosemary Peile. Her daughter Margaret has remained a constant and staunch friend ever since. I became even more acceptable when once again the Quaker network came into play and I discovered that the Peiles were part of the North Country Quaker network. I was a fourth cousin to Margaret's father. Once again the sherry decanter and a Quaker ancestry had proved an invaluable combination.

Floodlit gardens and moats, ballrooms in stately homes or marquees on lawns, and house parties did not always run smoothly. After a burst of debutantes' dances in the early nineteen sixties, I began to move out of the scene; but not before one of my last dances given by Dick and Betty Gurney, which was for their daughter Sally. I was duly summoned to Keswick Old Hall near Norwich on the Friday night, the dance being scheduled for Saturday. Saturday night's house party consisted of a number of guests but Friday was restricted to David Acloque, who was Sally's boyfriend, and myself. Dick Gurney's effort to bring his daughters out and introduce them to suitable men was a nonsense. Both Mary and Sally had acquired boyfriends before they did the season, and both subsequently have remained happily married to them.

I put in a tentative appearance in the kitchen on Saturday morning, thinking that I might thereafter potter around the garden and escape the inevitable pre-dance tension. There was to be no such luck, as Betty, looking out of the kitchen window, said to me 'Jones, here is a dustpan and brush. Go and sweep up the goose shit from my best car park.' The Gurneys had two Chinese geese known as 'the boys' who had been despatched to a stable along with the bantams for the duration of the weekend, leaving behind their droppings. With my dustpan and brush I set off only to be called back with the words 'Jones, there is a tiresome puddle. Please do something about it.'

There was indeed a rather large murky puddle which had made its appearance in the backyard, so I decided that a bit of syphoning might be in order. I acquired some hosepiping from Loose, the gardener, and using my experience of syphoning water butts at Spring House and my mild knowledge of physics, I sucked the hosepipe with the intention of drawing the water onto a lower level. My syphoning did not prove effective; and Loose raised some stones to discover that the Gurney drains were definitely out of order. I suffered no ill effects from sucking the Gurney drainage system; and Loose, Dick Gurney, David Acloque and I went to inspect the Gurney septic tank, which was topped by a rectangular nineteenth century brick construction. It was oozing black filth; and action had to be taken. Pickaxes and shovels were found; and the four of us dug a ditch from the septic tank into the nearby stream that flowed into the river that passed in turn through the centre of Norwich. A little mathematics involving two or three hundred guests flushing the Gurney loos two or three times a night meant that a certain amount of sewage would flow through the centre of Norwich. Betty rang the Norwich County Council and with her mischievous and innocent charm won the day. Dick Gurney struck the pipe which we had also exposed. David Acloque exclaimed 'It is just like striking oil!' as a stream of filthy black liquid shot into the air and eventually settled down into the ditch which we had dug. We covered our ditch with corrugated iron sheets; and Sally's debutante dance was to take place on the lawn at Keswick with an open sewer flowing two feet beyond the marquee. Happily any prevailing wind was blowing in the right direction.

I returned after my digging operations to have a bath only to find that the Keswick Old Hall water supply had cut itself off. The pump had failed. The indomitable Loose was able to fix it, so I was able to relax and later that evening took up a position behind Dick and Betty and Sally on their line of reception. I sat on a sofa to view the passing debutantes. I was allowed to make my choice. I did so and was able to smooch with the girl in the nightclub. Perhaps I was wrong to finish the smooching and to take her out early in the morning to catch tench on bait in a Gurney pond. She ignored me thereafter. However, I was not entirely forgotten, because I received an invitation to her subsequent dance which resulted in my unfortunate incident with landing a car on a garden wall.

In the meantime, life in the English countryside was changing dramatically. Long Burton in 1970 was a very different place from the Long Burton of 1960. Late on Christmas night in 1962 I put the dogs out into the yard for their pre-night-time pee. It had begun to snow. The dogs returned, those in baskets downstairs with the more favoured on the beds of my parents and myself upstairs. I recall listening to the wind buffeting the chimneys before falling asleep. I was woken by my mother at what I considered to be an unnecessarily early hour after a heavy and sybaritic Christmas. I was told to get out of bed and help Gavin dig out Foggy, our Jersey house cow. I remember swearing and muttering 'Who in hell left her outside?' My mother merely replied 'Get out of bed and go and help'.

Somewhat mystified I made my way to the bathroom, looking out of the windows to see nothing more than a light dusting of snow in the back yard. Having dressed, I went downstairs and out of the back door and was confronted by a remarkable sight. The wind had blown all the snow into a huge drift, covering a complete stable block. Foggy had not been left out but was encapsulated in her stable beneath the drift. The stable block on the other side of the yard was unaffected; and Gavin and I retrieved stable shovels and eventually dug our way through to Foggy, who seemed to be totally unaware of what was happening outside. There was another smaller drift by the gate leading into the yard from our lane which in turn led to the main Sherborne/Dorchester road through the village.

I was able to bypass the drifts and find my way onto the main road where further drifts of six to twelve feet high occurred every fifty yards with only a light dusting of snow in between. At the bottom of the village the drifts were even higher. It then snowed for the next two or three days, filling in the spaces between the drifts. The West Country was cut off; and although Long Burton was, somewhat surprisingly, possessed of a snowplough, this was of little effect. Dynamite was used on the road between Yeovil and Dorchester. It blew the snow into the air, but the snow merely returned to its previous position. Helicopters lifted out stranded motorists; but some had been trapped in their cars; and I seem to recall that a few were eventually found dead. The great freeze continued throughout that vacation and for many weeks after I returned to Cambridge. However, during that vacation I had spent many hours shovelling snow and in so doing became aware that many villagers still had outside privies or lavatories and were dependent on candlelight and had no hot running water.

The lane leading up to Spring House from the main road came to an end with a thatched stone cottage dating from about 1600. On the right at the end of the lane was Spring House itself and opposite on the left was our paddock. One half of the cottage was deserted; the other half was occupied by the Stainer family. Old Mrs Stainer lived there with her two daughters Bessie and Mabel. I would frequently visit them and became aware of their primitive existence. Their only supply of water was a tap outside the front door; there was no electricity; and they lived in the evening by flickering candlelight.

The privy was some fifty yards from the house through an unkempt garden. Those fifty yards I shovelled free of snow during that winter. So primitive was the existence of the Stainer family that I once had to answer a plea for help when old Mrs Stainer fell out of bed. I enlisted the assistance of John Ware and between us we lifted her up and put her back beneath her blankets. In doing so she became panic-stricken and was convinced that we were about to take her to the workhouse. 'Please don't take me to the workhouse; I don't want to go to the workhouse,' were her pitiful cries. It was deeply disturbing to discover that fear of the workhouse, which I had associated with the novels of Dickens, was still ingrained in a villager living in the second half of the twentieth century. Bessie Stainer, who worked as a seamstress for Sherborne Girls School, was the last of the family to die. I purchased the Stainer cottage from the Digby estate for two thousand pounds with a legacy left to me by Muriel. When renovating the property, wooden panelling was discovered behind the layers of plaster and newspaper used as wallpaper. Central heating has now been installed together with electricity and an inside lavatory. The outside privy is a garden shed; but the cold-water tap outside the front door still remains.

The nineteen-sixties saw similar changes to properties throughout the village. It also saw a mushroom growth of modern bungalows and houses; but the downside to this was the loss of traditional village country life. No longer did the villagers gather together once a week for traditional West Country dancing. I believe David Ware has collated and recorded something of these traditions, which hark back to Thomas Hardy with his Wessex novels. Otherwise I fear they are lost for ever.

The increase in population with new housing estates was to be matched by a corresponding decrease in the number of people going to church on Sundays. Perhaps one church turn-out that survived was Remembrance Day. This was of enormous significance to Gavin, who had lost so many friends in the First World War. Long Burton's Memorial Sunday was always to be special.

I was summoned each year for Remembrance Sunday to chauffeur Old Comrades into Long Burton from outlying villages and to draw chalk lines on the main road for those same Old Comrades to take up their position in front of the Long Burton memorial.

Unfortunately, I did not always live up to Gavin's expectations. Two occasions were a disaster; the atmosphere at Spring House was not exactly convivial as a result.

On the first occasion I had drawn up the chalk lines and enlisted Leslie Robbins, who was a Special Constable. The traffic could be stopped by Leslie and myself, but we had not allowed for Sam Harris's cows. Traffic could be stopped but Sam's fifty or sixty Friesian and dairy shorthorns could not. The resulting chaos can be imagined.

My second gaffe occurred some two or three years later when I was detailed to collect a Sherborne schoolboy who was supposedly a star in the Sherborne Combined Cadet Force Band. He was to sound the Last Post on his bugle outside the church door after Gavin had given the Remembrance Sunday words of 'They shall not grow old . . .' I collected the youth with his bugle in its box. The arrangement was that Gavin, having finished his words near the altar, would nod to me and I would then, from my position at the back of the church, nod to the youth who would duly play the Last Post. I was not entirely certain that Gavin's nod was necessary since I believed I had enough initiative to realize when he had finished.

However, he did nod and I, in turn, nodded to the youth outside; but nothing happened. Furious nods then followed to no avail. The service, in a somewhat disrupted state, then continued without the Last Post. It transpired that the youth had packed his bugle into its case but left behind the mouthpiece. Gavin was furious. It was all my fault. As I had been RSM of the CCF at Wellington, I ought to know that boys were unreliable, and I should have inspected the bugle case. The following year I am sorry to say that I made a firm excuse for avoiding Remembrance Sunday.

Subsequently I was to see Gavin through the service during his last years when he had become extremely frail; and everybody in church was just hoping that he could stand in the middle of the aisle and recite the Remembrance words. He did it; it was sad; but I remained proud of him. His sense of duty and the community spirit which it invoked with all those present is something that should not be lost.

Church attendance, country dancing and housing estates aside, cows in the village were now milked by milking machines, except the Spring House cows which continued to be milked by hand by

John Ware. Whilst other stables modernized, our horses continued to be denied the luxury of plastic; they were still fed from metal feed tins and watered from metal buckets with their hay in impossible hessian rope haynets. The hay was frequently cut on the premises with a minimal grass content. Our horses survived on dried thistle, white campion, dock and such as the increasingly rare cowslip and bugle. Ragwort was not allowed because of its poisonous nature. I had to pull up ragwort before the so-called hayfield was cut. This was a pity because it was a favourite food for cinnabar caterpillars with their delightful diurnal moths of red and green.

Now hay is cut as one hundred per cent grass. Perhaps the horses are happier. On that point I am not certain. What is certain is that the wildlife of England has greatly diminished; and species disappeared in the nineteen sixties together with the black and white woollen striped shirt that was worn by villagers cutting the verges or laying the hedges. The shirt was adorned with a collar stud. I have always assumed that the collar stud on the black and white striped woollen shirt had a collar attached for church on Sunday. The shirt was then used for working in the countryside during the following week. Nowadays, of course, washing machines have been invented, and shirts can be washed every day; jeans have replaced boots and gaiters; and the woollen shirt has been replaced by the T-shirt. Hooks, scythes and billhooks have disappeared and have been replaced by electrified trimmers and strimmers. Haystacks and corn stooks are no longer to be seen and the last of the horse drawn commercial traffic, the milk-float, has also disappeared.

Intensive farming with its selective weed killers and insecticides doubtless contributed to the destruction of wildlife which was so apparent in the nineteen sixties. However, this does not explain why wildlife also disappeared from woodlands as well as farmland. Later came the demise of such as the London sparrow and the starling roosts in Leicester Square and elsewhere in the capital. I think it unlikely that the activities of farmers were solely responsible for wildlife changes in urban areas.

In 1964 I took a rod on the River Frome near Dorchester. Initially the fly life was prolific; but within three or four years the position had changed dramatically. No flies hatched and no flies rose. Eventually I abandoned my rod. The same could be seen on the

River Avon at Salisbury. On a Friday evening during the train journey down the Sherborne in the early sixties, the water would be boiling with fish; and at the end of the decade all was still. I have never since seen any fish rise there.

During the great freeze of 1963, I fed apples to some twenty song thrushes and six mistle thrushes together with other members of the thrush family such as four or five fieldfares and three or four redwings. Five pairs of song thrushes nested in the garden; and there would be frequent sounds of them tapping open snail shells on the garden path. By 1970 both snails and thrushes had gone. The linnets, goldfinches and flycatchers were in decline. Only the magpie explosion and the sudden appearance of the long-tailed tit and collared dove went against the trend.

It is difficult now to realize that stripping away the turf at the base of an apple tree in 1960 would disturb a wide variety of insects while the same tree ten years later would yield nothing. Only the butterflies seemed to hang on at Spring House. In summers in the early nineteen seventies, it was still possible to walk around the garden with a pre-lunch gin and tonic and spot some sixteen species without any great difficulty. I fear that only the occasional tortoiseshell and holly blue now survive. I wonder who in the early nineteen sixties would ever have believed that the sight of a cloud of cabbage white butterflies would soon become a rarity.

With the destruction of the countryside and disillusion with the Sentinel, life needed a change. Following a suggestion from Henry Scrope, my Cambridge friend, I wrote to the College of Arms, hoping that my knowledge and interest in genealogy might be helpful. I was interviewed by Colin Cole who had recently become Windsor Herald. After a drink in the local Horn Tavern, I was employed as his assistant at the rate of two shillings and six pence an hour. I began work at the College in the spring of 1967. As Gavin somewhat facetiously put it, I was about to join *Alice in Wonderland*.

CHAPTER 10

The College of Arms and the Coati Sable

A BANDONING MY CITY BOWLER HAT and rolled umbrella, I took the Underground to Blackfriars and walked up Queen Victoria Street to the impressive wrought iron gates of the College of Arms. I then crossed the cobbled courtyard of the late seventeenth century building, mounted the Victorian horseshoe set of steps and went into the Earl Marshal's Court. The Earl Marshal's Court was once an active court room deliberating on the legal use of armorial bearings and allied matters. It now serves its purpose as the grand reception hall of the College which is the headquarters of the corporation of the Kings, Heralds and Pursuivants of Arms. These are the three grades of the Officers of Arms and are all known colloquially as 'Heralds'. Colin came to greet me with an armful of files: and I was placed into what is called the White Library.

My first task was to examine the documentary evidences to support a drafted pedigree of a distinguished Welsh family, beginning with fifteenth century effigy tombs in Llandaff Cathedral. Thereafter, like many other families, the pedigree reflected a rise and fall in fortune. The evidences piecing together each generation were rather weak in the early nineteenth century; and the agricultural labourer, who was soon to become familiar to me as the 'ag. lab.', made his appearance before the family rose again in status during the twentieth century.

Colin returned at the end of the day, after I had struggled with reading fifteenth and sixteenth century wills and puzzled over the documentary proofs of the family's suppressed period. I explained to him that I was not entirely familiar with late medieval and Tudor palaeography and found deciphering the documents somewhat difficult. In his good-humoured manner he picked up a will, looked at it briefly and explained that palaeography was easy once you had recognized one particular word and can then see how the writer wrote his vowels and consonants. This was, of course, very sound advice which I have always followed. However, Colin, continuing to examine the will over which I had been struggling, said somewhat expansively, 'You are lucky that this is not in Latin.' I looked at him and between us there was a long pause. He looked at the will again; and, after a further pause, he asked me what I made of the document. To this I replied, 'It is in Latin.' I then explained the 'ag. lab.' problem; and, somehow or other, I had passed my first test as a genealogist. I was removed from the White Library and taken into Colin's own chambers at the top of the east wing of the College where, in two small rooms piled with books, armorial porcelain, a multitude of papers and files and kettles with wandering leads and corresponding coffee cups, at least three or four staff all tried to grab a few square feet of working space.

This was a time when genealogy or pedigree tracing was bringing a quantity of business into the College of Arms. During my time at the College there has been a marked decline in such business. The reason for this is simply that there has been an increased public awareness of the availability of documentary evidences. It has become one of the fastest growing do-it-yourself hobbies, greatly aided by the internet. Unfortunately this gives rise to much amateur genealogy which is too often fraught with wishful thinking; and pedigrees are strung together on very scanty evidence. A burial of John Smith in 1800 does not necessarily prove that he is the same man who was baptized in the same parish as John Smith, the son of yet another John Smith, fifty years earlier. Further evidence is required to prove and link the baptism and burial beyond reasonable doubt.

Colin had numerous pedigrees for me to work through, to collate evidences and to present them to other Officers of Arms for examination. Before acceptance for registration, any pedigree collated by an Officer such as Colin goes through a process of being examined separately by two other Officers of Arms. The College of Arms is the official repository of pedigrees proving entitlement to armorial bearings. Many pedigrees are also registered which have no armorial content. Garter King of Arms, the senior Officer of Arms or Herald, is also responsible for the examination of evidences and the acceptance of a claimant of a title to be placed on the peerage and baronetage rolls held by the Lord Chancellor, now the Minister of Justice.

In preparing pedigrees for such examination, I often retreated from the sparse space and coffee cups of Colin's two rooms to the White Library. This was a room of unofficial books, largely printed parish registers and indexes of wills; but it also accommodated an expansive working table. It was not the holy of holies, which is the record room of the College, where the official pedigrees and office copies of grants of arms are housed. No person working in the College gains access to the record room without the presence of a supervising Officer until he or she has worked in the College for six months and been properly screened by Chapter. Chapter is the corporation of the Heralds or Officers of Arms in action as the governing body of the College of Arms. It is chaired by Garter and consists of their monthly communal meeting. In 1967 I was excluded from the record room; years later I was to find myself chairing those monthly Chapter meetings.

My humble escapes to the White Library, working through Colin's pedigrees, were interspersed by visits to Somerset House for birth, marriage and death certificates and wills, and further visits to the Public Record Office in Chancery Lane for even earlier wills and census returns. Colin had let me loose on genealogy; and I began to learn more about the College itself and those who worked there.

The thirteen Officers of Arms are appointed by the Sovereign on the recommendation of the Earl Marshal, the Duke of Norfolk. Chief among them is Garter King of Arms, or Garter Principal King of Arms, who is alone responsible for Royal heraldry and is the sole granting authority for the heraldry of peers of the realm. The insertion of 'principal' in his title vexes his Scottish counterpart, Lord Lyon King of Arms. In this ongoing, but usually friendly, rivalry, Garter can reply that Lyon has the superior designation 'Lord' and uses the royal 'we' in his letters patent creating new armorial bearings.

Garter is also party to all letters patent establishing new armorial bearings. He acts with the two provincial Kings of Arms: Clarenceux, whose jurisdiction is south of the River Trent, and Norroy and Ulster who prevails north of that river up to the Scottish border and also in Ulster. All three Kings of Arms exercise their authority jointly in the Sovereign's other realms and territories outside the United Kingdom, and in cases where honorary grants of armorial bearings are made in America and occasionally elsewhere, with the approval of the Foreign and Commonwealth Office and its counterpart in the country concerned. Canada is now an exception, as the Queen established a separate Canadian heraldic authority during my time at the College.

Grants of armorial bearings have been the responsibility of the Kings of Arms since the Middle Ages, and are conferred upon deserving individuals as a dignity. 'Eminence' was the criterion laid down by Henry VIII. In the twenty-first century there is a certain liberality in this interpretation; and anyone who has contributed to society as a whole is deemed eligible. The number of grants of armorial bearings has fluctuated over the centuries. A high point was reached at the end of the sixteenth century when it appears that something nearing two hundred grants of armorial bearings was made each year. A downturn after the Civil War reached its nadir in 1708 when no grants were made. Thereafter the granting activity of the Kings of Arms increased and, during my forty-odd years at the College, the number has settled at a little under two hundred a year, with the exception of the massive increase in corporate heraldry brought about by the Local Government Reorganization Act of 1972.

Below the three Kings of Arms rank the six Heralds and four Pursuivants. The term 'Herald' is often colloquially used to cover all thirteen Officers of Arms. Each of these runs his own private practice in matters concerning heraldry and genealogy. A rota system has long been established whereby they take it in turns to have a week 'in waiting'. During that week they receive all letters, e-mails, telephone calls and visitors with a wide range of queries, amongst these will be the occasional application for a grant of arms or armorial bearings. The Officer concerned will then be responsible for submitting the relevant petition and consulting with the grantee on the design, which is then sent to Garter for his approval. In general, grantees have little idea of heraldry; and a good or bad design generally reflects the creative ability of the Officer concerned rather than that of the recipient grantee. Over my subsequent years at the College, I can claim responsibility for the design of a little under a thousand coats of arms, which reminds me of Colin's misquotation from Tennyson 'A lovely lady in her charms is worth a thousand coats of arms'. As a bachelor, I would like to think that I will be able to compensate one omission in my life by achieving this magic figure.

My first attempts at design were not encouraged by Colin. He kept me firmly on genealogy and office administration, as when a somewhat eccentric secretary had left a message, which I retrieved early on a Monday morning, to say that she had departed for Africa to look for 'a blue hibiscus'. By the time Colin arrived at the office at lunchtime, I had approached an agency and a new secretary was sitting typing Colin's letters and answering the telephone. This was Caroline Calder, forty years later living in the South of France in the forests of the Dordogne, surrounded by stone walls to keep out the wild boar. The stone walls have been subjected to repair based on my experience of stone walling in Dorset. Unfortunately, there seems to be a difference between French and English stone; and my repairs have not always been successful.

Colin's refusal to allow me any heraldic input into his office was not helped by my comment on a certain coat of arms which he had designed. It consisted of a stag, above which was a chief or horizontal band set with two round garlands on either side of a ship's propeller. When I suggested this might appear to be a good advertisement for that particular brand of beef extract known as Oxo, Colin made sure that my heraldic contribution was kept to minimum. Recourse to heraldry was found elsewhere.

During these early days at the College of Arms drafting pedigrees from documentary evidences in the White Library, I examined the shields arms of past Heralds which adorned the frieze. I rapidly developed preferences and dislikes.

In consequence, I began to experiment with fictitious designs. Liz Gretton, a friend from debutante days, was working as an apprentice artist, and I gave her some of my efforts to work on, two shields of geometric design with two crests, one a blue anteater and another a black coati. My interest in natural history was about to make its impact on the College! The black coati was to prove of great personal significance.

My father's insistence on a Welsh squirearchal ancestry, complete with a lion rampant crest, was a nonsense; and Colin Cole insisted that I make myself properly armigerous. In other words, I needed to become a grantee of arms. It occurred to me that I could not do better than adopt the black coati crest which Liz Gretton had painted for me. It was sheer coincidence that coati could be taken as a pun on Coity, the place of origin of my known Welsh forebears.

I have much enjoyed my coati, the long-nosed, resourceful and inquisitive South American relative of the raccoon. I have had many encounters and adventures with them in Central America and have always been delighted to feel that in heraldic terms, at least, it is my own exclusive animal and much to be preferred to the sharing of the lion, stag or birds of prey with so many others.

In addition to running a busy practice at the College of Arms, Colin Cole was greatly involved with the City of London and was to become one of its Sheriffs. Double booking of engagements can sometimes happen; and shortly after I had begun working at the College, I was summoned and told that unfortunately double booking had taken place. I was therefore to take his place at a lunchtime City engagement in a church to address the assembled company on the topic of City heraldry. Thankfully, he gave me some props in the form of a number of wooden shields of the arms of city livery companies; and I was relieved when Colin subsequently told me that I had given a very passable presentation.

The College of Arms in 1967 was headed by the then Garter, Sir Anthony Wagner, a formidable scholar who remained aloof from the day-to-day life of the College. Access to Garter House, his chambers in the building, was difficult and further access to his own room, with its sumptuous red wallpaper decorated with garterial insignia picked out in gold and garter blue and with its baroque bookcases built specifically for their surroundings, was only negotiated by appointment made by one of his many secretaries. This was followed by a complicated entry involving a sequence of bells and internal telephones.

Anthony's intelligence did much to confound and even dominate some state and government departments; but it was possibly not to the advantage of the daily workings of the College of Arms, from which he remained aloof. The result was that the younger Officers of Arms formed what was to become known as the 'cabal' and pressurized for internal reform, advancing their own candidates for future appointment. Anthony's reaction was perhaps inevitable; he was not prepared to receive dictation from his juniors. As I was in the cabal camp, my chances of being appointed a Pursuivant were very much in doubt.

Matters came to a head in March 1970 when Anthony suddenly announced the appointment of four new Officers of Arms at the monthly meeting of Chapter held on the first Thursday of every month. Three other hopefuls linked to the cabal reacted and left the

The Youngest Competitor at the Meeting
He's 4½. But, in his red coat and jockey cap, he's as
comfortable and self-possessed as an M.F.H.

9. With Patball and my mother at Arborfield show in 1944.

10. *The Welsh Guards, Kings Birthday Parade 1932. The Prince of Wales between Chicot Leatham, Lieutenant Colonel commanding and first cousin of 'Banny' (left) and Gavin Young, Regimental Adjutant and my stepfather (right).*

11. *Blackmore Vale pony club hunter trials in 1957. In action on Goofa with Pat Young on Kilrush.*

12. *The main passage of the Anglesey with sundry school trophies and umbrellas. As head, standing in the centre and pointing to a notice board. Nicholas Tyacke in a white jersey stands in the background.*

13. My sister Alexandra.

14. *First appearance in a tabard as Bluemantle Pursuivant (standing) after the Garter Service, June 1973, with Theo Mathew, Rouge Dragon Pursuivant (sitting).*

15. As Lancaster Herald on the steps of the College of Arms painted by Dominic Ramos assisted by his father Theo.

16. *My mother and stepfather in 1978.*

College: one joined the Lord Chamberlain's Office, another became an Officer of Arms or Herald in Scotland, and the third simply melted away. Sir Walter Verco, who was then Chester Herald, came to see me as I sat poring over a pedigree in Colin's chambers. 'Good,' he said. 'Do not react; keep your head down and continue working; you will get there in the end.' It was good advice. Shortly afterwards, I was summoned through the process of secretaries and those security bells to enter Anthony's office where he told me that I was to be a probationer and considered for the next appointment. I was to cross the courtyard and to occupy a set of chambers which I furnished with sundry Harrison portraits, an early refectory table which I exchanged with Colin Cole for a backlog of payment, three sticks of furniture which I bought from a warehouse in the Fulham Road and a rather good but somewhat worn Axminster carpet belonging to Anthony.

On looking across the courtyard towards my new premises, I had observed a small trim figure striding over the cobbles with a jutting chin in grim determination and greying hair tied back in a bun with a black velvet bow. This formidable creature was Maria Chorley, employed as a secretary by Conrad Swan, York Herald and subsequently Garter King of Arms. He in turn was in partnership with Anthony Wagner, and as a probationer in the somewhat convoluted situation I was largely responsible to him. It was useful to have Maria on side.

Maria had had a series of husbands and had been the manageress of the Sydney Opera House in Australia. The current husband was less in evidence than her free-range budgerigar named Coopers. I was often to visit Maria's flat to encounter Coopers and his lack of domesticity. Maria's efforts to train him to defecate into the kitchen sink were never successful. In my experience, it is impossible to housetrain a bird. They always seem to be totally unconscious of natural bodily function.

Coopers played his part; but the alliance with Maria's determination and jutting chin became firmly and finally established with the appearance of the College flasher. Anthony had a long-standing and self assured secretary Diane; but this self assurance was undermined by the appearance of a flasher on St Peter's Hill opening his overcoat before unzipping his flies and exposing himself in front of her window in that part of the College known as Garter House. St Peter's

Hill is on the main highway between St Paul's and the current Millennium Bridge. Somewhat unnerved by several occasions of flashing, Diane had appraised Maria of the situation, who immediately expressed the wish to be informed of the next occurrence. It happened. The telephone rang. Maria grabbed her umbrella, and with chin forward, set off at a brisk trot across the College courtyard and around into St Peter's Hill where the flasher suddenly saw this diminutive but formidable figure waving a threatening umbrella followed by my pinstriped self shouting the occasional expletive and words of encouragement to Maria. This strange trio bought traffic to a temporary halt as we crossed over the main road south of St Paul's and disappeared into the Cathedral churchyard where we lost the flasher in the shrubbery. He never returned to terrorize the secretaries of Garter House.

Life as a probationer was not always straightforward; it was not merely noting armorial and genealogical entries in the official records of the College of Arms and then turning notes into an authoritative report. There were incidents which might have disrupted a probationer's career. I recall a certain dinner at St James's Palace with the officers of one of the regiments of footguards. After a somewhat happy evening, it was decided that I should be fully dressed in regimental uniform to inspect the guard on duty at Buckingham Palace late at night. It is the only time that I have worn a bearskin; but at the last moment common sense prevailed. I suspect that a somewhat inebriated inspection would have led to my dismissal as a probationer and might have had serious consequences for the officers of the regiment concerned.

High jinks were not confined to St James's Palace. The College of Arms had its fair share. I recall the heat of a stifling summer's evening being dispelled by a sudden thunderstorm. This induced two members of the College to strip off and pirouette in the cooling downpour by the College of Arms dustbins.

They may have remembered to take with them their glasses of alcoholic refreshment; but they forgot their keys. Even Lily Bowering, the long-suffering and motherly caretaker, long used to College of Arms antics, must have been surprised to be confronted by two shamefaced and naked members of that establishment covering themselves with dustbin lids, asking for readmission to the College.

It was one of this entertaining couple that sought to give me advice on how to run a future practice at the College of Arms. 'Always offer your clients a drink.' he would say and sought to persuade others of this wisdom. These others were perhaps too easily convinced.

A new Knight of the Order of the Garter had been appointed and came to see Anthony Wagner regarding his grant of Armorial Bearings. This matter had been delegated to one of the Officers appointed in 1970. Our companionable and entertaining and nakedly cavorting member of staff had persuaded this Officer that Knights Companions of the Order of the Garter should be offered a glass of sherry. The Officer concurred, and our friend duly ordered a dozen bottles which he then volunteered to store in his own office. The Officer expressed his gratitude and handed over the relevant cheque. The newly appointed Knight Companion arrived at the College a few weeks later and accepted the offer of a glass of medium dry sherry. However, when the store place was examined, only a dozen empty bottles were to be found. The embarrassed Officer could only offer the Garter Knight a cup of coffee.

Shortly afterwards our companionable rogue, who had purchased the sherry, left the College; but the Officer who had paid for the sherry naturally complained that he needed to be reimbursed. Our friend handed over a fistful of Nigerian banknotes, stating that they would more than cover the cost of the sherry. He had departed from the College before the Officer was able to pass the Nigerian currency to his bank. When he eventually did this, he was informed that the notes had long ceased to be valid currency.

The same member of staff did not confine himself to drinking sherry in private. Quadruple Cluny whiskies were his usual tipple in the Horn Tavern behind the College of Arms. On one occasion he had persuaded Walter Chattey, the College of Arms 'cofferer', to join him for Christmas lunchtime celebrations. I had struck up a good friendship with Walter; and we frequently lunched together. On this occasion I declined to join him.

Walter had been in the Army and had been captured by the Japanese after the fall of Singapore. Knowing him, I doubt whether he was a fantasist. So I believe that his tale of running a secret radio station in the prisoner of war camp with a number of colleagues was true. They were all subjected to the breaking of a bone or finger each day before final execution. Walter was the sole survivor and recounted how he was kept in solitary confinement, occupying himself by passing tomato seeds and growing tomato plants beyond his prison bars. Certainly his crippled hands showed that he had had broken fingers; but I do know whether tomato seeds can be ingested and collected at the other end for replanting. He was an old man for his age, arthritis forcing him to use walking sticks and vociferously voicing his disapproval of the reinstatement of the Japanese Emperor Hirohito as a Knight Companion of the Order of the Garter.

On the day in question, Conrad Swan, as York Herald, was 'in waiting', or the Officer on duty. His rooms or chambers were adjacent to the office of Walter Chattey; and it did not take long before Conrad had assessed the aftermath of the Horn lunch and rightly decided that Walter with his sticks was not capable of driving safely back to his flat in Swan Court, Chelsea. Reasoning with Walter under these circumstances was not an option. Conrad and probably a dozen others attempted this to no avail. I was summoned. When I saw that match and cigarette did not meet, I realized that Walter's lunch had gone a little too far and took what I considered to be appropriate action. I told the assembled company to keep Walter occupied while I went to the College of Arms courtyard, lifted the bonnet of his car and disconnected the leads. Unfortunately the determined Walter had cast aside Heralds, artists, scriveners, secretaries and others to hobble onto the courtyard, with his sticks and obstinacy. Unfortunately he saw me tinkering with his car. This did not help our friendship and jeopardized my proba- tionership as Walter screamed outside Anthony Wagner's window 'your bloody man etc etc'. Friendships go through these tiresome periods. This tiresome period lasted several years until he eventually accepted the fact that I had tried to save his life, and our friendship was re-established.

He retired from the College, typically expressing irritation that he had been given Anthony Wagner's learned work *The Heralds of England* as a leaving present and not a crate of whisky. He never returned to the College; but I used to regularly see him in his sadly declining state at Swan Court; and I believe that I and the actress Dame Sybil Thorndike and members of his family were the only people to visit him.

His funeral was on a Monday; and in one of those curious coincidences in life, a College of Arms radiator in the gallery of our important Record Room had leaked over the weekend. The floor of the Record Room was possibly a centimetre deep in water, which was also dripping through one or two presses of eighteenth and nineteenth century papers and collections of past Heralds. A successful rescue operation was put immediately into effect that morning with help from national museums; it was also the morning that Louise Campbell had taken up her position as the College of Arms Archivist; Walter Chattey's funeral went ahead under circumstances which would have given him a puckish chuckle. In the meantime I had survived his untimely shoutings from the College of Arms courtyard under Anthony Wagner's window as to my unsuitability for appointment, and was duly appointed Bluemantle Pursuivant of Arms in late March 1973.

It was during these uncertain years that I began to experience the loss of family. The first close member to go was Muriel, who died in 1966 on the twelfth of March, which so happened to be the birthday which I shared with Banny. As might be expected, Muriel left a whimsical will with forty-two legatees including the Dalai Lama. Many of the legatees were Central European aristocrats with whom Muriel had long since lost contact. The solicitor and executor, one Mr Maby, approached me on more than one occasion to ask whether I had any knowledge of the Princess of this or the Countess of that. The best I could do was able to point out that 'Mrs Pickle', mentioned as a niece in the will was really Lady Tickell, Violet's daughter. He also informed me that it had been Muriel's original intention was that I should return sundry figures of Buddha and other deities to temples in Tibet. As Tibet was politically disturbed at the time, I was spared this task.

The original will had allowed for her flat in Lennox Gardens and her house in Sidney Street to be shared between Dick and myself. Unfortunately she sold both before her death, and it was the residual legatees comprising three charities that were to benefit. However, I did better than my mother, who was left non-existent furs and jewellery. I must qualify this by saying I believe there was one fur slipper, a pair of wooden earrings chased with silver and suspended by long silver chains. There was possibly a fox fur. On the other hand

I received £1,200 and was able to put this towards purchasing the cottage that had been partially occupied by the Stainer family and had become vacant on the death of the surviving Stainer daughter Bessie.

The last of the Whitwell daughters to die was Banny, who suddenly sustained a heavy stroke at the age of 86. Georgina and I were summoned to nurse her at Harthover. Her mind became somewhat befuddled, but in typical style her last instructions to me were to place five shillings each way on the celebrated Lester Piggott who was racing at Zermatt. Clearly her two interests of skiing and racing had become confused; but her great character remained with her to the end.

Dick and I were with her when she died. We closed her bedroom and went downstairs to the drawing room where Bobby and Georgina were waiting. It was evening, so stiff drinks were thought appropriate. I poured everyone a good whisky; and while the four of us were beginning to relax, there was a stupendous crash from somewhere upstairs. We looked at each other in astonishment and with some alarm. I went to investigate and was relieved to find that Banny had not fallen out of bed. I closed the door once more and went on a tour of the other bedrooms. The cause of the crash was in my own bedroom where a portrait of Banny's erstwhile husband had dislodged itself from its two nails and fallen to the ground. It is tempting to think that this was some manifestation of the paranormal. It caused us all to titter somewhat nervously; but I have to admit that I had straightened Granpy's portrait that morning, and this must have been the cause of the portrait's dislocation. Others may doubtless see it as Granpy's signal of distress at the arrival of his estranged wife into the spiritual world.

Dick stayed on at Harthover after Banny's death, helped by a legacy of his Harrison aunts, Granpy's sisters, known to me as 'the Edginswell aunts'. I had only once met them because of the trouble between Banny and Granpy. Nonetheless the two sisters, Violet and Evelyn, always sent me a box of chocolates for Christmas and birthdays. On their deaths they had set up a trust to provide an income for Martin, the maid. Property was also left to their chauffeur. Eventually I received a small legacy when the trust broke up on Martin's death at the age of nearly a hundred. I had to spend my legacy on retrieving a rather good portrait of Violet and a further aunt which Martin had somehow acquired.

Dick did not have to wait for the breakup of any trust as he had inherited the Harrison family portraits. This was a good collection, in which Sir Joshua Reynolds and Sir Nathaniel Dance featured prominently. Dick inevitably wished to sell every picture. The solicitors informed me that there was arguably yet another trust set up by my great-grandmother, Sir Richard Harrison's widow. After somewhat heated family arguments during which I found myself isolated, an agreement was reached whereby the two more important portraits by Reynolds were sold; and I acquired the rest for a nominal sum. I have thereafter spent the rest of my life surrounded by walls of sundry Harrisons interspersed with the occasional Quaker forebear.

Dick spent the proceeds of the Reynolds portraits within a year or so and then was forced to sell Harthover and take up residence in the Wares' bungalow at Spring House which the Wares had vacated shortly before Gavin's death in 1978. I had cut-down copies of the two Reynolds portraits painted by Theo Ramos, an artist of the classical school, who was reputedly the Queen Mother's favourite portrait painter. He was to become a good friend and my chauffeur at my first official tabarded appearance as an Officer of Arms.

However, before any such tabarded appearances occurred I continued to reside in my bedsitting room in Evelyn Gardens, the address which I lent to debutante mother Betty Gurney. Betty took pity on my impoverished state and informed me that I should have a break in Ireland. I was to accompany her and her two daughters, Sally and Nicola, to Donegal to meet up with the Howard clan. Betty's brother John had married one Esme Howard; and Esme and her sisters had Donegal ancestry and continued to take a Donegal lodge each year. David Gurney had flatly refused to accompany his mother, claiming that she was always late on the fishing bank in the morning, being too busy digging up worms. Furthermore her endeavours to spin for a salmon on live worms usually attracted an eel, which took too much time to unhook and despatch.

I was happy to dig for worms at eight in the morning and to dispose of an eel when summoned by the shriek of, 'Jones!' from Betty, who was invisible behind one or two bends of the river from where I was chucking in a dry fly to catch unimpressed trout. I was an outsider in the Howard clan, which was dominated by one Alison Gibbons, know affectionately as the 'Mother Superior'.

The 'Mother Superior' was prone to rising early in the morning and taking a skinny dip in the bay with her younger sister Lindesay Beaumont. On occasion the local vicar would pass by; and the heads of the two sisters would bob on the water, hiding their nudity beneath the waves while they conversed with the unsuspecting clergyman. After breakfast the 'Mother Superior' organized sundry projects, us fishermen being exempted. While Betty Gurney and I dug for worms, the others were sent on expeditions to hoick for crabs in the rocks left by the retreating tide, to raise the lobster pots in the bay from the rowing boat and to gather mushrooms on the precipitous slopes and vertiginous cliffs of Horn Head.

Horn Head House had belonged to the maternal grandfather of Alison and her siblings. Permission had been given by the grandfather for the villagers to cut reeds between the sea and the house during the First World War. In consequence the house was exposed, the wind blew sand to smother the drive and house, so that today all that is left is a half-buried shell and tops of dead trees emerging from the now grass-covered dunes, trees which once lined an impressive drive.

The 'Mother Superior's' sister, Lindesay Beaumont, enjoyed an affectionate rivalry with the Gurneys who had conferred upon her the nickname of 'Queen Hornet'. Lindesay was in high spirits on our arrival, and the bantering between Gurneys and Beaumonts soon began. As a stranger to the 'Queen Hornet' I became an obvious pawn. At dinner that evening she insisted on addressing any remarks to me through Betty Gurney, so that the topics of conversation usually began 'Betty, will you ask your friend Mr Jones . . .' Not surprisingly I found this type of conversation a trifle awkward and caught the eye of 'Baby Hornet', Lindesay's daughter, who was sitting on the right-hand side of her mother. This was Nicola Beaumont who with her auburn hair, button nose, and apprehensive and sympathetic stare was to become one of life's collectables and an exceptional friend. At that moment I felt I needed an ally; and the fourteen-year-old Nicola became just that. The Gurneys remained highly amused at Lindesay's verbal thrusts and could only remark 'How typical!'

However, matters were to change. The following day the 'Mother Superior' had laid out pedigrees of the Howard family for the edification and education of sundry Gibbons, Bougheys and Beaumonts. As a genealogist from the College of Arms I glanced at these pedigrees. I was then able to remark to Alison that the Howards had been Quakers and in two successive generations they had married into the families of my own Quaker forebears; the 'Queen Hornet' and I were therefore cousins. The 'Mother Superior' reported this fact to her sister; and I was immediately upgraded. The next dinner I was no longer 'your friend Mr Jones' sitting at the far end of the table; but instead was invited to sit on Lindesay's right between her and 'Baby Hornet'. I was now 'dear Peter'. The Gurneys were left at the end of the table somewhat gobsmacked, wondering how I had managed such promotion. Genealogy can sometimes play a practical and rewarding part in life.

My fishing holidays in Donegal were my only journeys out of the United Kingdom during these years, covering the late sixties and early seventies, when Irish politics were somewhat explosive. The border between north and south had its memorable moments. On one occasion my map reading led us to an unauthorized crossing where an innocent country lane seemed to meander across the border. 'Keep going,' I said to Betty. 'Do not stop until someone starts shooting!' We sped on our way, and no bullets followed us. On a second occasion we did find an authorized crossing and when asked whether we had anything to declare, Betty said 'Yes, I have gunnera'. The border official was clearly bemused; there must have been a fair chance that he thought gunnera was to be identified with a sexually transmitted disease. He therefore sped us on our way very rapidly. Betty had in fact seen gunnera plants growing by the side of the road and had asked me to cut off one or two great clusters of seeds to plant around a pond at the Gurney Norfolk home, Bawdeswell Hall. For my part, I was conveying back to Dorset two or three young rowan saplings for my newly-acquired landscape gardening projects.

CHAPTER 11

Geese

A T SPRING HOUSE THE STABLES were gradually emptying of horses, and family equestrian interests were confined to building show-jumping courses, inspecting pony club camps and judging at sundry shows. Horses and ponies no longer grazed in the paddocks. The family cows were reduced to a single Jersey, and John Ware took on a job as groundsman as Sherborne School. He no longer milked cows morning and evening, and his growing fruit and vegetables in the back garden was abandoned with the arrival of the new Sherborne supermarket.

The consequence of these changes was that paddocks and garden were soon in need of attention. Nature needed to be kept in check; and this provided me with a new interest, which I alternated with fishing at weekends away from London. Fruit cages were demolished; vegetable patches were dug up; and I bought various books on gardening, which led me to plan an ambitious garden layout, even running to ideas for a lily pond. Although I managed to acquire considerable knowledge of shrubs, my success at growing them was somewhat limited. I spent money on shrubs which then inexplicably died or more visibly were attacked by the Spring House wildlife. In many parts of the garden the soil was very shallow and a spade-depth down hit solid rock. Between surface and rock there was a network of animal activity. In wet weather it was a sponge of vole tunnels, whilst the drystone walls held a large population of shrews that used to scuttle across the front path where the wall was broken by the front garden gate. The flowers in the beds in the front garden were frequently clipped by some small mammal, possibly the shrews; and I would watch the clippings being dragged away into the wall to be turned into nesting material.

The shrubs suffered particularly badly from the voles. I remember looking out of the bathroom window while shaving to see a choice daphne bush suddenly keel over. Its roots had been attacked by the vole population who also frustrated all my attempts to grow clematis up the apple trees and which seemed to consume every crocus bulb which I planted at the base of the apple tree trunks. The only successful clematis was a rampant montana which I planted at the corner of the house where the thatch dipped low towards the ground. This rampant montana took over the thatch; and I was repeatedly having to cut it down. It remains one of the few shrubs at Spring House which has survived my gardening days and must continue to irritate the present owners. The rowan saplings from Donegal dried up and died. The grass and weeds flourished.

Birds and butterflies were acceptable, particularly those sixteen species of butterflies seen whilst walking round the garden with a gin and tonic before lunch on Saturday; but the excessive sproutings of hemlock and cow parsley were another matter. Help was required to attack all the various grasses, weeds and umbellifers in the sundry paddocks, orchards and lawns. In midsummer it would take me nearly the whole weekend to cover everywhere; and I duly went on strike.

It was a Sunday lunch when I drew the attention of my mother and Gavin to the need for such help which I suggested might be in the form of a grazing animal. As this was no long provided by horse or pony, perhaps a goat would be a good idea. This was immediately dismissed as unacceptable. My friend Roddy Llewellyn already had a goat on his hippy commune in Wiltshire. Apparently this goat had caused problems of an unsocial nature, and Roddy informed me that it was being put into a trailer and sent down to Dorset. Parental disapproval meant that I had to act rapidly to forestall the arrival of Roddy's goat. Instead I mentioned sheep as a further possibility. My mother proceeded to give a lengthy lecture on sheep rot and bovine maggots. This was the first time that I became aware that my mother had any great knowledge of sheep.

If horses, goats and sheep were not possible, then I said it had to be geese. There was silence around the dining room table, which I took to be some sort of assent; and the following week I asked Conrad Swan to arrange for geese to be sent from Suffolk to the College of Arms. Conrad had a house in Suffolk and an interest in ornamental fowl.

In due course I set off for Liverpool Street Station to collect my geese, only to find that Nicola Gurney was meeting the same train to collect a nanny from the West Indies. The nanny was on the train, but my geese were not. After a few telephone calls I learned that the geese had come on an earlier train and were now in left luggage. I went there and collected two cardboard boxes, presuming that each contained one bird – a goose and a gander. I suspect that they were already traumatized before they were driven in a taxi to the College of Arms where they were to spend the night before being taxied once more, this time to Waterloo Station. I had been advised not to attempt to feed or water them. The geese therefore remained anonymous in their cardboard boxes, and they were placed in the luggage van to travel from Waterloo to Sherborne.

At Salisbury I suddenly noticed the two boxes on the platform as the train was about to leave. I yelled at a porter to put my boxes back onto the train. They were thrown into the luggage van as the train left the station, and the porter muttered some incoherence in my direction. This incoherence became clearer when I arrive at Sherborne Station. I moved into the luggage van to supervise the situation. As the boxes were lifted onto the platform, I was confronted by a station official who informed me that transport of animal life in the United Kingdom required a licence. As I did not have a licence the geese would have to be returned to Suffolk. I have no idea whether this was United Kingdom or European legislation; but I was aware that some animal life at least moved around the country without any such bureaucratic nonsense. When I pressed the official on this point, he explained that no licence was required on a train for dogs, cats or birds in a cage. I exclaimed 'These are birds in a cage', picked up each box and walked out of the station to the car park where I found my waiting mother, placed the boxes in the boot of her car; and we drove back to Spring House with two traumatized geese without their licence.

In the meantime, I had abandoned the idea of a lily pond and had dug a goose pond in the paddock opposite Spring House. I had also rabbit wired the paddock to prevent escape, so all was set to open the boxes and release their content. I opened the boxes by the side of my back-breakingly dug pond and two grey-brown bodies with black heads and necks with white bibs shot out and lay gasping among the umbellifers. These were Canada geese, alien river bandits from North America, but were nonetheless more attractive than the traditional heavy and low-slung greylag goose and its farmyard derivative. I needed to establish a working relationship with these foreign and distressed strangers who were intended to keep the Spring House grass under control.

Having released the geese into their rabbit-wired paddock with its pond, I returned to the front garden seat outside the Spring House dining room window with a glass of gin and tonic in hand. A few sips later, there was a sudden plop and a goose appeared on the lane in front of Spring House. My rabbit wire had failed. John Ware and his wife Verna were customarily eating their lunch in the kitchen. John was immediately summoned and the two of us gave chase; he caught the gander on the Sherborne Dorchester highway and gave chase to the goose through sundry Long Burton back gardens where he eventually trapped her. I fear my contribution to this operation is memorably negative.

The two geese were put into the walled back garden where they promptly disappeared under a honeysuckle bush only to re-emerge for some tentative nibbling at the lawn some twelve hours later. In the meantime, I had erected a pen of galvanised tin set in a two-foot perimeter around the paddock pond and subsequently put them in this enclosed surrounding. For five days I sat with them writing and dictating various heraldic articles and becoming goose-oriented. However ridiculous it may sound, I leant the basic language of goose honking, high and low pitched, quick and slow; and its use was remarkable in establishing a closely-knit gaggle of three, goose, gander and myself. It is an ignorant presumption prevailing among human beings that their pets and animals should respond to the English language. Little old ladies in countless suburban houses chatter to their budgerigars in English and farmers swear at their pigs and cows in the same language without for one moment considering that they might obtain a greater rapport if they used budgerigar or pig language. My honking, which I also extended to goose behaviour generally, was one of my life's most rewarding experiences. Behaviour extended to sharing varied bobbings and watery bouncings in the pond.

Sally Binding, who was working for me at the College of Arms, had named the geese Llewellyn and Louise after our two respective second Christian names. These two geese never related to other human beings; and even my mother, giving them additional grass cuttings, would be greeted with a hiss. On the other hand, they recognized my car arriving late on a Friday night from London, and I would never be allowed to go to bed without crossing over the front lane to the goose paddock to respond to their honking. They would rush from their roosting place at the side of the pond to greet me. I would honk, they would honk and there would be a prolonged greeting which might last for some twenty minutes. No touch was allowed except with Louise who would gently tweak my nose with her beak, which I reciprocated with my fingers.

The only physical contact with Llewellyn came with his somewhat aggressive behaviour in the spring. He decided to lower his head and give me a formidable peck. Being goose oriented, I bent down with thumb, forefinger and index finger forming a beak and pecked back at him. We had two such pecking sessions which established the goose gaggle order. Llewellyn's peckings were thereafter reduced to a sly stalking as I was gardening. He would then lurch for my shirt-tails. This was a macho goose; and he enjoyed nothing better than a good tug-of-war. It was good for both of us; but he knew who was boss.

Louise was perhaps more feminine. I worked with her and arguably taught her to respond to my pointing. I would indicate the existence of a dandelion with a forefinger, Louise would look at my forefinger, gently peck at it and then between us we would find the dandelion. I cannot claim that I actually achieved a fully-trained pointing goose, but we came very near to it. This was strengthened after Llewellyn was decapitated by a marauding Blackmore Vale fox. My mother telephoned the College of Arms; and I issued the instruction of 'Catch her and put her in the stables'. Louise was never allowed back to the fox-prone paddock.

She took up residence beneath the kitchen window; but at weekends I took her down to a second pond in a second paddock. It was new territory for her; I would have to go into the water first, making my own splashes, before she could be coaxed in. Thereafter she could be left to swim and dive, splash and flap, but it was essential that we kept in contact. Wherever I was in house or garden, it was necessary for me to keep up a honking contact. If she honked and I did not reply, goose panic would set in; and she would wander around the paddock honking frantically. I suspect she was not a happy bird living under the kitchen window waiting for my arrival at weekends. In addition to her pond splashings on these weekends she would come with me for a walk. There was then an uneasy stand off between Louise and the poodles, who were more interested in chasing rabbits. Louise would walk along happily behind my heels until she decided she had had enough when she promptly sat down and refused to move. She was waiting for me to pick her up. She spent the rest of the walk happily tucked under my arm.

Her death has always remained a mystery. Goose feathers were found over the stile on the far side of the main road passing through the village. As Louise never ventured anywhere near the road, I can only surmise that a Blackmore Vale fox had found her and she gave him a jolly good chase. We can all look at Canada geese as bandits of the waterways, and two flocks fly impersonally over my flat in Chelsea; but thanks to Louise and Llewellyn I am aware that those flocks contain great individuals with very different and special personalities.

Years later I was to spend nights in Bath, the historic home of Blackbeard the Pirate, on the banks of the Pamlico River in North Carolina, where someone had shot one of a pair of Canada geese which had attacked his dog. The surviving goose honked painfully on that shore night after night, searching for its mate. I was reminded of Louise and the failure that humans have in trying to communicate with animals on their own animal level.

With the death of Louise, grass, cow parsley and hemlock sought to re-establish themselves, but I persuaded my parents to employ a gardener, paid for by me out of the rent from the Stainer cottage. I was not prepared to re-burden myself with excessive gardening duties, for I was now Bluemantle Pursuivant and had a practice at the College of Arms to establish and run.

CHAPTER 12

Bluemantle

MY APPOINTMENT AS BLUEMANTLE PURSUIVANT had taken place shortly before the Sherborne one-day event where Gavin was organizing either the show-jumping or the dressage or possibly both. Resigned to his stepson joining 'Alice in Wonderland', he had arranged for unexpected interviews with sundry journalists. Their articles even extended into South Africa, where my real father was walking his dog when he was confronted by fellow dog walkers informing him that his son had become news in the South African press. I think and hope this news provided him with social ammunition to add to his tweed-suited charm with the ladies on the Kenilworth Racecourse and the cocktail party circle of the Cape peninsular.

As Bluemantle Pursuivant, I immediately discovered that I had inherited Bluemantle's Cricket Club; and Herbert Hunter, the secretary, telephoned me to give me details of the fixture between 'the Patron's Eleven' against 'Bluemantle's Cricket Club'. I was therefore to raise the Patron's Eleven. Trying to arrange a cricket eleven was not something I had expected on my appointment as an officer of arms. I soon discovered that my few cricketing acquaintances would only play cricket with others whom they knew and with whom they could indulge in pub drinks between and after forays onto the field.

I telephoned Philip Letts, my old housemaster, who had once been responsible for making me games prefect. It is possibly the only occasion that I knew Philip convulsed in laughter. I reminded him that I had been elected a member of the MCC at the age of fifteen by courtesy of my uncle Ted Leatham. My early membership was a mistake. Ted had put me down at birth but shortly afterwards the rules allowing for this had changed. I had been overlooked and in consequence became possibly the youngest member ever to be elected. Gavin had intervened and tactfully written to the MCC to point out their error. I was re-elected shortly afterwards and was able to sport the gaudy red and yellow tie of an establishment in which I fear I really had little interest. I remained a member of the MCC, but eventually concluded that the expense of belonging to a club to take friends to watch two schools playing against each other once a year was unnecessary; particularly as I had been at neither school. I therefore resigned. However, Bluemantle's Cricket Club was now a different situation. Philip thankfully rose to the occasion and over the years I was able to gather together some sort of side which eventually revolved around Nigel Wilkinson, who had captained the Uppingham School side. Nigel took charge of the situation, which continued until I ceased to be Bluemantle Pursuivant and become Lancaster Herald in 1982.

Cricket teams and even race meetings with their Bluemantle Stakes aside, I began practising as an Officer of Arms in October 1973. I had been held back from practising for six months until suitable chambers had been found for me within the College. This was a ploy of Anthony's to keep me within his own practice, which I refused to accept. It was all go, as eventually Anthony released me, and I was permitted to sit in the waiting room or reception area of the College of Arms to receive and talk to potential clients. In my first week, Monday, Tuesday and Wednesday each provided four paid-up cases with cheques of £25 over the counter. On Thursday I received £100 for genealogical research from a future cabinet minister; and on Friday I received my first application for a grant of armorial bearings. These were all members of the public calling at the College of Arms in person. The greater number of enquiries came by letter. Cases would, of course, consist of members of the general public, including a high proportion of Australian and American tourists, calling in and asking whether or not they had a coat of arms. Others would write in, anxious to trace their pedigree or for an identification to be made of armorials on silver, in bookplates or other items of domestic use.

The initial answer to these requests was to suggest a search being made among the official records of the College of Arms in order to see if the armorials were authentic and if so to whom they had been properly granted or confirmed. At the same time searches could be made to see what relevant pedigrees had at any time been recorded. These searches and subsequent reports attracted fees, which were set by the Officer in waiting. In 1973 I would charge £20 or £25; and it was this type of work, which provided two thirds of the income for my practice. It was not a huge amount; but after five years it enabled me to move from my bedsitting room in Evelyn Gardens into a small flat in Chelsea; and 79 Harcourt Terrace, irritating though its small size may be, has remained my residence ever since. However, it does have a roof garden; and my lost youth from Dorset is recaptured by sundry plant pots and bird feeders. There is also a goodly colony of holly blue butterflies which I suspect is totally unappreciated by my urbanite neighbours.

The official records of the College of Arms date back to the thirteenth century, the thirteenth, fourteenth and fifteenth centuries being represented by mediaeval rolls of arms. However, it was not until the fifteenth century, following royal directives, that the granting, control and regulating of armorial bearings became vested in the Kings of Arms. In the sixteenth century there was prodigious granting activity, starting with Sir Thomas Wriothesley, Garter King of Arms, at the beginning of the century, and culminating with Robert Cooke and William Camden who were successively Clarenceux King of Arms at the end of that century.

It was also during the sixteenth century that the Heralds, on behalf of the Kings of Arms, conducted their visitations, which were systematic surveys of all the counties of England, summoning, under Earl Marshal's warrant, all those considered to be 'gentlemen' or entitled to armorial bearings. Proof of entitlement, either by long usage or specific grant, was required before an official entry of the armorial bearings and the pedigree of the family entitled to the them were entered in the visitation books. Supplementary papers relating to these visitations show that those officers acting on behalf of the Kings of Arms must have had an enjoyable time. If they were not staying in private houses, they were put up in the local hostelry and surviving bills of fare show that 'capons' and 'lapins' were washed down by considerable quantities of mead and claret. Claret was measured in pints. The tip left for the serving maid sometimes far exceeded the cost for full board and lodging; and I wonder what service she was providing.

The visitations ended with the seventeenth century. Thereafter proof of descent establishing entitlement to armorial bearings was placed on a voluntary basis. However, it is not possible for an Officer of Arms today to provide a painting of armorial bearings certified in the name of a person unless that person has been properly recorded. A similar situation prevails with peerage and baronetcy titles, where rolls of the same are kept with the Ministry of Justice. A peer may not be deemed such until he or she has proved succession to the satisfaction of Garter King of Arms and thereby placed on the Peers Roll. I worked to establish a Royal Warrant to create such a roll on the abolition of the hereditary peers in the House of Lords. Without such a roll, the peerage would have degenerated, ultimately attracting frauds, con men and crazy eccentrics claiming to be Lord this and Lord that, supported by unscrupulous solicitors and others seeking to make sizeable amounts of money by acquiring so-called titles for their clients. The now discredited sale of lordships of manors falls into this category, as does the changing of a name by deed poll, thereby introducing the style or title duke, marquess, earl and so on. Happily, such changes of name by deed poll are now rejected for registration as being deceptive.

All grants of arms continued to be recorded and indexed in the official records following the cessation of the visitations after the Civil War. Pedigree registrations on a voluntary basis have also continued, with each pedigree being supported by contemporary documentary evidences. It is not until a Pursuivant and a Herald have examined the pedigree against these evidences and accepted the same that the pedigree goes forward for engrossment in the relevant book of record. Engrossment is by pen and black ink, skilfully employed by the Clerk of the Records and his assistant. The dedication of these two is remarkable.

The Clerk of the Records, Keith Evans, came to the College some fifty years ago and has given me invaluable support and advice as Garter. His assistant, Amy Hunnisett, is equally capable with pen and ink and provides me with a humorous annual outlet with the hanging of her Christmas stocking. Amy's stocking with sundry beasties on sticks, chocolate whizzgos, flamboyant pink fluffy feathered flamingoes or bouncy Father Christmases containing chocolate buttons in their stomachs has become a College of Arms annual event and a garterial outlet for artistic imagination and amusement.

If the £20 or £25 gathered in waiting did not reveal anything of relevance, I would explain in my report that in view of the disappointing results I had extended my searches beyond my original undertaking. This meant that I had consulted such as indices of wills or miscellaneous marriages in order to pinpoint a particular surname or the family in question, hoping that this would lead on to a further cheque for outside genealogical research and tracing a pedigree.

Genealogy or researching a pedigree has received considerable publication in recent years; and an increasing number of evidences have become available on the internet. In consequence genealogical commissions at the College of Arms have diminished; but in 1973 I was attracting sufficient work to employ my own genealogist.

Contrary to a popular view of British ossified class structure, British society has always been remarkably mobile. In general, the Victorian gentry were not the gentry of the visitation period. However, this is not a lecture on genealogy; it is sufficient to say that my practice as a junior Pursuivant attracted genealogical research which was frequently interesting and sometimes surprising. I had, for example, to break the news to a certain admiral that his father was not his biological father; but unknown to himself he was an adopted child. I also was able to trace a master butcher in Rochdale, Lancashire, back through the male line to a blind fiddler in Whitchurch in the eighteenth century and thence back again, legitimately and patrilineally, to one of our ducal houses. It was Grosvenor, the family of the Duke of Westminster.

Sadly, genealogy often attracts the deluded. Alabama has produced at least one 'George VI', who was not concerned about his throne but simply demanded the return of his crown and sceptre. Ireland yielded a fantasist who stormed into my chambers claiming to be the daughter of Queen Elizabeth, the Queen Mother. She explained in great detail that she had given multiple births, the figure of some twenty or thirty at a time being comparable to those fanciful reports of mediaeval monks. In an endeavour to resolve her problems I asked her age. When she volunteered this, I consulted the printed *Burke's Peerage*; and drew attention to the Queen Mother's age and suggested that it might have been impossible for the Queen Mother to have given birth at the age of ten or thereabouts. This proved not to be a good tactic. She seized my *Burke's Peerage* and flung it into the air, while I was subjected to a torrent of verbal abuse. I hastily retreated into saying, 'How very interesting. Now let us consider this quietly.'

In the meantime I discreetly telephoned the hall porter and said, 'Please come'. Thankfully, Harry Bowering, the porter, knew me sufficiently well to realize from the tone of my voice that something was wrong. He recruited the assistant hall porter; and both of them climbed up the stairs to my rooms, frogmarched the lady out of the College of Arms and promptly locked the gates. She sought to climb over the gates, yelling and screaming that we were 'in league with that bloody woman in Buckingham Palace'. It is easy to chuckle and relate such a story thirty years on; but it is touched with sadness. I often wonder why life has been so cruel as to drive these people into their nightmare world. Curiously, these fantasists have declined over the years; and my file 'nut cases' has received little recent replenishment. I have no immediate explanation for this. There is no doubt that the effects of the Second World War impinged on mental stability. Modern medicine has had a mitigating effect, and the internet has kept others fully occupied.

Colin Cole used to misquote Tennyson saying 'A lovely lady in her charms is worth a thousand coats of arms.' My first week in waiting gave me my first grant of arms which set me on my way to Tennyson's attributed target. I remain on course to achieve this by the time I retire. Tennyson in fact wrote 'A simple maiden in her flower is worth a hundred coats of arms'. I prefer Colin's version.

Heraldic design is, of course, largely subjective but I would like to think that my thousand designs will have some influence in the long history and development of heraldry which stretches from the twelfth century renaissance down to the present day. The most satisfactory designs are probably those that occur spontaneously. The grantee, either by correspondence or personal interview, is invited to make suggestions. In general, their ideas are limited; and in consequence I can claim responsibility for the great majority of my one thousand designs. Unfortunately there are a handful that I look back upon with some reservation; whatever entered my mind when I thought up that particular armorial!

My first thought in reaching a design is to find an animal for the crest, trying to avoid the over-used and ever popular lion, stag and birds of prey. My childhood interest in natural history has enhanced the heraldic menagerie as crests of a punning nature have introduced a wide range of wildlife. I have found that puns and occupations are usually rewarding. However, I have yet to recruit the giant anteater as a crest. After several attempts I have persuaded one peer to have a pair of giant anteaters in suitable heraldic tincture as his supporters, anteater being a pun on his forename of Anthony. Although I have used crickets as an allusion to the game, Colin Cowdrey being an example, I have not succeeded with the scarab or dung beetle. I am still hopeful that a football player will accept a green dung beetle rolling its ball of dung, suitably depicted in heraldic gold, as a desirable crest.

I have been rather more successful with the armadillo for masters of the Armourers and Braziers Company and military grantees involved with tanks; and I appear to have acquired a certain notoriety for the unusual with the crest of a rabbit-eared bandicoot, granted to an Australian, with the bandicoot playing bagpipes.

Centuries of heraldic design and tradition allow for my bagpipe-playing bandicoot to be preferred to a polecat talking on a telephone. I firmly refused the telephone; and the polecat crest came into existence cheerfully playing a flute rather than using an item of nineteenth or twentieth-century technology. I feel such technology does not integrate well with heraldic tradition. The balance of originality, tradition and modern technology is not always easy. However, some chemical symbols, for example, lend themselves well to heraldry. On the other hand, it must be remembered that speed is timelessly represented by the arrow or the swallow, whereas a representation of the latest rocket from NASA could soon become outdated. It is this timeless quality which needs to be retained in heraldic design.

Once the crest animal, whether bandicoot, armadillo or anteater, has made itself apparent, I will then turn my attention to the shield of arms. I have always found it difficult to arrange numerous devices in any form of satisfactory design; and I have criticized much twentieth century heraldic design as being similar to a badly arranged shelf of antiques in the Portabello Road. Ideas and allusions need to be condensed. Very often the same charge can be made to double up as a pun, occupation or hobby. For example, I once designed a badge for a cat-loving chiropodist; the heraldic badge simply featured a cat's footprint within a circular surround. The roadrunner, that splendid ground cuckoo of cartoon fame found in the American south west, entered heraldry with two wavy blue bars on a white background, representing the River Thames. These were set between three roadrunners in suitable heraldic tinctures as an allusion to the London Marathon. In my search for simplicity and distinctiveness, I have a tendency to stay with the geometric. Instead of a cricket bat or pads, I have tended to use three vertical bars or pallets to suggest stumps. Roundels or spheres suggest cricket balls. Conjoined chequers outlined on three sides with a different tincture can suggest football goalposts; I would not entertain the idea of football boots in heraldry. Other chequers divided diagonally in blue and white can suggest white sails on a blue sea, hence providing an allusion to sailing better than a representation of a yacht.

My friend Sir John Stuttard, a past Lord Mayor of London, wished to have a skiing lion as a crest. Rightly or wrongly I insisted that the skis be removed. The ski sticks remain; and I certainly objected to the idea of bobble hat and goggles. I sometimes wonder whether I was too strict; but it has given John great delight; and his skiing lion and my objections have featured in many city dinner speeches. John's Arms consist of black pallets or vertical bars on gold surmounted by four red roundels, the whole suggesting an abacus and hence his career. However, condensing and doubling up of devices might have been suggested by John's surname of Stuttard and his interest in skiing. Diagonal and indented bends i.e. stripes might have suggested a 'stuttering line' and also skiing slopes. We decided instead to allow his career in financial matters to dictate the nature of his shield of arms.

In addition to the day-to-day running of a practice in heraldry and genealogy from my chambers in the College, there were the state ceremonials. My first wearing of buckle shoes, tights, black breeches and tailed red tunic was at the 1973 annual Garter Service in St George's Chapel, Windsor. I was the last officer to pay for his own uniform. Denis Healey, subsequently Chancellor of the Exchequer, was to take pity on the heralds; and the Treasury came to the rescue of my juniors.

That first ceremonial outing was a hot day. I recruited Theo Ramos, the copier of my seventeenth century forebears painted by Reynolds. Chauffeur Theo turned up at my bedsitting room in Evelyn Gardens with his silver Bentley and conveyed me down to

Windsor. Heralds picnic at Runnymede meadows on the banks of the River Thames with umbrellas, game pies and champagne. Heralds' wives and staff bring goodies out of the boot of their cars and colourful parasols are set up. It is a precursor to Ascot week; and the groups of Heralds and their friends provide a flavour of British life to the bemusement of American tourists cruising up or down the Thames. Tempted though I was, I refrained over the years from taking a rod and flicking a dry fly over the Thames when bedecked in court dress.

On a more serious note, my chauffeur-driven silver Bentley swept me to the State Entrance in Windsor Castle. Windsor Castle, like the House of Lords and Buckingham Palace, is a somewhat mystifying labyrinth of grand rooms; it is advisable to know the whereabouts of loos and to acquire friends and allies among the staff.

On this occasion, Theo left me at the State Entrance; and for the first time I met a tabard, which is the panelled coat comprising the Royal Arms back and front and also on the sleeves. It was heavy; and it was not until I put on middle age weight that I lost the dreadful throbbing in the shoulders which I was to experience on subsequent state occasions, particularly the Opening of Parliament.

The Heralds lined up in St George's Chamber in front of the Garter Knights. The Queen arrived at the far end of the chamber. Garter Wagner signalled with his sceptre; and we began to process through the chamber down the Grand Stairs, out of the State Entrance and into a sunny afternoon where the Heralds met up with the Military Knights of Windsor. The whole procession then continued past cheering crowds lining the route through the lawns and courtyards of Windsor Castle. After the Military Knights of Windsor, I led the Heralds' section of the procession with Theo Mathew, Rouge Dragon Pursuivant. The crowds cheered, I kept my sergeant major face, learned at Wellington, straight ahead. My mind wondered why I had suddenly gone back into prep school shorts. The sense of the tabard ending just above the knee occupied my thoughts as I tried to become accustomed to this new garb. It was almost a mystic occasion as we entered the chapel to the blast of state trumpeters and made our way up the aisle to the quire of St George's Chapel at Windsor. Mystic it may have been until we turned right towards the altar for the reciting of the creed. Thin soles and a measure of nerves, combined with a hot day, left a nice wet footprint. I suspect that this right turn with my wet footprints and a line of other similar footprints on the floor of St George's might have delighted some mischievous photographer.

The Garter Service was ended. Members of the Royal Family, the Garter Knights and Heralds stood on the steps as their cars arrived in turn. Although I was obviously at the end of this procession, Theo and his silver Bentley provided a certain stylish twist to its tail. That twist was destined for humiliation. After a champagne reception in a summery garden outside Windsor, Theo and I journeyed back to London; but somewhere in the suburbs the morning-coated Theo, the silver Bentley and Bluemantle Pursuivant in court dress found their convivial return to London brought to a sudden halt. The Bentley shuddered, stopped and emitted vast quantities of steam. Theo, whose car mechanic abilities are as doubtful as mine, muttered something about boiling engines. Leaving our erstwhile distinguished vehicle to cool down, we decided to repair to the local transport café where we enjoyed fried eggs and bacon. Theo has always recounted what then happened. Apparently in court dress and with sword I brushed against some rather more normal occupant of the café who exclaimed 'Hey, you 'ave an offensive weapon'; referring to my sword. Theo always maintains that I replied somewhat pompously saying, 'Do not worry my friend, I have a licence!'

Ceremonial duties have sometimes necessitated this carrying of a sword in public. The Lord Chancellor, Derry, Lord Irvine of Lairg, expressed horror when I told him that I would walk down the Earl's Court Road with a sword. I have on occasions done this; and thankfully London has never questioned or threatened such mildly unusual behaviour. A court sword is perhaps rather different from gang-related flick knives; and Earls Court Station is easier to find than seeking a taxi in the rush hour in order to travel from the Earls Court area to the College of Arms near Blackfriars. Bear in mind a uniform will fit in a suitcase; but a sword will not.

CHAPTER 13

North America

IN ADDITION TO BUILDING UP a genealogical and heraldic practice at the College of Arms, interspersed with the occasional ceremonial, lecturing and writing were part of my life as Bluemantle Pursuivant. Writing was confined to now long-forgotten articles and dual authorship which included a book entitled *Mediaeval Warfare*, a subject where I have to confess my knowledge was somewhat limited; but it was a coffee table book, selling well for two or three years. Lecturing was to become much more rewarding and exciting. In February 1980 I set out to cover nineteen American cities in twenty-one days, travelling into or through thirteen American states. It was to be my first heraldic tour of North America; and, five minutes from my London flat, the handle of my suitcase snapped.

My conscientious Secretary, Joyce Carter, had noted that New England was gripped in frostbite weather, so I had been duly equipped with a furry hat made from Canadian beaver, gloves, sheepskin liners and other warm but heavy items of clothing. A dinner jacket and suits, including the inevitable tweed suit for Boston, were also necessities. Even spreading the load between two suitcases, a briefcase and a box of carouselled lecture slides, the weight proved too much.

Later that day I risked frostbite in Boston to purchase rope and made a passable attempt at lashing a new handle, drawing on my experience with rope and knots with the 'tweenies' at Wellington. That particular suitcase subsequently survived eighteen cities and corresponding air flights; but then, alas, I watched it coming down the baggage collection chute at Syracuse Airport with an eighteen-inch slash on its topside through which my shirts and underpants were seeking to escape.

That February and March saw the first of a number of trips to the United States which allowed me to visit all fifty states of the Union. I soon learnt that a Herald travelling in the States on heraldic matters should not expect luggage to lighten as the tour proceeds. Letters

Patent of Armorial Bearings can be thankfully shed at handing-over ceremonies; but in return the Americans are ever generous and often impractical in their gifts. Six glass tumblers suitably engraved were presented to me on the east coast of Florida. I managed to juggle with them and the rest of my luggage across that state and with some relief was able to discard them with my next host and hostess.

Books are a great favourite; no less than five were presented to me in Savannah, Georgia. The kindest and most improbable gift also came from Georgia. My itinerary was altered in order that I might be driven fifty miles or more to receive a special Georgian country delicacy. I was presented with a large jar of blackberries! The presentation was made by a local Georgian farmer who showed me his blackberry bushes with considerable pride; and we discussed the wildlife of his 'yard'. He explained to me that snakes were a frequent problem. He had long disposed of them by picking them up by the tail and cracking them like a whip, thus breaking their necks. Recently he had misjudged his technique and ended up with an angry rattlesnake in his hands. He had flung it over the wall before it had time to bite him. We discussed how he might deal with his snake problem in the future; but reached no satisfactory conclusion.

Formal presentations of Letters Patent of Armorial Bearings and lecture occasions are normally predictable except for the unexpected intrusion of God and country. Saluting the flag and singing the *Stars and Stripes* is easy to accept, and in return American audiences seem prepared to sing *God Save the Queen*. However, lecturers in the South must be prepared to sing *Dixie* while little old ladies in long white dresses attempt to hold back their tears at meetings of the daughters of this or that group of historical dames.

Those going to Canada need not be concerned with learning the Canadian national anthem. In October 1983 I went to Victoria, Vancouver, and felt it necessary to spend hours memorizing *O Canada*. I spent hours pacing up and down my room in the imposing Empress Hotel learning both this anthem and my speech for the following day. The next morning I stood in morning coat in the hotel foyer while bemused American guests were held back. A convoy of limousines and motor bicycle outriders drew up outside. Officials came to shake me by the hand and I was introduced to my ADC. I still do not know what duties the latter was supposed to perform. I was ushered into one of the limousines; and taken off to inspect a guard of honour.

Thereafter the Deputy Governor of British Columbia, the Mayor and myself mounted a dais in the civic centre for the handing over of the Letters Patent ceremony. The band struck up with *God Save the Queen*; and all the assembled company sang lustily. After a brief pause there followed the Canadian national anthem. The audience remained silent; and I proved to be the only person present who knew the words. I gave up after the first line, somewhat irritated that my hours of memorizing the night before had been wasted.

In general, American patriotism is acceptable and unalarming. The real problems can arise with God. I soon learnt the necessity of being prepared to say grace. Fortunately my memory recalled that used at St Andrews: 'For what we are about to receive may the Lord make us truly thankful.' I have frequently used this, holding my neighbours hands as I speak. This often happens with outstretched arms so that my head has been bowed in suitable humility over my food. Well can I remember trying to prevent my nose bobbing down into the black-eyed peas and turnips tops in a plantation house in Louisiana while this typical Southern fare was duly blessed.

Such a simple thing as a pocket proves to be a desirable receptacle for visiting cards and also choice linen napkins often embroidered with personal monograms or state flowers and birds. These accompany heavily iced drinks. This napkin and ice etiquette, unfamiliar on this side of the Atlantic, leaves me placing discreetly the napkin into a pocket with the embarrassing consequence of clearing pockets on my return to London and wondering whose embroidered cardinal or dogwood is a missing item in an American napkin set. The pocket is not confined to secular drinks. The church is also involved; and God can again be problematical.

On being presented with a palm leaf on arrival at St Thomas's Church, Bath, North Carolina, I folded it up neatly and placed it in my pocket and then endeavoured to make polite conversation to the North Carolinian church congregation who, as ever, expressed their charm at having met me before any other exchange of words had taken place. I have always found this Southern effusiveness a trifle embarrassing. I am afraid I seldom progress beyond giving a wry grin and a few muttered words of something or other. I have never ever been able to formulate any standard form of natural and sincere response. Thankfully, North Carolinian friends are fully aware of this; and in this instance Josie Hookway was able to guide me through the Bath congregation to enter the church for the service. Taken by surprise, I found this entry was to be in the form of a procession. 'Where is your leaf?' enquired Josie. Hastily extracting my folded leaf from my pocket, I processed to my seat in the front row, holding it in a horizontal zigzag position. Everyone else's leaf was upright. It was Palm Sunday. My leaf was not a souvenir to be retained. I left it behind on the pew.

Churches in the Bible Belt of America are packed. Churchgoing in the Bible Belt is a social occasion and must bear similarity to that of Victorian England. The congregation is dressed in its Sunday best; and, driving to church with Eleanor and Leon Bradshaw in Salisbury, also in North Carolina, I have become conscious that there are as many churches as there are pubs in an English country town. The Bradshaw church has a particularly vertiginous balcony and their favoured position is in its alarming front row. Here too my pocket proved a problem. Being taken unawares, I suddenly had to dig into it to find a note. As all banknotes in America are green, it is easy to make a mistake. I was immediately convinced that I had donated one hundred dollars. Eleanor Bradshaw, who has long kept a motherly eye on me, noting my quizzical expression whispered 'What is wrong with you now?'

'I think I gave a hundred dollars'.

'Do not worry,' she assured me. 'We will get it back afterwards.'

A Baptist reunion day in Georgia sounds harmless enough. On that occasion God-fearing Baptists had made their way from all over the United States and come back to their home roots for the event. I had been invited to the gathering, and after an early morning religious discussion group, to which I unsurprisingly contributed little, I made my way into a packed church. The minister from the pulpit welcomed guests. Then a cold sweat began to trickle down my spine as I heard the words 'and among our gathering today there is a special guest from England'. All eyes sought me out; and I was invited to address the assembled company for five to ten minutes. I eventually became used to such introductions and have encountered these on such improbable occasions as Chapter Meetings of Daughters of the

Confederacy to an evening of Scottish reels in a Polish dance hall in upstate New York.

I have found that family genealogy has proved particularly useful on such occasions. I explain that the first of my forebears to come to America was shot in the rump by an Indian poisoned arrow during the American War of Independence. This was a Colonel Alexander Patterson who was defending his estate outside Montreal. The arrow killed him; and the family returned to London, not to come back until the American Civil War when Alexander's great-grandson, Richard Harrison, returned to North America, as a Military Observer for the British Government. He was mistaken for a spy by a Southern picket. A noose was slung over the branch of a tree; and he was about to be strung up when a timely messenger arrived to say that he was to be spared. He recalled the incident in his autobiography and repeated it in an article on his experiences in America for *Blackwood's Magazine*. Not surprisingly, the family avoided North America thereafter until Richard's great-grandson, namely myself, made his appearance.

I then find it expedient to thank the audience for their welcome and hospitality, pointing out that they have more than made up for the disgraceful behaviour that their American forebears meted out to my own ancestors. In this way, I have found that ancestors can actually be put to practical use!

Impromptu speeches, television and newspaper interviews, and chairing seminars at universities and problems in church all lay in the future, as I landed at Boston's Logan International Airport to discover that my Bostonian friend with whom I had arranged to stay for three nights had suddenly gone to the West Indies with her new boyfriend. In consequence, she had booked me into the Copley Square Hotel. On enquiring of my taxi driver, the latter informed me that this hotel was only used by 'little old ladies'. In spite of this inauspicious start, I soon found myself caught up in Bostonian social life, thanks to the English Speaking Union and to Tom Parker, the director of Boston's State House Museum who was responsible for my first impromptu speech after lunch for some literary club. I had to speak in reply to the Chilean Ambassador. I believe this was the first time that my ancestors were called upon to provide 'speech material'.

After three nights in Boston my lecture tour was scheduled to begin with my first presentation at Yale University. The train journey from Boston to Newhaven gave me my initial impressions of the American countryside and its people. Two of these impressions have proved lasting, the size of the houses and the quantity of trees. I was not to see a single field on the east coast until I neared Baltimore long after Newhaven; and I still believe that a bear could walk from the Canadian border to Florida without leaving woodland except to cross the occasional road. One thing which I did not notice on this first tour was the size of the American people.

Subsequently I have become more and more aware of this and find American obesity both grotesque and sad. I once had to travel overnight from Rocky Mount, North Carolina down to Miami. I sat next door to an ample black lady with her paper bags, out of which came a non-stop supply of junk food which she ate throughout the night. It was hardly surprising that I felt more and more squashed into my corner window seat. I fear this is typical of far too many Americans, particularly young girls whose thighs seem welded together with fat and who are only able to waddle from the knees down. Unfortunately thirty years later the British seem to be following suit.

My first address at Yale University was marred by the absence of any workable projector. As heraldry is essentially a visual subject, slides are vital. Wine flowed freely until a projector was eventually found. I was learning another lesson; it is necessary to try and check equipment well in advance of delivering a lecture, otherwise bulbs may not work and electrical leads may be too short. The endless jamming of a machine can keep you on the podium for no less than two and a half hours, as I discovered in Cleveland, Ohio. Worse still, a projector in Oklahoma City gobbled up each slide in turn and spewed it out onto the floor in tiny shreds of celluloid. Happily this last disaster came towards the end of my first tour; and I had been wise enough to keep some slides in reserve.

Newhaven and Yale were followed by New York, Baltimore and Columbus, Ohio. For me Columbus was particularly notable for my first sight of the cardinal: the scarlet bird with crest and black mask ranks as one of my great first birding sights as it flew through snow-laden gardens of the graceful Columbus suburbia.

Columbus also yielded the Harmons, who remained good friends until they died. Cosme Harmon was subsequently responsible for introducing me to old people's homes in Santa Barbara, California. I stayed with her in one such home and was introduced to playing scrabble with 'the little ole ladies' of that establishment. I do not think that I have ever come across such blatant cheating and viciousness. In spite of being a guest, English spelling was disallowed; and I was able to convince myself that the absence of 'little ole men' was caused by the bullying and harrying of their wives which drove them into an early grave.

Cleveland followed Columbus; and then came Memphis where I had a day off duty. In a letter to my mother I find that my 'so-called day of rest consisted of breakfast in a place overlooking the river, a visit to a cotton-weaving factory, a drive over the river into Arkansas, lunch with some genealogically-minded group, a press conference, tea with another group, dinner (Mississippi frogs' legs), followed by a concert.' This so-called day off was followed by Oklahoma City, Tulsa, Kansas City, St Louis, Indianapolis, Chicago, Milwaukee, Buffalo and back to New York. Each day normally began with an early flight to the next destination. There was then either a press conference or a reception followed by lunch. The afternoon would consist of a visit to the local attraction such as the Oklahoma Cowboy Hall of Fame, the bridge at St Louis swaying in a snow storm, the arboretums at Milwaukee or the Niagara Falls near Buffalo. There would then be a return to the house of my host and hostess for that night in order to change prior to a further reception, dinner and my presentation.

1980 was followed by a second tour exactly a year later. This covered Virginia, the Carolinas, Georgia, Florida and a return visit to Kansas City. North Carolina provided me with long-term friends. There was Ralph Rives of Enfield who greeted me at Greenville Airport with the words 'Thank God you do not look like your photograph'; and subsequently bounced me into forty-five minutes talking on 'Being British' at East Carolina University in North Carolina. There were Eleanor and Leon Bradshaw of Salisbury who invited to dinner two 'suitable' women. The first was an elderly Admiral's widow on two sticks whom I had to help down the steps into the sunken dining room. The second had been a girlfriend of President Woodrow Wilson. This situation was rectified the follow-ing morning when Sally Hibbert, in her twenties, was produced from the house next door. She too became a great friend until her untimely death in an air crash outside Jacksonville in Florida, shortly after she had been staying with me in Dorset with her fiancé, Paul Greenwood. Paul was ultimately to be responsible for my forty-eighth state, Vermont, which we visited together on a birdwatching expedition.

The 1981 tour ended in New York at a small dinner party attended by an English woman whom I vaguely recognized. It soon became clear to me that her wits may have been confused by the gin bottle. During the course of dinner, conversation turned to Dorset; and thinking that we might have mutual acquaintances I mentioned one or two of them to her. I was surprised when she told me that the only people she knew in Dorset were Gavin and Daphne Young and then went on to say that Gavin had recently been particularly busy with horse events. When I informed her that Gavin had died three years previously, she refused to accept this information and announced to the assembled company that her great friend Daphne would have told her of this and that Daphne had recently been embarking on a series of wildly extravagant shopping sprees.

When I let her know that Daphne had died a year previously, she insinuated that I was talking rubbish. Eventually she posed a question 'Anyway, how do you know these people?' To this I simply replied 'You are talking about my parents.' There was a stunned silence around the dining room table; and I changed the conversation immediately.

My introduction to the western half of the United States came in 1983 following an exhibition of heraldry in New York. Following New York came my presentation in Chicago and then my efforts to learn *Oh Canada the Fair* in Victoria, British Columbia, before spending two nights with the Mormons in Salt Lake City.

I had been reassured that my host in Salt Lake City was not a Mormon, because I have difficulty in coming to terms with the Mormon faith. It then transpired that the reason why my host was not a Mormon was because his views were so extreme that he had been ejected from the church. These views included plural marriage. One wife had died; and, although currently married to a pretty young blonde, he was seeking a further wife or wives. The blonde informed me that she was perfectly happy with this situation. The problem with plural marriage is that it encourages breeding; and the house, which was furnished with psychedelic carpets and starry wallpaper, was full of uncontrollable Mormon children. I slept in a room next door to children pillow-fighting late into the night, interspersed with their frequent visits to the 'bathroom'.

The next morning I was taken up into the mountains to visit the vaults containing Mormon records. At least three vast portcullises sealed the entrances to the mountainside. As we drove up, a voice boomed out demanding that we identify ourselves. This done, one portcullis rose; and I and my excommunicated Mormon host went through a tunnel to be greeted at the end by armed guards. I believe I was only the fourth or fifth non-Mormon to be allowed into the mountain that year; and it was now October. Computerization of records was everywhere apparent; and the whole structure was designed to withstand nuclear warfare. I refrained from commenting that I thought the area was also prone to earthquakes for which there seemed to be no contingency plans. That evening, I delivered my address to repeated interruptions from members of the audience who saw Mormonism in every heraldic device; esoteric arguments developed as to Christ's marriage at Cana in Galilee. The number of Christ's wives and marriages increased as the evening moved on.

A visit to the main library in Salt Lake City revealed that some of my Harrison forebears had been 're-sealed' as Mormons. As this included three generations of seventeenth century clergy, I wondered why re-sealing was necessary for them to obtain salvation. It transpired that the person responsible for this re-sealing was no member of the family. I therefore queried why an outsider should take it upon himself to interfere with the salvation of my forebears and asked whether I could have them un-sealed and returned to their former spiritual state. This was not well received.

Denver followed Salt Lake City. My hope that I would be able to relax with a single lecture to the Denver branch of the English Speaking Union was dashed. My host was a professor at the university and had lined me up to chair a seminar on Britain's position on the nuclear bomb. I have always found that American students or undergraduates are very different from their British counterparts. Whereas British undergraduates can hold strong opinions, which often lead to belligerency, the American student, in contrast, seems hesitant to come forward; and when he or she does so it is always with extreme politeness and deference.

Denver was no exception; and the bland nature of the seminar was only rescued by one girl who had been very forthright and held strong anti-bomb opinions. She approached me afterwards and apologized for being too outspoken. I was able to tell her, with sincerity, that she was the best thing that had happened to the seminar. It was a pity that some of her fellow students did not differ from American government policy. Their attitude may have been the result of ignorance, but I sense it may have been a form of patriotism which does not allow for disagreement with any current administration's policy. Possibly the British Monarchy assists in keeping a greater distance between British patriotism and the dictates of any Foreign Secretary.

Denver was followed by Mobile in Alabama where I was one of the patrons of the British Fair. This meant giving two presentations a day and receiving a park on behalf of the British people, given to us by the citizens of Mobile. A proper English town crier had been produced; and after suitably disclaiming, Edwina Sandys, my fellow patron and the granddaughter of Sir Winston Churchill, and I took possession. Unfortunately, the park seemed to be a disused and deserted downtown plot, but presumably the idea was to plant it up with trees. I do not know whether Edwina has ever returned to Mobile; but I have not.

Mobile was followed in quick succession by Shrieveport (Louisiana), Jackson (Mississippi), Birmingham (Alabama), Montgomery (Alabama), Chattanooga (Tennessee), Atlanta (Georgia) and Cochran (Georgia). This was a trip which did much to increase my knowledge of Southern food. Whilst I was able to appreciate the quail, champagne and strawberries for breakfast in the Napier household outside Montgomery, I developed a particular dislike for grits. This is often served at breakfast and consists of a coarse oatmeal. Grits presented me with problems in Cochran.

I had been lent a charming antebellum house named Ebenezer Hall, complete with my own manservant. This was on campus at Middle Georgia College in Cochran. The College was being made suitably armigerous. Apart from handing over the Letters Patent and receiving the citizenship of Cochran, I had agreed to give a series of talks on heraldry. On my first morning at Ebenezer Hall, my manservant served a gargantuan Southern breakfast, complete with the inevitable grits. I managed to eat most of the breakfast, but left some toast and the grits. This greatly upset the well-intentioned manservant. I explained to him that I found grits difficult and expressed the hope that they would be omitted from my breakfast in future.

The following morning I overslept. Not wishing to cause further offence, and being in a hurry to reach my first lecture, I took my breakfast to the 'bathroom', tearing up the toast and fried bread and disposing of them down the loo. All disappeared until I came to the fried eggs. I flushed and for two seconds they went away only to reappear sunny side up. I had blocked the loo. During the later morning break, I repeated flushing and succeeded in bringing the water over the seat. I was reduced to mopping the flood with towels. A wire coat hanger proved useless in acting as a drain rod and served only to etch grey squiggles on the porcelain.

I did not have the courage to explain to the Principal of Middle George College that I had blocked his drain; but, happily, I was able to persuade him to take me into Cochran, whose citizens had kindly presented me with the Freedom of their city. The Principal was somewhat bemused and explained to me there was little or nothing of merit for me to see in Cochran. I persisted, saying I wished to absorb 'my city'. I succeeded in my ploy and found myself left alone in the high street. Assistants in the hardware store in a small Georgian town had probably never met an Englishman, let alone an English-man asking for a plunger. The charming and helpful assistant found me a plunger and even wrapped it so as to disguise its exact nature. I am happy to report that the plunger did its work and is probably still to be found packed at the back of the cupboard beneath the kitchen sink in Ebenezer Hall.

My relief was not to be entire. Two days later a grinning girl approached me on campus and said that she had heard I had been in Cochran. It transpired that her sister was the assistant in the hardware store. I was caught out. The news of what had happened doubtless spread throughout the College.

I left Cochran and from Atlanta flew to El Paso, West Texas. My friends, and great benefactors of the College of Arms, Ian and Anne

Robinson had lent me their house at Ruidoso in New Mexico to relax for a few days before returning to London. At El Paso I hired a car. As I have recounted elsewhere, my driving is perhaps a little lacking in experience and practice. It was the first time that I had driven in America; and I had no previous experience of automatic gears. In consequence when I put my foot onto what I presumed to be the clutch the car stopped abruptly, giving rise to a number of exasperated hoots from cars behind.

Eventually I led a line of cars out of the airport and onto the El Paso strip. Somehow I kept going, along what seemed to be the longest strip I had ever encountered; but eventually I found myself alone on the road leading through the Chihuahua desert with its yuccas and prickly pears. I was just beginning to relax when I was waved down by a policeman. Fully expecting to be fined or worse for some driving misdemeanour, I was therefore pleasantly surprised to discover that he was checking for 'wetbacks' illegally crossing from Mexico. He was equally surprised to discover that I had an English accent, which he seemed incapable of understanding; and this understanding seemed also to extend to knowledge as to England's location in the world.

This is not as far fetched as it may at first seem. On more than one occasion I have had to explain that I come from England, only to be greeted by a puzzled expression and the suggestion that 'Gee, that's somewhere north of New York ain't it?' The accent can also be tiresome.

Although not in America, I was recently travelling on a train in Germany with my Herald Painter Gillian Barlow when a pretty blonde came aboard, dragging after her a heavy backpack liberally covered with the stars and stripes. On observing her difficulty, Gillian made an overture to assist by saying, 'That looks rather heavy'; to which the American replied; 'I am so sorry but I don't speak German'. Gillian replied; 'I know, that is why I addressed you in English', and received a somewhat puzzled 'Oh'. In consequence I am afraid we both left her to manage her own backpack.

Thankfully my policeman on the Texan/New Mexican border accepted my accent; and I sped on my way to Ruidoso for a few days of relaxation and bird watching. The absent but ever-generous Robinsons had invited me to help myself to all food and drink; but I felt the drink supply must at least be replenished, so I took my car down the mountainside into the main street of Ruidoso where I parked. As I was still mastering the technique of driving an automatic car, I considered that shopping on foot might be wiser. This caused considerable consternation at a drive-in liquor store; and I had to negotiate my way in through the staff entrance. My first visit to Ruidoso was extending my knowledge of the American way of life.

My second visit to Ruidoso in the fall or autumn of 1985 brought me into contact with Native America. Ian and Anne's house was on the edge of the Mescalero Apache Reservation, which included the Sierra Blanco Ski Resort and the Inn of the Mountain Gods. Anne and Ian had bought a small ranch outside Ruidoso and shortly after their arrival had gone to the Inn of the Mountain Gods for a meal. Ian had a liking for pottering around shops and, finding a shop in the inn, had engaged the girl behind the counter in conversation. Ian explained that he and his wife had recently bought a nearby ranch and asked her advice about shopping in Ruidoso. On being asked where she did her shopping in the town, she replied 'We don't'. On enquiring further, she explained to Ian that she and her husband did their shopping in Paris. Ian subsequently told me that 'the conversation then changed gear'. The girl was Rita, the vivacious Navaho wife of Wendell Chinot, the President of the Mescalero Apaches. The Robinsons and the Chinots became great friends and in consequence during my 1985 visit, I returned to the house in the middle of the morning to be told that Wendell had invited me to lunch. When I commented that Wendell was some one hundred and fifty miles away in Albuquerque, I was informed that he had sent his private plane. Ian and I went to the airport to board Apache I, with its plush leather seats and cocktail cabinet. The pilot flew us to Wendell's own private gate at Albuquerque Airport.

The principal purpose of this lunch was for me to design armorial bearings for the Mescalero Apache Tribe. This I did before lunch over a gin and tonic. Thinking that a European shield would be somewhat incongruous, I decided to use a round Apache shield upon which I placed the traditional four-pointed Apache star between four crescents. The supporters on either side consisted of Apache spirit dancers; and the shield was crowned with an Apache spirit dancer's headdress. On my return to London I persuaded Colin Cole, in his capacity as Garter King of Arms, to accept this design.

An arrangement exists whereby the Kings of Arms may devise armorial bearings for American corporate bodies, provided agreement is obtained from the Governor of the state in which that corporate body is sited. This was not necessary in the case of the Mescalero Apache Indians whose reservation, with other Indian reservations, does not form part of any state. The devisal of arms was eventually handed over to Wendell Chinot at a dinner in Claridge's; and I understand that the document is now a prominent exhibit in the Mescalero Museum.

My encounter with Apaches was not confined to Wendell and his wife Rita. Anne and Ian were largely based at their home, Kilcoy Castle, near Inverness. Their house in London and their ranch in New Mexico were visited less often. The ranch was a relatively modest establishment; and the half dozen or so horses were looked after by one Ted who was Wendell's horse keeper. Ted had a particularly attractive Mexican girlfriend called Esperanza whose responsibility was to look after the Robinson house. I recall arriving at the house after Ian, Anne and myself had spent a few days in the Big Bend National Park where Anne and I had been heavily into migratory warblers. I noted that the large vase of flowers on the mantelpiece of the Robinsons' house was in need of attention, as it contained two very dead and bloated mice. The next day at the ranch, Ian and Ted were discussing horses while Anne and I climbed up the hill to the corral. On the way I spotted a horse's foot; and on our return comment was passed to Ian who asked Ted what this meant. Ted replied that there was nothing to worry about as it was the remains of a wild horse, brought in by the coyotes.

I had observed that none of the Robinson horses appeared to have only three feet; however Ted's explanation did not seem to me to be very satisfactory. I murmured to Anne that it must have been a somewhat peculiar wild horse, as there was a shoe on the foot.

Perhaps the above were indicators as to what later transpired. Ted and Esperanza duly produced a child and announced their marriage. Anne and Ian decided on a wedding present. The happy couple were to be flown on Concorde to London where they were to stay at Claridge's. They were then to go to Austria where I seem to recall the Robinsons had purchased a property. This was to be followed by a visit to Kilcoy Castle and a return flight on Concorde to New York and thence back to the reservation. Any problems at Claridge's would be referred to me at the College of Arms. The couple did indeed turn up at the College, complete with baby or papoose slung over Esperanza's back. I sorted out one or two minor problems, but both Claridge's and the College of Arms must have been reminded of that film *Crocodile Dundee*. Once back on the reservation, I understand that Esperanza hopped over the border and disappeared with a rich Mexican businessman. The marriage had apparently never taken place. Nonetheless the papoose was accepted into the tribe, which was one happy ending to this saga.

I was to become much involved with the Heraldic Exhibition in New York which opened in 1984. This was an opportunity to have an office outing. Julia Hett and Louise Campbell were then both working in my office. All three of us flew to Seattle in September 1984 and toured the northern Rockies, becoming experts on the difference between pine, spruce, hemlock and fir. In absorbing spectacular scenery, we encountered cowboy culture. Louise's father had been a cook on the cowboy waggon trail and had eventually settled on his own homestead near Spokane. Louise had moved from her homestead background through university into the archival world and had then been taken on as the College of Arms archivist. She was then subsequently purloined by me to assist with various projects in my office. Her uncle lived at Yakima in the state of Washington and was able to explain to us the finer points of cowboy culture at the Yakima Rodeo before we attended the annual buffalo roundup at Missoula in Montana.

I was intrigued to notice that the dog of the Wild West was clearly the poodle. Pick-up trucks containing the carcase of deer would frequently accommodate a poodle guarding the would-be venison; and poodles were to be seen running along behind their cowboy masters as they crossed the range. It was curious to see poodles following the horses, something for which the Spring House poodles had never shown any inclination. It was the rabbits which had held their attention.

Perhaps somewhat disappointingly, the cowboys themselves appeared lacking in vitality. A typical bar in the Wild West would contain cowboys slumped over the counter, nursing a glass of their chosen liquor. It was at Deer Lodge in Montana that Julia attempted to liven proceedings. Leaping onto the bar, she proceeded to lift up her skirts and hopscotch over the glasses along the length of the counter. It was to little avail. One or two of the cowboys lifted their heads with little or no expression of surprise before returning to their slumped positions. Arlene, the barmaid, was the only person to respond to Julia's antics. She suggested that a repeat performance might not be a good idea as it could lead to violence.

Ten days later Julia endeavoured to waken up Keystone in South Dakota by sitting crossed legged in the middle of the road. This too produced no response from the local inhabitants; and Julia had to accept that the only reaction she was going to get from the Wild West was from an irritated Englishman who was anxious to get back into the car, drive on to the nearest motel and have a good night's sleep. Night drives should not involve sitting crossed legged in the middle of the road but should be looking for porcupines, skunks and other wildlife.

There were plenty of porcupines and skunks in the next two or three days. Dusk and nightfall are rewarding with porcupines in particular coming out in the evening and possibly trying to take salt or some mineral from the road. The problem is to try and cut them off before they disappear into a storm drain. Leaping from the car, I endeavoured to head them off; and Julia was able to take good photographs of a porcupine on the road between us, sitting up in agitation on its hind legs. I had run the risk of breaking my neck in a hidden storm drain; and both of us had run the risk of being heavily punctured with porcupine quills with the animal using its defence mechanism of charging rapidly backwards. My sole defence was the sole of my foot; and I am not certain what Julia had apart from a flapping handkerchief.

This particular trip ended at Sioux Falls in South Dakota. I flew back to New York to attend various functions in connection with the Heraldic Exhibition. At a cocktail party that evening I was asked about the flight from England and the weather in London. When I replied that I had not come from London but had flown in from Sioux Falls, it had a stunning effect. Manhattan society could not conceive that anyone could wish to visit Sioux Falls, wherever that was. I might as well have come from Mars.

One disappointment in this tour of the North West was the absence of bears. We worked around Glacier and Yellowstone

National Parks looking for bears and moose to no avail. The moose situation was eventually rectified in the Grand Tetons where the three of us were observing a Brewer's blackbird. I inadvertently swung my binoculars left; and a bull moose with cow and calf in tow came into view. In our excitement we moved forward and flushed two further moose who had been lying some twenty yards in front of us. There were further moose sightings that glorious autumn day. Beaver and bald-headed eagles were also apparent, but bear remained elusive.

It was not until August 1994 that I had proper encounters with the American black and grizzly bears. Louise by then had returned to Washington; and I went with her and her husband to the Canadian Rockies where we found black bear on more than one occasion by the roadside. Grizzlies followed after Louise had put me on a flight from Seattle to Ketchikan in Alaska. Alaska was to be my forty-fourth state, and far from being full of ice and snow, the temperature was in the high eighties. That evening I was able to write to the College of Arms to say that I had met my first Alaskan. She was a striking blonde with a commanding presence who sat next to me on the ferry from the airport to the mainland. She informed me that she had been visiting her son who was at university in Florida. I found this rather difficult to accept as I placed her in her mid twenties. Possibly the son was a stepson. During the course of the conversation I learnt that she lived in Ketchikan; and when I asked her what she did there, she replied that she was a striptease dancer in the Marine Bar. This too was reported in a letter to the College of Arms that evening: 'Guess what, I have met my first Alaskan; she is a striptease dancer . . .'

The following morning a P & O cruise ship berthed and spewed forth a high percentage of its two thousand odd passengers into the relatively small town of Ketchikan. I promptly disappeared through a tunnel into the rougher side of town in order to escape this invasion. I was immediately confronted with the Marine Bar. Although I had been warned that Alaskan women were not to be considered attractive, this warning was unjustified; and, although my particular friend was not working that day, her fellow dancers were certainly memorable.

A voyage of peaceful serenity on the State Marine Ferry took me from Ketchikan to Skagway. The waterway passed through pristine landscapes, and the only disturbance was the chug of the engine and breaching humpback whales. Skagway was the base town for the Klondike Gold Rush, the home of the outrageous Soapy Smith who exploited all the miners before they dragged themselves and their provisions over the White Horse Mountains into the Yukon. Soapy Smith was shot in 1898. The railroad subsequently came to Skagway; and I was able to cross the mountains through spectacular scenery in the comfort of a train before bussing on to White Horse, the Yukon capital. Apart from being dive bombed by a nesting glaucous gull on the banks of the Yukon River, it was intriguing to discover that this capital of a vast territory had only ten buildings on the side of a main street leading from river bank to wilderness.

After this Yukon detour, I returned to Alaska to catch up with grizzlies in Denali National Park and on the Kenai Peninsular. Like all bears, they are curiously nervous and skittish. With the exception of the polar bear, human beings are not high on bear menu. It is therefore only necessary not to disturb or alarm them or to provoke attack by taking food into the forest. When walking through grizzly bear territory, it is wise to make sufficient noise to ensure that the bear is aware of human presence. Some people walking in the wilderness will do this by tying bells around their ankles. I did not bother, but merely made a mental note that I should try to avoid approaching any bear nearer than twenty yards, or fifty yards in the case of a sow with offspring. I was able to watch a number of bears who were attracted by the upstream migration of salmon. The grizzly is a surprisingly aquatic animal; and I remember one in particular who spent most of his day in the nearby sound diving for his fish.

Bears' skittishness is not restricted to the grizzly. I have spent time in a hide in Riding Mountain in Manitoba where dog food was spread on the forest floor and deep-frozen beaver staked out to attract the American black bear. In this instance the bear was cinnamon coloured and, being frequently fed, might have become well used to human presence. On the contrary, the slightest noise would send it back into the deeper forest or to seek safety in the nearest tree.

My Manitoban host also provided me with a horse which had been schooled to a European style of saddle and European riding, suggesting a British rather than an American influence in the wilds of Canada. In addition to riding through country where moose and beaver were frequently encountered, we also drove south into North Dakota, bird watching lakes as we went. This allowed me to visit my forty-ninth state. I recall being charged some ten dollars at the border. I have crossed from Canada to the United States on many occasions and have never before or after encountered such a charge. I am convinced it went into the immigration officer's own pocket.

Crossing the border, it was immediately apparent that I was back in the United States for there was a huge model turtle in an outsize snowmobile. We dined in Bottineau, a small prairie town surrounded by sunflowers. Remarkably, the Scandinavian restaurant produced an excellent meal, far superior to any restaurant that might be expected in rural or Wild West America. It also yielded postcards of Tommy the Turtle and his snowmobile which I was able to send to American friends, stating that North Dakota did indeed exist and was in the forefront of American culture, drawing their attention to turtle and snowmobile. This was in the summer of 2000.

American culture also extends to embrace death. My friend Ralph Rives purchased his own tombstone, obtaining the same at a cut price when his mother died. The tombstone has been lying in the ground, suitably inscribed except for his year of death. He has accepted that this may not have been a good idea as members of the family at Christmas lay floral tributes on the tombstones of other members of the family, leaving his own unadorned. In consequence he has considered it necessary to purchase flowers to decorate his own stone so that passers by should not wonder whether his stone might not be for the forgotten or undeserving. Unfortunately there is now an ongoing problem with the cemetery gardener chipping the corner of the tombstone by over-enthusiastic use of his motor mowing machine.

Another American with whom I stayed for several nights filled the basement of her farm with Nicaraguan refugees. The basement also contained a large aluminium tank. I was led to believe that in this tank was preserved the body of her husband. The family burial plot was full; and I was invited to wander the sizeable garden to decide on a suitable site for her own burial in due course. Preferably it should have a good view over the rolling countryside; and when she had decided where she herself might be buried, then her husband's prolonged stay in the basement could be terminated; and he would be interred in advance of his wife.

It was not until the summer of 2004 that I finally managed my last and fiftieth state of the Union. After twenty-five years visiting America, Michigan had remained elusive. Julia, who had hop-scotched over bars in Montana and sat cross legged in the middle of the main road in Keystone of the Cop fame, agreed to come with me to Detroit before she went to stay with friends in Canada, and I departed to Wyoming to become a cowboy. I doubt whether many people decide to choose Detroit for a summer holiday; but the world-famous Detroit Zoo was of particular interest. I had read about it when I was a child and once again I was convinced that keeping animals in captivity is not always cruel, not least because wildlife freeloaders were clearly making use of its amenities. The amenities of Belle Isle also occupied us for the rest of a weekend where we studied American black weddings being processed in various tinctures of lilac, primrose and turquoise. Bridesmaids, ushers' waistcoats and stretched limousines with appropriate rosettes were all adorned in the chosen wedding colours. Sadly, we noted a measure of inebriation and a number of brides of unhappy appearance. Thereafter we flew to Copper Harbour on the banks of Lake Superior and ferried to Isle Royale, an island which is Michigan's only national park. It proved to be a wildlife disaster; migratory birds appear to fly east or west of it and sedentary birds appear to avoid it. We were reduced to walking the trails, learning the multitude of berries and identifying various conifers, becoming expert at the difference between fir and spruce, with cones up or down. Julia then departed to Canada; and I went to Twin Creek Ranch in Wyoming to be a cowboy.

After some thirty years, I had renewed my acquaintance with the horse in India. During the 1970s and early 1980s, I sustained a number of dislocated bone problems, largely brought on by child-hood riding. I had been warned by an osteopath that I should never ride again. However, I chose to ignore this and returned to the horse in India with its European style of riding and well-schooled Arabs. In 2002 I had summoned up equestrian courage to stay for ten days on Bellota Ranch in Arizona, taking in Forth Worth Zoo on the way. Bellota insists on taking 'experienced' riders only; and on my first excursion in a Western saddle, I was deliberately tested for my ability, I was relieved to find that I passed the test and even had to give a lead when my tester's horse became difficult. Thereafter, I was released with Jeff my wrangler to ride a mountainous and rocky range, two days of which were spent searching for a mare who was thought to have produced a foal. Apart from aching knees, I developed a reasonable relationship with my horse Bart. I wrote back to the College of Arms to suggest that Bart ought to be short for Baronet, but I assumed was short for Bartholomew.

In 2004 Twin Peaks, Wyoming, was rather different; and I was made to 'push' cows from nine to five without even a break for lunch, under the watchful eye of a Shoshone Indian named Peewee who had little patience for the ageing and unfit! I was sent up steep sagebrush slopes to retrieve wayward cows, swearing at horse and cow alike. Driving animals out of a creek, my cows would inevitably jump the creek and set off in the opposite direction. Curiously, the knees which had suffered in Arizona survived this ordeal; but every other bone in my body ached, and my voice was hoarse from shouting at both horse and cow. The unfamiliar Western saddle discovers muscles and positions unknown to anyone brought up riding in the English fashion. Neck reining is acceptable, but riding continuously on a loose rein is distinctly unnerving. In cowboy country the horse picks its own way; and in consequence I have difficulty in accepting that horse rather than rider controls the situation. This difficulty can lead to argument which is not advisable on the sagebrush slopes of Wyoming's Windrush Mountains, and certainly not when sagebrush turns into precipitous rocky drops into cottonwood creeks. Nonetheless, I returned to the College of Arms having visited my final state in the Union and fulfilling a childhood dream of being a cowboy.

What had begun with a lecture tour in 1980 had led on to additional tours combined with visiting friends and exploring the Wild West. When California came in, surprisingly late at state number forty-two, I decided that all fifty states should be visited. Perhaps I had returned to my childhood with its collation of lists of monkeys or Knights of the Round Table; and I felt a considerable satisfaction when number fifty was achieved.

CHAPTER 14

Mexico

I SPENT THE MORNING OF MY fortieth birthday in Tulsa, Oklahoma;
by lunchtime I was in Kansas City telephoning Dorset to check on
my mother; and in the evening I gave an address to members of the
Kansas City branch of the English Speaking Union before staying
with a retired horse judge, Colonel James Parker, with whom I
seemed to share many friends and acquaintances on both sides of the
Atlantic. A week later I returned from my first American tour, having
shed a good stone or fourteen pounds in weight, and went
immediately down to Dorset. It was March; in January my mother
had been diagnosed with motor neurone disease. Thankfully this
advanced rapidly. She was only to live for a further six weeks and
died on 3 May aged sixty-nine, having survived Gavin by a mere two
years.

At the same time Dick Gurney fell from his horse onto a Norfolk
road and died that night in Norwich Hospital. His daughter Mary, in
an unforgettable act of kindness, wished to be with me to give
support at my mother's memorial service and to stay with me at
Spring House. We juggled dates. Norwich Cathedral overflowed for
Dick; but the church service in the parish church at Long Burton for
my mother was more modest. The villagers had brought in flowers;
and I stood and spoke, explaining the nature of the service. I drew
attention to the organ music taken from the musical *Salad Days* to
reflect her early flapperish life. The first of the three hymns was *Cwm
Rhondda (Guide me O Thy Great Redeemer)*, the great Welsh rugger
hymn which had so often disrupted the drawing room at Spring
House when the television was turned on for rugger matches; and
Gavin would rise from his armchair and start singing lustily. It had
become the family national anthem; and I assume will in time be
played at my own funeral. Her second hymn was also poignant and
at her request, *Onward Christian Soldiers*, which she had muttered
under her breath as her horses took a fence either at a point to point
or on the hunting field. Lastly came *There is a green hill far away*. This

was her third choice and reflected her late afternoon walks to find a silent spot where she would look across at distant misty hills in the late evening, listening to the songs of birds and surrounded by her dogs. Her ashes joined those of Gavin at the head of the nuns' cemetery in the local Roman Catholic girls' school, where they had both helped with the riding and enjoyed walking the dogs in the extensive grounds overlooking the Blackmore Vale.

When Gavin had died, the Reverend Mother had called to extend sympathy; but my mother was not in the house as I had sent her away for a few days. This gave me the opportunity to give the Reverend Mother a glass of sherry, to enlist the school's aid in providing a choir for Gavin's Memorial Service in Sherborne Abbey and to ask whether his ashes could be interred in the nuns' cemetery. He had expressed the wish never to be buried in Long Burton churchyard as he did not want to be disturbed by farmer Sam Harris's cows depositing cow pats on top of him. He would prefer his ashes to be buried with the nuns, many of whom had been the subject of his teasing over the years. The Reverend Mother was enthusiastic: 'We would love to have the Colonel buried among our nunny buns!'

Some weeks later I placed the urn containing Gavin's ashes in the ground in the cypress surrounded cemetery with its nuns' gravestones. My mother with Gavin's favourite poodle on a lead and other family members stood by before returning to the main school buildings for tea and biscuits. Meanwhile, the Reverend Mother and I went down on our knees. This was not to pray, but to scoop the soil over Gavin's resting place. The Reverend Mother muttered something about 'foxes'; but I am not certain that a fox can break into an urn or that it would be interested in ashes. When my mother died two years later, the nuns dug up the ground again in preparation for a second internment. The nuns were kind enough to show their affection for my parents by putting up and paying for a brass plaque, the plaque being attached to the cemetery's crucifix. So ended my family life; and I was now on my own. The fox too had played its part at their end; and both Gavin and my mother would certainly not have objected.

I then set to work sorting out Spring House, despatching worn out horse blankets, dog baskets and opening up the dairy room, that repository of old fishing rods, First World War military equipment and trunks of family papers. In the course of the revamping of Spring House, I accepted a reverse telephone call from South Africa to say that my father had died and had been buried a few days earlier, a curious twist in my relationship with my paternal family. I suspect that the acceptance of a reversed charge telephone call to be told of a father's death is unusual.

Driving from London down to Dorset on a Friday evening became an impossible nightmare. I do not understand how people have second homes. Seven roundabouts on a Friday evening had to be negotiated before meeting the motorway. This was followed by a morning with my inherited daily, old Mrs Male, one of the last real villagers, who would cook me lunch and expound on local village gossip. We would agree that the countryside had disappeared; but I declined to examine the gallstones of her husband Percy which were kept in some bottle or jar as the Male family heirloom.

Thereafter there was Jerry the gardener. We would work cheerfully together revamping the Spring House garden in my determination to create a result worthy of Thomas Hardy's Wessex with a cottage-type garden in front of the house with its stone and thatch. Jerry and I were not assisted by some of my guests who all too frequently plucked up newly embedded plants, mistaking them for weeds, and leaving the latter. Other difficult guests suffered asthmatic problems from the dust created by the builders and decorators. It was back to London on a Sunday evening with another two and a half hours' tedious driving. Retaining the old homestead in Dorset was becoming increasingly difficult.

I held on to Spring House for a few more years; but after a serious burglary which relieved me of a quantity of swirling Dresden figures, clocks and, somewhat irritatingly, the first two cups which I had won on Diddles and Patball many years before, I sold it. I did however retain the Stainer cottage, renamed Well Cottage, and the Ware's bungalow, which was now occupied by my uncle Dick.

Dick was somewhat distressed at my sale and suddenly began to complain of stomach pains. He drove up to Scotland to paint grouse moors; but within twelve weeks he was dead. He was the last of my most immediate family.

At the end of the year of my mother's death I escaped to India, which has opened up a new dimension in my life. By the age of thirty-nine I had been tiresomely jilted or rejected by two or three girls and had decided that marriage with the risk of a scolding wife and reactionary children with the certainty of nagging and draining school fees might not be the answer to life. I had therefore decided to travel.

In the autumn of 1979, I had already embarked on international expeditions. My initial choice was India; but this was interrupted by my first lecture tour in America which diverted my new-found sense of adventure towards Mexico. I went to New York to arrange my first lecture tour and then went Mexico-bound to JFK Airport. I immediately learned that airports, airlines and I would never have an easy relationship. I was held back at the check-in desk to be told that my travel agent had failed to confirm my flight on an overbooked plane. At the last moment I was released and told to hurry. Seizing a fistful of passport, tickets, boarding pass and other documentation, I took this advice and started running. I promptly went through the wrong door and set off all the alarm bells in the airport. Setting off alarm bells in JFK Airport with all officials homing in as if I was a potential terrorist can presumably bring the whole airport to a juddering halt. Perhaps because I was British and was able to explain the situation I was allowed on board, being the last passenger to take my seat. I assume that JFK Airport returned to normal.

On arrival in Mexico City, I found a further problem which can confront the independent traveller. My local agent never appeared; and, apart from one or two telephone calls, I received no communication from that agent during the next three weeks. In consequence I had no vouchers and had to argue my way at each hotel. Eventually I was even reimbursed for my taxi fare from Mexico City Airport to the Hotel Reforma, where I arrived several hours after the alarm bells had rung at JFK Airport and half an hour after I had despaired of a travel agent and been forced to find my own taxi.

It is perhaps hardly surprising that after a little tidying up, I went straight to the bar for a stiff drink, bent on trying a genuine Mexican margarita in Mexico City. At the bar of the Hotel Reforma I encountered one Mario. Together we drank vicious margaritas and listened to a sinuous brunette cabaret girl singing a song whose main line was 'Push push the bush'. Mario then suggested I might like to see something of Mexico City at night. This proved to be an exotic and erotic experience as we went from nightclub to nightclub. During the course of much conviviality, a telephone call was made; and Mario's sister Bertha came to join us. I subsequently found myself in an awkward situation in a nightclub in the Zona Rosa when I bought a red rose and presented it to Bertha. Everyone in the nightclub stood up and applauded. It appeared that I was now seriously committed, if not engaged, to Bertha. Unfortunately, I did not find her attractive. In the early hours of the morning I managed to detach myself from Mario and Bertha, and gay propositioning waiters at nightclubs who had expressed the wish to sleep with me rather than the more attractive nude blondes in the Zona Rosa back rooms. I returned to the Hotel Reforma with a throbbing head. Risking the threat of Montezuma's revenge, the euphemism for violent diarrhoea, I drank quantities of tap water and rose three hours later with a clear head to take the hotel bus to the Teotithuacan pyramids of the sun and moon, where I found the prolific hatchings of Meso-American butterflies in November as exciting as the pyramids themselves.

The next day I took a tourist bus to Taxco, a town of white stuccoed red-tiled houses of Latin American charm. Taxco is a town famed for its silver and discovered by the conquistador Cortez. Half way between Mexico City and Taxco my bus stopped at some tourist emporium which sold everything from Mexican silverware to plastic Mexican donkeys. Within a minute I had wandered off and seen my first hummingbird, a small green hovering something which I was totally unable to identify from my field guide to Mexican birds. At Taxco my fellow tourists were once more organized and subjected to the tyranny of a tourist guide. Among the thirty or so tourists were included a lesbian couple from the Channel Islands of some intelligence, a charming Spanish Countess who had come to see how the ex-Spanish colony was progressing and an embarrassing English football fan from Newcastle who had never been abroad before. The latter's unbelievable behaviour made it somewhat awkward to be British. I was led to understand that he regarded the basin in the bedroom in the hotel at Taxco as a lavatory seat and brought the basin and himself to the floor. I somehow directed a rescue operation; and together we pacified the hotel authorities.

I joined my fellow tourists on the bus into Taxco the following morning; but sought to make an escape when they stopped at a silver store in the town. The tour guide grabbed me, as I refused to enter the store and started to explore Taxco on my own. As I was not a paid-up member of the group, I told him to go away. I then learned that tour guides can be aggressive. He attempted to manhandle me into the store; but I managed to shake him off, explaining that I was not really part of his group, and ignored his protests. I made for the cathedral, which was typically Spanish with two towers on the front facade and weeds sprouting luxuriantly from the roof. Inside was another tour guide; and listening to him I learned that the cathedral was exceptionally lucky in its possession of a picture painted by Peter Paul Rubens of St Bernadette of Lourdes. It was a somewhat indifferent painting, typical of those found in Latin American rural churches.

Gullible tourists may be taken in by an erroneous attribution to a major European artist of the seventeenth century; but how he came to paint a relatively modern saint who lived some two hundred and fifty years later, with a picture appearing in a cathedral in Southern Mexico somewhat stretches the imagination. It is distressing to think that Americans and other tourists, who pay considerable sums to travel abroad, are captivated by this deeply distressing rubbish. I recall that when the Channel Island girls and the English football fan eventually caught up with me as they entered the cathedral, I warned them of the St Bernadette picture and disappeared into a Taxco cobbled courtyard where a group of children were playing football. One of them stopped to ask me where I came from. I replied 'England'; once again in my life I was emphatically informed that England was somewhere north of New York.

Two days later I encountered another child. I was sitting having a meal with two American couples in an open square in Oaxaca when a girl aged about six appeared with her arms full of bunches of roses which she was trying to sell. I allowed myself to succumb to her appeals, bought the roses and, remembering my trouble with Bertha, decided not to present them to my American companions. I looked at the child who looked at me and with her smattering of English asked who the lucky recipient might be. I said; 'They are for you'. There are special moments in life which remain memorable; and that moment was one of them. The child's face changed from puzzlement to astonishment and then huge delight as she skipped off down the road, clutching her roses shouting 'Mama, Mama!' in her ecstatic excitement.

The following day I took a local bus for several hours drive through mountainous countryside where I recall counting seven ranges of hills, one behind the other, each set with pencil-like cactus. I had already encountered that somewhat uncouth English tourist; but I was now to discover his female counterpart. Creating a scene, she forced the bus driver to stop so that she might collect a tampax from a suitcase which was outside in the bus's storage compartment. In the meantime she had made her problem all too clear to everyone in the bus. Not surprising the Mexicans were astonished; and I was deeply embarrassed; I felt that I was party to an attitude which had established the British Raj in the nineteenth century! The British could not care a damn what others thought and did exactly what they wanted to do. This latter-day specimen of the British Raj, having stopped the bus, went outside, rummaged around in her suitcase or backpack before disappearing into the cactus. During these proceedings I recall another hummingbird; but species of Mexican hummingbirds were all beginning to look somewhat similar. It was to be many years before I mastered hummingbird identification.

My bus trip took me to San Cristobal de las Casas and Trudi Blom at Na Bolom, 'The House of the Jaguar', a converted monastery or convent, run by Trudi as a scientific and cultural institute, where I enjoyed her invitation to visit her private garden with further hovering, darting and unidentifiable hummingbirds. Sitting next door to Trudi at strictly teetotal meals, I was mesmerized by her ever-changing hair colour. At one meal she would be bright purple and at the next primrose yellow with various shades of orange and lilac in between. The lurid hair colour was supplemented by varied examples of Meso-American silverware which dangled from her ears. She was a woman of considerable presence and charm; and when I broke away from her and turned to my neighbour on the right, I would find a native American woman with breast exposed, suckling a baby. The alcohol situation was rectified in the evening by the Mexican Minister of Agriculture. From somewhere he produced bottles and like my first night in Mexico City, I probably deserved a hangover; but like Mexico City no hangover occurred. I returned to my room which was full of Indian artefacts and a resident colony of paper wasps. Happily paper wasps are inactive at night, and I was left to sleep in peace.

Shaving the following morning was another problem as the wasps were nesting over the mirror above the basin. Being somewhat cumbersome members of the wasp family, I was able to demolish a number of them. Eventually I decided that a sting from a wasp twice the size of English wasps was not worth it. I brushed the fifty or so which I had slaughtered on one side, went to breakfast, largely unshaved, and requested that my room be properly de-infested.

After three hours sleep following my last drinking session with the Minister, I was taken to the airport, only to find that the airport staff were on strike. I enlisted myself as ground staff and recruited two girls in their twenties. They were travelling together; one was a cropped-haired blonde Canadian and the other a long-dark-haired Indian. Together we pushed the plane out of the hanger. I noticed that it seemed to be held together with leather straps. I sat next to the pilot with the two girls behind me; the plane was at full capacity; and we set off with an alarming shudder, appearing to head straight towards the mountain. At the last moment we rose into a thunderstorm and ultimately descended into what I thought would be my first excursion into Amazonian tropical forest. Sadly Palenque Airport was set amongst green fields and cows. However the spectacular Mayan remains at Palenque, some distance removed from the airport, had been left in a small patch of tropical forest where every tree was smothered with bromeliads, lianas and other springing, sprouting, climbing and shooting plant life. It was even more luxuriant than I had expected.

It is difficult to realize that in Amazonian-type forests there is a greater quantity of animal life than anywhere else on the planet. It is silent except for such as the occasional shriek from a distant piha bird or the musical call of the tinamou; and movement seems restricted to the large blue morpho butterfly that will suddenly flap across the trail with its six-inch wingspan. Signs of wildlife become more apparent with a survey of leaves which are eaten, nibbled and generally attacked in a manner unseen in any English wood. Clearly things happen in the Latin American forest. Patience is required; and exactly like fishing, something happens every half an hour; I have always likened fishing to watching wildlife in these forests. At Palenque I was rewarded by the sight of something perched on a branch. My immediate reaction was that it was a monkey, possibly a marmoset or tamarin. Even in my comparative ignorance of Latin American forests, I then realized that the marmoset was not a possibility. It suddenly occurred to me that this was a trogon. The bird's grey back should be hiding a brilliant red and white front. For the first and only time in my life I was able to call a trogon and induce it to turn round. I was exactly right; and the pigeon-sized trogon turned and revealed its spectacular front. My identification was correct; and it was a slaty-backed trogon. Unfortunately, life moves on; and, years later, I now treat the many species of trogons in the tropics as being as commonplace as the song thrush in Dorset or the long-tailed tit in Chelsea.

Later that same evening at Palenque I went into a thatched cavernous barn with a dirt floor. At the far end there was an unattended bar. Between the bar and myself was a table with two burly moustached men sitting on either side of a black howler monkey. I enquired in English whether it was possible to obtain a drink; and one of the men replied, 'Thank goodness you spoke, as my friend here was about to shoot you.' He went on to explain that his friend's wife had run off with a man and that he had mistaken me for this man. He further explained that the monkey belonged to his friend, the bereaved husband, and that they were all on their way to seek consolation with a local prostitute. I accepted their invitation to join them in consuming the contents of their bottle, but declined to share any delights on offer from the ladies of Palenque. I have often wondered how the howler monkey fared in a brothel.

From Palenque I returned to Na Bolom. Trudi as ever was powering national events in Mexico. There was a conference of doctors. They were to return by flight from San Cristobal de las Casas to the Caribbean port of Villahermosa. I too was returning to Villahermosa by a series of taxis, buses and flights; in fact I had about ten or twelve legs of varied transport. The doctors joked, saying that Mexican transport would be such that I would arrive at Villahermosa several days later. I had chosen to travel in this way as I wished to enjoy mountain scenery which I had missed during the evening darkness of the day of my arrival at Na Bolom. The laughter was eventually on them as I arrived at Villahermosa Airport shortly before the doctors whose flight had been inexplicably but unsurprisingly delayed. All of us then spent the next hour or so catching black fly in test tubes from the airport windows. This was supposedly in the interest of science; but it seemed to cause consternation among the airport staff until we eventually persuaded them to join in. From Villahermosa, the doctors returned to Mexico City; and I went to Merida to enjoy the Mayan remains of the Yucatan Peninsular.

From the Yucatan I was to return to Mexico City. Mexican airlines decided to go on strike, so once more I was backed up in a queue. Chaos resulted as passengers remonstrated with airport staff. In the chaos I was exchanged from one list to another. Eventually my name was called from the top of the new list. I was not simply the Señor Gwynn-Jones. I was Señor and Señora Gwynn and Señor and Señora Jones. I had met up with my Canadian and Indian friends from San Cristobal de las Casas Airport. They were way down on the list and would never have made it on their own, so I grabbed them as my two wives, Señora Gwynn and Señora Jones. We went on board leaving scores of stranded passengers to an indeterminate future at Merida Airport.

My Mexican experience, as an individual traveller, introduced me to incompetent airlines and confusing airports. Over the years these have never improved. Mexico also introduced me to the difficulties of identifying the transitory hovering and darting of the humming-bird. This has proved a much more exciting challenge; and I can now claim to be a little more proficient at hummingbird identification. Watching them feed on spiky yellow-orange heliconid flowers in the Latin American forests is rather more tolerable than the dreary interior of a dreary airport with delayed flights and mislaid baggage.

CHAPTER 15

India

LECTURING IN AMERICA WITH ITS diversion to Mexico and the death of my mother had deferred my arrival in India where the *Jungle Book* stories of Kipling and my great-grandfather Harrison's part in the Indian Mutiny has always beckoned. It was in November of 1980 that I eventually arrived early in the morning at Delhi Airport. The plane was late. This was the old Delhi Airport before its modernization. There were huge scuttling cockroaches the size of mice and large black witch moths flapping into various corners as dawn rose. I collected my baggage off the carousel where it was accompanied by packages of many shapes and sizes in cardboard or plastic wrapping tied with a variety of strings, ropes or strips of yet more plastic. This was India; and my luggage, consisting of a suitcase and zip bag, was for once easy to identify.

As I was to learn over the years, flights into India are inevitably delayed; and once again my travel agent failed to meet me. Outside the airport building, I was immediately assailed by a sea of enthusiastic faces bobbing above their white–clad bodies; and there was that pervasive Indian smell. Indian towns and cities are at best like an ants' nest; but for some strange reason the ants congregate more thickly in a baffling confusion at airports. The smell remains pervading; even after a bath followed by solitary relaxation in the bar of one of Delhi's posh hotels, it seems impossible to remove. Scientists can analyse it; but I suspect that the burning of cow dung is a major ingredient.

Amongst the confusion, I picked out a taxi driver. We drove to the Taj Mahal Hotel; and through the early morning mist hopped crows and myna birds, spindly legged Indians rode on wobbly bicycles, the occasional cow stood by the side of the road and white buildings streaked with lichenous grime stood set back from the dust which made do for a pavement. The occasional bus or truck, spewing forth plumes of black diesel fumes, passed by or was overtaken, their rear end painted with the words 'Horn Please'.

Driving in India involves a horn culture; and I have even seen a truck adorned with the words 'Toot a Hoot'. There is one toot to request overtaking; there is a second toot from the second driver to invite overtaking; there is a third toot from the first driver to thank the second driver; there is a fourth toot from the second driver to thank the first driver. All such etiquette is complemented by general tooting telling humans and animals alike to move out of the way. This can even be directed at the inanimate with a stray rock in the middle of the road attracting its own particular toot.

On arrival at the Taj Mahal Hotel, I thought to take two or three hours nap to recover from a sleepless overnight journey. However, I looked out of the window. There were soaring pariah kites, screeching rose-ringed parakeets and a flock of white-backed vultures roosting opposite my window in several large mango trees. The ubiquitous common Indian myna was pecking about wherever pecking was possible. This was too exciting. I abandoned the idea of sleep, summoned a taxi and spent the rest of the day touring the sights of Delhi.

My first impressions have remained lasting for twenty-five years. The all-pervading smell, which I now find as welcoming as an old friend, and the decrepit state of once-glorious buildings. This is probably as much due to the replacement of the princely classes as it is to the endless battering by monsoon and traffic pollution. There is doubtless a connection between lichenous grime and weed-sprouting rooftops and the monsoon season.

There was also the impossible traffic, dominated by the three-wheeled motorized rickshaws disgorging black plumes of diesel fumes and intermingling with bicycles, cows and motor bicycles driven with fury by young and old enthusiasts alike, many with a girl or matron sitting sidesaddle in her sari behind him. Anything goes and anything forces its own way through the mêlée, including the occasional elephant, my first elephant sighting being opposite the Red Fort as it barged through the traffic bearing a load of sugar cane and being driven by the inevitably spindly-legged Indian wrapped about the waist with his white dhoti. It is even possible to see something like a motorized tea chest on three wheels with its front cut open to allow its driver or manipulator to peek out and play his part in the traffic chaos.

I was not unduly disturbed by Indian poverty. Of course, the standard of living is generally lower than in the west; but stand in the streets of an Indian village or the suburb of an Indian town with its discarded refuse, piles of rubber tyres, building rubble and indeterminate stacks of metal, and all around will be beaming faces, in stark contrast to walking to Earls Court Underground Station in London on a Monday morning where the faces are generally glum. It is the animals which I have found more depressing. The diseased dogs of India and the three-legged cows and other horrors are, in my experience, only matched by the dogs of Sri Lanka. I soon learnt to avert my eyes from the worst horrors and direct them towards the astonishing grace and beauty of Indian women in their colourful saris. India is a land of ever-surprising contrasts.

My first day in India was a full day of culture shock; and that evening I departed on an overnight train, bunkered up with Punjabi businessmen. Between us we consumed my duty-free whisky; and I listened as they expounded on the war between Iran and Iraq and the rise to power of Ayatollah Khomeni. I listened to their intriguing conviction that the Ayatollah regime in Iran had been placed there deliberately by the Americans as a foil to the Communist Bloc. Eventually my companions fell asleep and snored as only Indians can snore. I have been on many overnight Indian trains and can speak with some experience on male Indian snoring habits. Indian women, in contrast, arrange themselves gracefully, often resting their head on the hand with a crooked elbow. They remain stationary for hours on end, not even a hiccup, let alone a snore, is to be heard.

Early the following morning I arrived at Jammu and was taken by taxi and shikara, Kashmir's canopied equivalent to the Venetian gondola, to the houseboat owned by the Gandhi family on Dal Lake, to spend three or four days exploring the Vale of Kashmir. During my childhood I had so often listened to grown-ups talking about the vale with great affection and nostalgia. These romantic ideas inspired by the remnants of the British Raj were to be immediately modified by the impossibility of escaping the entertaining and persistent Kashmiri salesmen. Relaxing in a bath after a day's riding or after an evening reclining in my shikara on cushions under a canopy, being rowed through lotus and heavily kingfishered backwaters, there would be interruptions. The door would burst open with a Kashmiri salesman insisting on unrolling carpets to test Sahib's sensitive feet after his bath. Banishing that salesman, I would return to my bedroom to find 'Mr Tailor of Taste' going through my sparse wardrobe and explaining that a suit could be run up within twenty-four hours, backing this up with a list of his clients which did credit to *Burke's Peerage* or *Landed Gentry*. I did eventually fall for some beautifully painted Mogul-type pictures which I have never regretted. I brought them back to adorn the drawing room at Spring House; and they are now interspersed and form something of a relief from family portraits, sporting prints and Janet Whitwell's watercolours. Sadly politics and religion have interfered with Kashmir's economy. 'Mr Tailor of Taste' and his fellow Kashmiri craftsmen have moved south to cater for tourists in the rest of the Indian sub-continent. They will probably never return. Tourists are notoriously bad at discerning real crafts-manship, tempting the craftsmen to churn out cheap and simple rubbish for high-spending Europeans and Americans. Kashmir and all of us will be the losers. The Kashmiri on the other hand is being superbly entrepreneurial and exploiting a gullible market.

I returned from Kashmir, and like so many tourists went on to 'do' the golden triangle of Delhi, Agra and Jaipur with an extension to Udaipur and Bombay.

Unlike my great-grandmother, Janet Whitwell, I removed my shoes to enter and enjoy the Taj Mahal. Unfortunately, in descending into the crypt in a queue of silent and respectful tourists who were almost exclusively Indian, I hit my head against the marble lintel. There was a resounding boom, much to the consternation of all. I fear I had done little to repair my family's relationship with that magical building. I walked back from the Taj Mahal to explore the gardens of my hotel and spotted a brownish bird with a dark, slightly crested, head. I pursued this bird through frangipani, hibiscus and bougainvillea. The bird checked and gave me a chance to swing my binoculars onto it. As I had hoped, I discovered that beneath its tail it had a scarlet backside. This was the red-vented bulbul, one of India's commonest birds. As I was to become more sophisticated in Indian birdwatching, I now dismiss the red-vented bulbul as a 'trash bird'. It does not detract from the excitement of my first sighting. Excitement was further enhanced at Bharatphur, midway between

Agra and Jaipur, a watery game and bird sanctuary where past Maharajahs and British Viceroys would account for thousands of birds in a single day's shoot. In spite of nights rendered sleepless by the sudden and spontaneous outcry of jackals, I have managed to identify one hundred and sixty-four species of birds on one of my subsequent brief visits.

I had employed a young boy to row me out to the nesting sites of stork, ibis, spoonbill, and other water birds that were roosting in acacia-type trees on the mud islands in the lagoons. My youthful companion was pulling up lotus roots, which are something of a delicacy, when I spotted a small but very black cloud on the horizon. This began to grow at considerable speed; and I drew the boy's attention to it. He abandoned his lotus roots and rowed rapidly towards the shore. We were able to reach the park offices before a stinging sandstorm swept in. It became as dark as night; and the one or two jeeps used by park rangers were forced to use their headlights. The sand was followed by heavy tropical rain.

Within twenty minutes the skies were again clear; and the sun came out. The ground was flooded; but I found a raised dyke which led back from the park offices to the forest lodge where I was staying. I suddenly found my way blocked by a sounder of some six wild boar. This was my first encounter with boar; and I wondered how they would react. I stood still and watched as they dropped off the dyke and splashed their way through the flooded scrub, scurrying into deeper undergrowth.

The following morning I had another new wildlife encounter which enabled me to put my bushcraft to the test. I had been tutored in the rudiments of bushcraft in Africa.

Two years previously I had paid a brief visit to the Gwynn-Jones family in South Africa and taken the opportunity to spend ten days in the African bush. At Londolozi and Mala Mala private game parks I had pestered the Varty brothers of Londolozi and Maurice, a guide at Mala Mala, to teach me about bushcraft. This was an unusual request from a tourist and provided them with something different. I was taken off in an individual jeep down the dirt tracks of the bushveld. I was no longer confined to a tourist jeep looking for the 'big five', lion, elephant, buffalo, rhino and leopard. The intercommunication between my individual jeep and the other tourist jeeps would come into operation. Maurice and I would be asked, 'Where on earth are you?'

Maurice would then reply, 'In the rubbish dump'. We were both wearing goggles, poking around with sticks in the debris and turning over galvanized tin sheets looking for snakes and other goodies such as 'scorpies'. The goggles were prevention against ringhals, the spitting cobra; but we collected less harmful snakes, placing them in jam jars and bringing them back to the camp to exhibit to somewhat apprehensive guests.

On another occasion Maurice radioed through to nearby jeeps with the message, 'You might be interested to know that Peter and I are watching a flock of wattled starlings'. After a somewhat noncommital response he was asked whether there was anything else of interest and whether we had seen a herd of buffalo which had been reported in the vicinity.

'Oh yes,' replied Maurice; 'the buffalo are all around us. That is why the wattled starlings are here.' Jeeps in the bushveld immediately changed gear and rushed to find us. Unfortunately no one was interested in our wattled starlings. We were 'bloody fools' not to have reported the buffalo herd. Maurice and I were very happy not to have done so, so that we had a good ten minutes of both starlings and buffalo to ourselves.

It was with Maurice and the Vartys that I explored the bushveld picking up a spoor or footprints here and there, identifying droppings but more importantly learning about the brushed grass, the clipped bush or the smooth entry to a termites' nest which might indicate anything from the passing of an elephant to snake occupation. We usually found the elephant but avoided the snake.

It was in India at Bharatphur with its low scrub jungle and lagoons that the tuition received from the Varty brothers and Maurice paid off. Spotting some unusual spoor, I used my African bushcraft and set about tracking the animal, looking for signs of swept grass and further footprints. I was eventually rewarded by entering a clearing to be faced with a magnificent male black buck. We stared at each other for a good ten seconds before he dashed off into the bushes. Bharatphur was full of sambhur and chital deer and also the nilgai antelope, but I was not expecting black buck. On subsequent visits, I tracked down the occasional herd of black buck; but sadly I believe they are now, like the Siberian crane, no longer present in the reserve. Unfortunately England is not the only country which has suffered a depletion of wildlife in recent years.

That first visit to Bharatphur also saw my return to the bicycle. The admirable Dharmendra Sharma, an expert ornithologist, had suggested to me that I might like to leave the park to visit some nearby grassland to pick up plover and lark. He presented me with a bicycle. Unfortunately, the sacred cow had been to work on the seat and had chewed off all the leather, leaving only the uncomfortable framework of metal springs. It was some thirty years since I had ridden a bicycle; but we set off and joined the chaotic traffic on the main Jaipur Delhi highway. It was then that I discovered that the brakes were little better than the seat. Out of control, I rode into the back of a flock of goats, which scattered in consternation, causing further traffic confusion and a highly agitated Rajput goatherd. I was relieved to meet a roundabout and take a minor road to the successful viewing of our intended birds.

Re-entering the park at Bharatphur, I was again thankful to leave behind the traffic of the highway; but I had not made allowance for the occasional pothole. I encountered one of these, collided with Dharmendra's bicycle and landed in the ditch, which contained a cow carcass and a flock of vultures. Having waited thirty years for this adventure, it would be another twenty years before I ever took to the bicycle again. This was to be a rather more leisurely and safer ride in Cornwall with a relatively comfortable seat undemolished by the sacred cow and workable brakes.

On that first visit to India, I was driven from Bharatphur to Jaipur, arriving before lunch in time to enjoy a pre-prandial gin and tonic in the Polo Bar in the Rambagh Palace Hotel. While sitting at the bar, I noted a couple sitting by the bar and overheard their conversation. They were having difficulty in identifying a bird which they had seen. Having with me a field guide, I approached them and, acknowledging that I have been listening to their conversation, suggested my book might be of assistance.

'I am so glad you have come to talk to us,' said Fabian. 'I wanted to ask you whether you were having lunch in the Mount Nelson Hotel in Cape Town two years ago'. My father, my sister Alexandra and myself had indeed lunched at the Mount Nelson, a few days before my flying to the bushveld. I asked Fabian how on earth he knew this, to which he replied that once he had seen a face he never forget it. Clearly the Gwynn-Jones trio at the Mount Nelson must have been something of a spectacle; but I do not know whether his attention was drawn to our lunchtime table by Alexandra's film star looks or my ugly mug. Whatever the answer, Fabian and his wife and myself spent a happy next day exploring Jaipur and its surroundings before I continued on my way to Udaipur, Bombay and the south, eventually arriving at the West End Hotel in Bangalore where I encountered the Indian caste system at its worst.

The West End Hotel is one of the five-star Taj group; but outside my cabin a dog had been squashed by a car with guts and entrails spread out before my front door. I enquired of the management whether these canine remains might be removed. It became apparent that only lower caste could perform this menial task, and endless negotiations and difficulties seemed to arise. Crows and vultures arrived on the scene before any human was able to sort out the problem. In consequence, I repaired to the bar and struck up one or two heavy-drinking acquaintances. I awoke the following morning with an appalling hangover.

I had a long drive from Bangalore to the Nilgiris Hills with a driver who was more horn orientated than most. My head was banging; and it was not helped by my driver who tooted his horn at a tortoise crossing the road and even at a stationary rock. We stopped in Mysore where I joined the jostling, pushing and chattering throng in Mysore's equivalent of the Garter Service. The twentieth-century Mysore Palace set with its thousand of light bulbs at night on a somewhat gothic facade was now the backdrop of painted elephants, golden umbrellas and sword-bearing attendants with bangles and annulets on arms and legs. Indian legislation may have tried to abolish the Maharajahs and the Princes of India; but they and their pageantry have often survived.

Leaving Mysore, I headed for the Nilgiris Hills and tried desperately to avert my eyes from oncoming trucks and buses which hurtled down the middle of the road to bypass slow-moving bullock carts. At the same time, I attempted to block my ears from the ever-irritating horn and hold my breath as we swerved around a truck or bus which was discharging plumes of vicious and acrid black diesel fumes. As is typical in India, there were always intriguing road signs; there is one outside Mysore which states firmly 'Beware, vertical bend ahead, keep left'. I am not sure about vertical bends; nor do I fully appreciate road signs in Kashmir which say firmly 'It is forbidden to fall asleep while driving'.

I arrived at the gate of Bamboo Banks Farm in November 1980. The gate was not only electrified to keep out marauding animals but was also hydro-mechanical. The rope pull lifted weights which disgorged water from various containers which in turn disrupted an equilibrium and a rock-weighted rod lifted the gate. This consisted of an electrified pole from which were suspended strips of metal that clanged together as they reached the vertical position. A car had approximately two minutes to pass underneath. Thereafter the hydro-mechanics went into reverse and the gate automatically lowered itself. This was no mere whim of its inventor, Siasp Kothavala, the proprietor of Bamboo Banks. Thirty years later the gate has featured in articles in American and British newspapers; it remains in full working order, keeping animals at bay and avoiding the necessity of staff running from the house or the inconvenience of anyone leaving the car to open the gate.

Once through, my car went up the drive where there was a low-slung single-storey house with a wide verandah which could be glimpsed through varied shrubs and creepers. Down the steps leading from the verandah came a confident teenage girl. This was Shahanaz Kothavala. I must have muttered something to the effect that I had come to stay for four or five days and hoped that I was expected. According to the Kothavala account, Shahanaz returned to her mother to report that there was another Englishman outside who had come to stay, and enquired 'Are the English all so peculiar?' This problem was compounded by Shahanaz reappearing and saying 'Would you like a swim?' In her view I was clearly stamped as British Raj when I dismissed this invitation with the words, 'I would prefer to have a beer.' My head was now clear from the hangover; but I was left with a considerable thirst.

This is Shahanaz's account, but I am sure she is correct as the request for a beer was not unreasonable at twelve o'clock in the morning. This was more desirable than the proffered swimming which consisted of a water tank overhung by trees and occupied by a semi-habituated water snake named Sydney. It is only in 2008, some thirty years later, that Bamboo Banks has acquired a proper swimming pool; but the first day it was full and open, a colony of frogs moved in overnight, together with a soup-plate-sized turtle, presumably migrating from Sydney's tank. In the meantime Sydney or his descendants have continued to enjoy the tank, swimming amongst white waterlilies for the planting of which I can claim some responsibility.

After I declined a swim and requested a beer, Shahanaz's mother, Zerene, came down the creepered steps of the verandah to greet me. Apparently I had arrived a day early; and her husband Siasp was in Bombay. He was expected back the next day. Zerene Kothavala was not only confronted by a 'peculiar' Englishman arriving on the wrong day, but an hour or so later there was another unexpected visitor. This visitor claimed to be a Kothavala and a cousin of the family. He was the father of two daughters. The eldest daughter had lost her virginity at university, causing great disgrace to the family. In order to prevent his second daughter following her sister's example, he had walked across India to arrange her marriage with Zerasp, the son of the Kothavalas of Bamboo Banks.

Later that evening Zerene and this unexpected cousin conducted a conversation behind a screen in the long drawing room, a room with oriental carpets, heavily carved ebony furniture, Anglo-Indian ornaments, sporting prints and even a Privy Councillor's sword. I have been responsible for adding to the sporting prints over the years; The sword, which is identical to a Herald's sword, had belonged to Zerene's grandfather who had been a Privy Councillor. By the time that Zerene had embarked on her conversation, I had moved from declining the invitation to join Sydney in his water tank, had familiarized myself with the birds of the heavily-wooded coffee plantation, noted the Mawara Arab horses in the stables, and moved on to an evening whisky. As I sipped my drink, voices behind the screen became somewhat heated. According to Zerene, my face suddenly appeared and I said, 'Mrs Kothavala, if you need any help please let me know'. Zerene always said that from that moment I became a great friend.

The next day her husband Siasp arrived; and the unexpected cousin was put into perspective. This so-called relative seeking an arranged marriage proved to be a con man. In the meantime, Siasp and I established another good friendship; we discussed hunting in India and the whereabouts as to where you should put a stirrup on the foot; we drove through the forests of Mudumalai and were charged by elephants coming from two directions at once.

'What happens if we meet another herd of elephants around the corner?' I asked.

'We get out of the jeep and run. Hopefully the pachyderm will be more interested in the jeep than us.'

I disagree with Siasp's elephant etiquette, in particular the standing still and clapping of hands at truculent members of the species. I run. This has included a rapid scramble up a rocky hill face in western Nepal where the elephants are particularly noted for their size. I suddenly found myself face to face with one of their massive bulls. His tank-like face suddenly rose out of the bamboo within about five yards. I retreated rapidly up the rockface behind me grabbing hold of thorny shrubs and prickly bushes to take me to safety.

Elephants aside, Siasp and I discussed matters that included his silkworm farming. In consequence we sought to arrange a business deal with my kindergarten friend Robert Goodden who was running Worldwide Butterflies and had taken on the Lullingstone Silk Farm, which produces the unique English silk used for the last two coronations as well as the Queen's and the Princess of Wales' wedding dresses. The bureaucracy, both Indian and European, scuppered the enterprise.

We passed a rock with an overnight daubing of white paint stating 'Christ says Lo I come quickly'. Quick as a flash, Siasp, who had never seen this graffiti previously, remarked, 'Peter, there is one of your lot who is concerned with Christ's sex life.' The conversation then turned towards fishing. I was aware that he hunted with the celebrated Ooty Hounds and had shot tiger. I asked whether fishing was on his agenda to which he replied, 'Peter, fishing is a line with a worm at each end. The only fishing I have ever done is with dog and dynamite'. Writing with hindsight on past conversations is seldom easy. What was said can become distorted. However, what I call 'Siaspisms' are not easily forgotten and have not been exaggerated!

I left Bamboo Banks to return to the West End Hotel at Bangalore. Siasp had informed me that his elder daughter, Dinaz, was a receptionist there; and he instructed me to give her a spank on the bottom. The foyer of one of the Taj Hotels in India is a formal place; and relaxed western ways are not always appreciated by eastern decorum. However, I noticed that the receptionist wore around her neck the faravahar, the winged god symbol of the Parsees; this must be the Kothavala daughter. She turned to retrieve my key from a cubbyhole on the far wall. I leant over the counter and smacked her. There was an instant reaction, and I was confronted with an utterly horrified face. We stared at each other; she aghast and I trying to place a slight twinkle in my eye. I won the staring match and at last, she exclaimed, 'I know where you have been!'

My relationship with Dinaz formed into a close friendship over frogs. On a subsequent visit to Bamboo Banks, Dinaz was there with her daughter the newly-born Tanisha. Her husband Prio was at sea. Dinaz was taking a very aloof view of the tourists in the guest houses; but she seemed to accept me as an honorary member of the family and continued to deplete my cigarette supply. It was not until I was asked to share a bathroom with her that a real friendship formed.

We did not actually share a bath together; but on the first occasion I used it on my own she enquired afterwards whether I had found the bathroom acceptable. I remarked that all was well except for a frog which had hopped across the floor. I was then informed that this should not be a problem as frogs did live among the aspidistra. That night or the next day I asked Dinaz whether she wanted to use our shared bathroom, as I would like to have a bath before dinner. She assured me that she had no need for the bathroom at that time. Shortly afterwards I returned to my room and collected a change of clothes and towels before going to the bathroom where I began to turn on a tap. I then noticed not one frog hopping across the floor but fifty little brown frogs in the bath itself. There was also the sound of the tittering of an Indian girl outside the bathroom door. The ice was broken. Sadly Dinaz was not to live long. Gastroenteritis caught up with her diabetes; and I received the sad news of her death by telephone during a meeting with the Earl Marshal at the College of Arms. She had died the day before. Two days later she had been destined to fly to London and was becoming vexed at the idea of wearing 'closed shoes' as opposed to sandals.

Dinaz left behind a husband, a daughter Tanisha, then aged about six, and a golden cocker spaniel with a white quiff called Scamper.

Her husband had a career at sea so Tanisha was immediately absorbed into Shahanaz's household at Mysore where she was a little younger than Shahanaz's daughter Vashti and a little older than Vashti's brother Yzad. Scamper took up residence at Bamboo Banks. He had not been allowed to accompany Tanisha to Mysore, where he was in disgrace. On a previous occasion Scamper had been invited to stay. Shahanaz, then pregnant, and her husband Raian had two great danes. The great dane bitch had come on heat; and the great dane dog had been sent to kennels. The arrival of small Scamper caused no great concern, the great dane being some two feet or more taller than the spaniel. In due course Shahanaz gave birth to Vashti; that very same evening Raian started to act as midwife to his great dane who then produced a dozen puppies, all through a rather harrowing night. Scamper is responsible for an intriguing minority canine population in Mysore known as 'daniels'.

Scamper was not permitted to meet his descendants. On Dinaz's death he was banished to Bamboo Banks to join Budmarsh, a yellow labrador, Cuddles, another supposed labrador, and the self-considered aristocrat Victoria whose labrador lineage was clearly mixed with some rather more humble blood from the local village of Masinagudi, as manifest by her mix of brindle, black and white. Victoria was the matriarch of the Bamboo Banks pack. Once a sheep chaser, she had been caught committing that sin and beaten to death's door by Siasp. She never chased a sheep again. Her attention was directed instead towards 'natives'. Victoria was certainly a racist. Siasp and I watched from the outside breakfast table as a timid Tamil negotiated the hydro-mechanical gates and made his way up the drive towards us past a snarling Victoria who had despaired of further snacks from the breakfast table and was having a morning snooze. However, Victoria decided that a snarl was sufficient; snoozing was to be preferred to a charge and a grab at a Tamil buttock.

The Tamil declared himself to be a Jesuit priest and asked Siasp to contribute towards a loudspeaker for the local Jesuit church in the village. He explained that the two Hindu temples had loudspeakers; and the muezzin at the mosques were equally equipped. It was therefore necessary for Christians to be able to compete with this din. Siasp reacted as I had hoped; 'Go away you stupid man, God is not deaf'. Victoria snarled again; but it was not until I was left in charge of the dogs that I fully appreciated her racism.

Siasp and Zerene had gone up the forty-two hairpin bends to Ooty, the rather ramshackle hill station left by the British; but it has a certain charm. Snooker was invented at the Ooty Club; and the walls of the dining room are hung with photographs of past presidents and chairmen of club and hounds, all failing to resolve the correct position of stirrup and foot. This somewhat esoteric equestrian controversy consumed hours of my childhood around the Spring House dining room table.

With Siasp and Zerene at Ooty, I was left in charge of the Bamboo Banks pack. I had been informed that Scamper would not take part in any run around the farm. Scamper would be too idle and would remain dreaming of Mysore great danes somewhere near the outside breakfast table. Siasp and Zerene had underestimated the bond which I had established with this dog. He was delighted to come for a walk; and it was Scamper who led the way. The farm is some forty acres, enclosed by a massive trench to keep out elephants and the occasional cow owned by local villagers. It does not keep out wild boar, deer or leopards, the latter having acquired a taste for Bamboo Banks foals. Basically it is grassland with trees and bushes, stands of bamboo by the nearby river and the coffee plantation near the house which is also thick with sal and other local Indian trees. The sandalwood has long since been poached.

My dog walk with Scamper leading the way was far removed from taking rabbit-chasing poodles through patches of brambles and muddy Blackmore Vale pastures. My pack put up a blacknaped hare. They gave chase; and Cuddles eventually emerged from some stinking cesspit dripping in black gunge. In the meantime Budmarsh discovered an unwanted buffalo which had strayed in from some village compound. Budmarsh went at the buffalo; and the buffalo went at Budmarsh; and I was left shouting and yelling before Scamper and Victoria appeared at my side both hopping along on three feet. We were now in an area which has since seen some doubtful and truculent wild boar with one stinking dog, another which had seen off a snorting, head-swinging buffalo with formidable horns, and two dogs suddenly hopping along on three feet. I have since discovered that this pathetic hopping, lifting one useless leg in the air, is caused by a burr which eventually shakes itself out. I was just returning home when Victoria shook out her offending burr and, hearing local natives on the boundary track, suddenly shot off through a hole in the chain-link fence to attack the tribals who were innocently carrying brass water pots on their heads to and from the river. There were sundry shrieks and yells and a few flying pots before I was able to bring her to heel. My pack of four may have enjoyed their walk; but I did not. I have since gone on strike and refused to take on dog responsibilities.

My small friend Scamper came to an untimely end. A pair of cobras had taken up residence among the shrubs and creepers of the verandah. Normally the dogs are wary of cobra and the cobra run. The dogs will bark and pursue them but keep a wide berth. However the verandah was rather too near to home, and both Scamper and Budmarsh were bitten. Zerene and Siasp were in Poona; but the Bamboo Banks staff fed the dogs with white of egg. The aged Budmarsh lived on; but Scamper did not survive his cobra bite. Subsequently I made it clear to Siasp that if I was unfortunate enough to be bitten by a Bamboo Banks cobra, I would need something more than white of egg as an antidote. In the meantime Zerene informed me that if she was born again she would wish to be a Bamboo Banks dog; that is an appealing thought.

Dinaz also left her daughter Tanisha, petite with huge almond eyes, who has inherited much of her mother's character. The last time I saw Dinaz I went to her flat or apartment in Mysore for lunch before driving on to Bamboo Banks. Little Tanisha was very aloof until, behaving like her mother with the frog episode, I was suddenly zapped by a water pistol as her small face appeared cheekily from behind the sofa.

I last saw Tanisha on another sofa at Bamboo Banks where she had come in dressed in a child's sari, had stretched full length on the sofa, arranging herself with various cushions, and eventually gave her instructions; 'And now Peter you can read to me'. I do not know what I was reading but I was soon firmly ticked off. Thankfully Siasp interrupted us and, hearing his granddaughter criticizing my pronunciation, admonished her firmly and said, 'Do not tell an Englishman how to pronounce English; it is you my dear who are wrong'. Nothing more was said; but Tanisha's face acquired a somewhat subdued and puzzled expression. With my pronunciation of the English language in doubt, we put Beatrix Potter aside and took to the horse instead. Incidentally Indian children are steeped in English literature from Beatrix Potter through *Alice in Wonderland*, Winnie the Pooh, *The Wind in the Willows* and on to Harry Potter, Philip Pullman and Tolkien.

Tanisha was a very good rider; and she and I went out into the jungle that stretched beyond the farm. The jungle consists of stands of sal trees, thickets of lantana and open areas cropped by villagers' cows and deer with the occasional dangerous signal of fresh elephant droppings. On one particular occasion that Tanisha and I were out with the Bamboo Banks syce or groom, Tanisha suddenly swerved out of control on the permanently pregnant Bamboo Banks horse, Betty, towards a herd of elephants as we were cantering after a pack of wild dog, the dhole. Betty swung a wide circle and for once the elephants were unperturbed. The dholes are still there; Betty has convinced me that there is no such thing as an equine menopause; and Tanisha remains unforgettable for our other sorties into the forest to play 'I Spy', with her ayah or Indian nanny totally befuddled as to the exit of her charge into the jungle with a strange European man. We had great fun; and both of us cheated like mad! I suspect the ayah must have been appalled.

1980 saw my first visit to India. Thirty years later I am probably more familiar with the birds and butterflies of Bamboo Banks than I am with those of childhood Dorset. It has become my midwinter home where I spend Christmas and the New Year. Siasp and I still ride around the farm; the grandchildren are growing up; there is a new generation of labradors of suspect pedigree and everything is kept ticking by Tamil staff seemingly ageless and perennial.

CHAPTER 16

A duke, a Texan, Latin America and sundry Australians

B ACK AT THE COLLEGE OF ARMS, 1980 was a relatively uneventful year; but I was aware of certain subtle and subterranean movements. Rodney Dennys, Somerset Herald, had been House Comptroller, managing the College on a somewhat loose rein with the aid of a laid-back architect. Anthony Wagner had paid little attention to the College as a building. Colin Cole had taken over from Anthony as Garter in 1978. Rodney immediately began a campaign to appoint me as House Comptroller; I launched a counter campaign. The outcome of this manoeuvring was a Chapter meeting whereby Conrad Swan was appointed House Comptroller; and I was appointed his deputy. Immediately afterwards Conrad said to me, 'Let us go and have a drink'. Over a whisky we immediately agreed that a bursar was necessary. The result was the arrival of Graham Beck and the resignation of Conrad as House Comptroller a year later, leaving me in charge with a one million-pound restoration programme to put the College of Arms in reasonable physical condition to celebrate its 1984 quincentenary. Also in 1981 I was appointed Lancaster Herald, although this effectively made little difference to my heraldic practices.

Thanks to King Richard III, who had incorporated his heralds in 1484, there was a measure of urgency; and thanks to Graham Beck in his new appointment as Bursar there were alarming discoveries of what needed to be done. Graham and I discovered huge fungiform growths the size of footballs as we lifted reading shelves in the basement library and discovered large chunks of masonry at roof level about to descend on unwary visitors to the College. We started work and had a portacabin lifted over the wrought-iron railing of the College into the courtyard whence I directed operations. Director I may have been, but the practicalities were the responsibility of Graham; and the money was raised by the ever indefatigable Christopher Mann who was enlisted as fundraiser. Officers were shunted into 'Wendy houses' or partitioned cubicles at different levels in the Earl Marshal's Court, the main reception area of the College; and by 1984 our quincentenary year we had a building in sufficient order to receive the Queen and for the Heralds to process in style across Queen Victoria Street into our church of St Benet for a celebratory blessing.

House Comptrolling at the College of Arms brought with it a close association in England and adventures in America with Miles, Duke of Norfolk, the Earl Marshal. The Earl Marshal acts, as it were, as moral supervisor of the College of Arms. He is not a member of Chapter, the governing body of the College. However, he is responsible to the Crown for its general well being and the behaviour of officers. Miles took an active interest in the restoration of the College and signed numerous letters, drafted by Christopher Mann, requesting funds towards the restoration. Letters would come back, 'Dear Mr Norfolk, we regret . . .' etc. Christopher would seize the opportunity with gusto, 'We fully appreciate . . .' etc 'PS. Incidentally you may wish to know that you addressed "Mr Norfolk" incorrectly; he is in fact the Duke of Norfolk' etc. A letter of apology would be received accompanied by the desired cheque.

Fundraising had involved the setting up of the College of Arms Foundation in America. This was to be a charitable organization to enable Americans to pass money to the College without payment of tax. In addition to helping with the fabric, it was hoped that the Foundation would sponsor heraldic exhibitions and officers' lecture tours. It managed an exhibition for the 1984 quincentenary; I had spent two weeks working on the exhibition in that February, searching for suitable exhibits and crossing a snow-bound Central Park each morning and evening to and from the New York Historical Museum and the apartment of my friends Pete and Mary Hamilton in Park Avenue. I learned that Americans are perhaps not always as hardworking as generally thought. The curator, a certain American senator, had to be replaced before I achieved any modest action. I also had to threaten to withdraw the College of Arms from the whole exercise unless such action continued.

The exhibition at the New York Historical Museum opened the following year with moderate success. I have always felt it was something of a missed opportunity and would like to have seen select exhibits mounted in facsimile tournament tents. A colourful mediaeval splash combined with heraldry from the twentieth century would have appealed to the American public rather more than a somewhat dry academic display without any catalogue.

Tournament tents aside; I fear my attempts to provide a popular appeal to heraldry have not been over successful. Bernard Miles, the founder of the Mermaid Theatre in London, and I wished to have open air productions of Shakespeare in the courtyard of the College of Arms. The horseshoe staircase and parapet with windows above lend themselves to Mark Anthony disclaiming from the top of the horseshoe steps, battle scenes from Henry V along the parapet, Falstaff cavorting with his friends and making full use of steps and parapet alike, Juliet doing whatever Juliet should do from a Garter House window, and Prospero taking centre stage on the small flat roof above the main College of Arms entrance. Unfortunately, Bernard and I were not to fulfil our ambitions; I have never ever been able to mount tournament tent exhibitions in New York or Shakespearean productions in the College of Arms courtyard. I regret the failure of these enterprises; but I am aware that this failure has brought a sigh of relief from the majority of my colleagues.

Shortly after the exhibition in New York, I dreamed up the idea that universities in America might be prepared to offer funds in return for the College providing student access to genealogical and historical records for research. The College of Arms Foundation and the Earl Marshal seized on this idea. I claim responsibility for what proved to be a complete disaster. American universities do not have funds available for such research; but this did not prevent the Foundation from sending Miles, Graham and myself for two weeks in the States to visit universities, principally William and Mary College in Virginia and the University of Texas, to seek these student funds. A limousine cruised around Chelsea, collecting each one of us in turn, and we were duly driven to Gatwick where we were placed in a VIP lounge.

There were no long airport waits and shortly afterwards we were told it was time to board our American Airline aircraft to Houston, Texas. We were escorted out onto the tarmac where I noticed another limousine with bunches of flowers on the back window and by the front windscreen. When I enquired of the American Airline official as to whether they were taking a coffin to America, she replied, 'It is for you, sir'. Accordingly the three of us entered the flower-strewn but coffinless limousine and cruised to the aircraft which had by then left the gate, moved towards the runway and was awaiting our arrival. Miles and Graham sat together by a window; I was across the aisle next to a business man from Omaha, Nebraska. Somehow we seemed to receive our champagne before everyone else in the first class compartment; and, on arrival at Houston, everyone was told to remain seated until the three of us had left. I had engaged in conversation with the Nebraskan businessman from Omaha. I did not explain fully who or what we were but, on answering his query, I merely said that I was a historian. I think he was as puzzled by our VIP treatment as I was by why he had to fly to Houston to reach Omaha, Nebraska.

The three of us were therefore the first to leave the plane. I led the way and was greeted by an airport official who enquired whether I was 'the Duke of Wellington'. I replied that I was not; 'You want the Duke of Norfolk; he is the one behind.'

With the identification of dukedoms and individuals sorted out, which took ten seconds of humorous conversation, we avoided all immigration officials, waiting for luggage at carousels or other tiresome airport formalities or requirements and were ushered onto an interconnecting flight with fewer flyers but more champagne on to Austin, the capital city of Texas, where we were escorted to a long stretched limousine. The three of us tried to pretend that we were used to such vehicles and refrained from helping ourselves immediately to the cocktail bar. Miles was rather keen on trying to use the intercom to the driver. He considered this a late twentieth century improvement to an otherwise booming general from the Brigade of Guards shouting orders to a taxi driver seated some considerable distance in front of him. To be truthful, I think both cocktail cabinet and intercom were untested by the three English trying to be English in the Lone Star State.

There followed two weeks of receptions with our presentation. Miles kicked off with ten minutes on the Anglo-American special relationship. This was followed by me talking about the work of the College of Arms and Heralds with sundry heraldic slides. Graham completed our presentation with a plea on behalf of the fabric of the College. All three of us were up early in the morning either at the Inn of the Four Seasons in Austin or at the Williamsburg Inn. At Austin, Miles and I spent much time leaning over the bridge watching species of Texan turtles, discussing the College of Arms. I became aware that I was not destined to remain Lancaster Herald.

I discovered that top class American hotels are incapable of boiling an egg to the satisfaction of an Earl Marshal. Neither Miles nor I had any clue as to how many minutes it should be; but I suggested roughly three. It never worked; and on our last day at the Inn of the Four Seasons, Miles accepted my suggestion that scrambled eggs might be better. Moderate success; but I dread to think what would have happened if we had asked for poached, baked or coddled. American eggs seem to be fried with the universally accepted qualification of 'easy over' or 'sunny side up'; expressions which seem to have spread world-wide.

I became aware that Americans are not always well disposed to providing funds to their pleading British cousins. On our last day we gave a lunch in New York. On my right was Mrs Oscar Hammerstein. Rodgers and Hammerstein music has always been about the summit of my musical enjoyment. On my left was Steven Runciman, later Lord Runciman, the scholar of the crusades. I remember asking Steven Runciman how he had become interested in the crusades. His father had been in the British Embassy in Istanbul. This coincided with Great Uncle George's ambassadorship. Our conversation changed gear, when he discovered that I was a great-nephew of George and Muriel Clerk. During our exchanges of reminiscences and gossip I fear Mrs Hammerstein may have been somewhat ignored; but I glanced across the room and saw another couple not speaking to each other. This was Miles and Anna Glen Vietor.

Anna Glen had clearly been placed next door to Miles Norfolk as a possible source of funds. Anna Glen was a staunch Anglophile with money stemming from the Black Ball Shipping Line, which operated between Liverpool and New York in the days of sailing ships. Anna Glen knew exactly why she had been placed next to the Earl Marshal; she did not like it; and Miles was finding it heavy going. It so happened that I had stayed with Anna Glen on my first lecture tour in America. We had then and since established a good friendship; and at this lunch in New York we caught each other's eye. I went over; there were warm embraces, to Miles's astonishment. Afterwards he confided he had had a very difficult lunch. Unfortunately the Foundation had failed with Anna Glen; but my friendship survived and shortly before she died she gave me a special party in her New

York apartment. Fifty or more people drank champagne surrounded by oil paintings of the Black Ball shipping fleet. It was on that occasion that I flew back to England, sitting next door to a fellow passenger who was researching eighteenth and nineteenth century shipping lines. She knew all about the Black Ball line, such is the small world; and I was able to put her in touch with Anna Glen. I believe it gave them both great pleasure during the last few months of Anna Glen's life.

Our American experience confirmed that American individuals are understandably reluctant donors and that American universities do not have the funds available for student research at the College of Arms. There were two spin offs of our visit. Firstly Miles was subsequently bombarded with American requests for seats at the State Opening of Parliament; and I was sent a graduate from the University of Texas who was researching Tudor England in order to write a whodunit novel. The arrival of Virginia Clegg, an infectious Texan, was to teach me much about my own country. She took up residence in my flat for some two years, was party to the development of the Globe Theatre and enabled me to see much of London and England which otherwise I might have missed. Contrary to all my predictions, the Globe Theatre has survived.

Ginny showed me that most of England consists of dirty stonework repeated in houses and walls throughout the country, and a nationwide, albeit fragmented, flock of sheep.

'What's that creek?' as we sped over a bridge.

'That', I replied, 'is the River Thames.'

'What's that town we have just been through?'

'That is Stratford upon Avon'; and I hastily added, 'and we are not going back!'

I tried to teach her to fish in Northumberland. She never caught a fish; but the knots in her cast must have broken many records. Ginny eventually returned to Texas where fishing has not featured in her life; but the Globe Theatre continues to flourish, as has her induction into birdwatching and my coati crest on the ring on her signet finger.

House Comptrolling at the College of Arms prepared me for experiences with the British Press. Misrepresentation, the taking out of context and general misreporting is exasperating but is probably the price that we pay for free democracy. Too often I have been quoted in the press using words which do not even feature in my vocabulary. On one or two occasions I have had to resort to the dictionary to discover the meaning of the word which I am supposed to have used. It was one evening that I bought an *Evening Standard* to discover that I had ruined the College of Arms. The facade of the College of Arms had survived the blitz, including its steps, which were now being replaced by modern steps totally out of keeping. I had achieved what Hitler had failed to do. I do not know who was behind this rubbish. I can only say that the stone steps which I replaced dated from the nineteen fifties. The stone used for replacement came from the identical quarry. It is sad that irresponsible reporting is undermining the principle of freedom of speech. Where freedom of speech involves downright lies, I fear there is a problem. However, I have learned subsequently that it is wiser to shrug the shoulders and ignore it.

Sometimes the press can get things half right and half wrong. When Harold Wilson was elevated to the peerage, I was the Officer in Waiting. The telephone rang. It was a member of the press, who in a general way enquired as to who might be eligible for a grant of arms and how was a design agreed. I was then asked what might be suitable for a parliamentarian. On the spur of the moment I mentioned that 'the collective noun for rooks is a parliament' and I suggested that a rook might be a suitable crest. Unfortunately, it also has other connotations, with the suggestion of rooking people off; and this was promptly given wide airing in the press. The waggish Lancaster Herald featured prominently in the *Evening Standard*, causing considerable amusement to the regular train travellers down to Dorset that Friday evening. I did not share that amusement; but I had learnt to be very wary of the press and the tricks it can play. Harold Wilson did not have a rook as crest. He settled for a lighthouse as an allusion to his love of the Isles of Scilly.

Five years after my Mexican experience, I decided to penetrate further into Latin America. It was, of course, Latin America that was the home of the coati, the long known relative of the racoon, that was my crest.

I first encountered the coati in Santa Rosa in Costa Rica. Walking beneath the wide-spreading guanacaste trees above short grass, I noticed a movement. I swung my binoculars, thinking that it must be a squirrel, but across the branch, staring at me, was a coati, and in nonchalant fashion it dropped to the ground and walked off with tail erect. He was a male and did not realize that he was my special animal. The coati features in my signet ring, Ginny's signet ring, photographs of coatis from Latin America are sent to me by archaeologists of Mayan remains, there are coati hospitals, and it is curious that one of the world's most apparent and resourceful mammals is almost totally unknown in the United Kingdom.

I had seen a tame coati suspended by collar and lead from the hand of a village girl in Mexico. As nonchalant as my first coati, it appeared unconcerned at being hung by the neck with all four legs waving in faint protest waiting for its child owner to return her attention, which hopefully had sustained only a temporary distraction. In Peru I was to draw a coati blank; it was not until Santa Rosa that I saw my first coati in the wild. In the meantime I had widened my Latin American experience with an expedition to Peru in the spring of 1984.

I made contact with an agent in Lima and worked out a three-week itinerary. This itinerary broke down at its inception. A Wagner cousin of Anthony was Foreign Minister; and arrangements had been made for me to have dinner with him at my hotel. However, unbeknown by me, my agent had changed my hotel; and in consequence I missed what might have been an interesting evening. I taxied in irritated mood the following morning to downtown Lima to view the sights and see the puzzling casket containing the body of Pizarro, the conquistador. This seemed to be some two feet long, suggesting that he must have been a tiny midget. I then set off south, noting that my agent had given me a driver with an entire tourist minibus to myself, thus explaining why the trip was so expensive.

We drove through the aridity of the Atacama Desert where no blade of grass or spike of cactus will grow except near the banks of rivers which flow at intervals from the Andes. Remarkably the Atacama contains the celebrated Nazca lines, the huge animal linear formations in the desert and mysterious elongated trapeziums made by past Indians moving the stones to expose the sand beneath, which enabled them to create the largest human works of art on earth. I was able to fly over the Nazca lines in a small aircraft, but unfortunately my next-door passenger was an ageing American matron who was

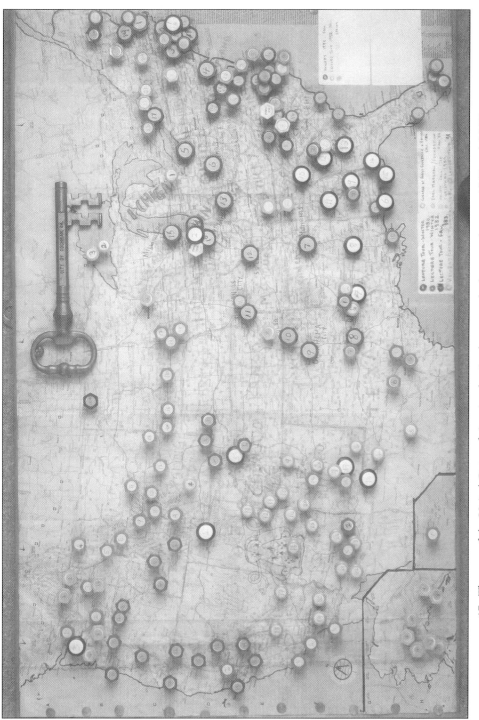

17. *The map of the United States of America showing lectures and adventures between 1980 and 2005, including Alaska, Hawaii and the key to the city of Cochran, Georgia.*

18. *Virginia Clegg, 'Ginny', being literary in my bush hat.*

19. After receiving the CVO in 1998 with (far left) Nicola Harker (née Beaumont), (left) Stephen Dickinson and (right) Mary Dickinson (née Gurney).

20. *Into the jungle for birdwatching and bughunting at La Selva, Costa Rica.*

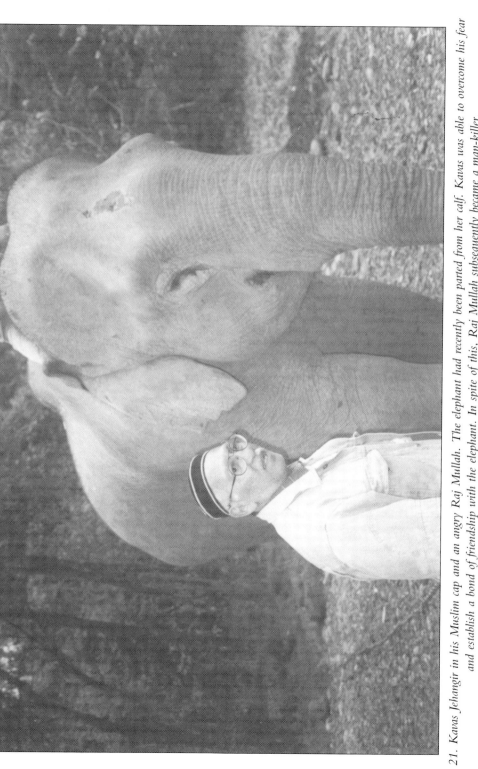

21. Kavas Jehangir in his Muslim cap and an angry Raj Mullah. The elephant had recently been parted from her calf. Kavas was able to overcome his fear and establish a bond of friendship with the elephant. In spite of this, Raj Mullah subsequently became a man-killer.

22. The stalwarts of Garter House: Judith Hardy (centre) adviser on Peerage and Baronetcy claims, legal matters and genealogist; Gillian Barlow (left) my personal heraldic artist; Julia Hett (right) research assistant.

23. *Out riding in India with Siasp Kothavala, accompanied by Louise, canine daughter of Victoria.*

24. *Heraldry is fun. The Princess Royal in Garter's Office 2008.*

promptly sick; and I had to help administer sick bags whilst trying to take fleeting glimpses at the desert works of art below; and in consequence I somewhat regretted not being allowed a second Nazca flight.

Apart from past Indian civilizations, the sole human activity in the Atacama at the time of our visit appeared to be the rearing of chickens. The birds were housed in vast batteries and fed with fishmeal which in turn was the product of the teeming waters of the Pacific. Millions of fish not only fed the chickens but also supported Peru's shoreline mammals and birds.

I set my eyes firmly on the small of the back of my guide as he led the way down a vertiginous forty-five-degree salt-baked slope of sand to a cliff edge where I found relief from my vertigo in a makeshift wall some six feet long and two and a half feet high composed of loosely piled rocks. Vertigo is compounded by looking through binoculars over a barren cliff edge. Thanks to my small precarious wall, behind which I crouched, I was able to overcome my vertigo and enjoy the rocks and surf, which interacted with fur seals and sea lions. Dolphins, frigate birds and boobies were in attendance.

These were the cliffs of Paracas, giving a wildlife spectacular which was enhanced the next day by my trip to the Ballestas offshore islands where thousands of seabirds massed onto the rocks. Being gorged on the fish they are the source of one of Peru's major exports, guano. Serried ranks of fur seals and sea lions, the one stinking and the other being relatively non-odorous, jostled and packed coves and rocks, with some breaking rank and bobbing in the sea. There was barking, grunting and other deep mammalian noises echoing around the caves. Boobies, frigate birds and the spectacular Inca tern packed themselves on every ledge, nook and cranny above. At last I found it. It was my first and only penguin, Humboldt's penguin, lurking sorrowfully at the back of a cavern. Three thousand species of birds later, this lonely specimen remains my only penguin sighting.

Departing from my penguin, I re-engaged with my agent and somehow or other the sights of Peru came and went. I suspect that my impressions of such as Cusco and Machu Picchu were much as other tourists. I eventually arrived for ten rather disappointing days on the Amazon where ovate leaves and the occasional iridescent blue hand-sized morpho butterfly flittering across the trail introduced me to the dense greenery of Amazonia, where you can stand on a trail thinking that nothing happens until you realize that most of those leaves have been eaten and plundered. Wildlife is at work. The elusive wildlife made an unexpected appearance when Angel, my guide, took us in his outboarded canoe to his wooden house on stilts where his mother gave us an Amazonian packed lunch.

A small smoked fox, smoked catfish and smoked armadillo were on the menu. The fox meat was gamey; but I was slightly put off by the fox's head being attached to my proffered meal, complete with charred whiskers. The catfish was forgettable; but the smoked armadillo was delicious. I am convinced that the cow is responsible for the destruction and devastation of much of Latin America. It is unfortunate that Peru and its neighbours cannot develop their own endemic meat and have armadillo farms thriving in Amazonian forests.

The last night of my scheduled itinerary in Peru was to be spent in the Hotel Amazonas in Iquitos, the Peruvian port on the Amazon. The following day I was to fly back to Lima to catch an Air France flight back to Europe. I had come earlier that afternoon on a two or three-hour motorboat journey accompanied by Amazonian Indians and a quantity of chickens. We chugged down the River Napo into the Amazon with a vast expanse of water at the confluence, traditionally the home of super-sized anacondas. The Amazon itself at Iquitos is sufficiently wide that it takes an Indian in his canoe an hour to paddle across it. Further east at Manaus in Brazil it takes the ferry well over an hour to cross from bank to bank. Rivers are big in South America.

My 'supposed' last night in Peru saw me going to the bar in the hotel before dinner. Sipping my drink at the bar, there were two or three girls perched on bar stools to my left. I did not take much notice of them until they began to engage me in conversation; and one of them said that she would like to dance with me. Somewhat reluctantly I took this dusky maiden in her lurid tangerine lycra shorts into the adjacent nightclub. My dancing abilities, such as they were, became lost by the late nineteen sixties; and the detachment from your dancing partner where you wave arms and legs about to thunderous music preventing any form of conversational contact has become one of my pet hates. On this particular occasion, Maria, the dusky Peruvian, and I were able to overcome some of my dancing difficulties and struck up a friendship. We exchanged addresses. It transpired that she and her friends lived in Lima and had merely come to Iquitos on a long weekend to see the Amazon.

The next morning my agent took me to Iquitos Airport in order to fly by Air Fawcett to Lima. There I was to catch an apex Air France flight back to Europe. My agent left me at Iquitos Airport, ignorant that Air Fawcett had rescheduled its flights. Hours passed as I sat frustrated on a green plastic seat. Eventually Air Fawcett arrived. I scurried frantically on board, leaving behind a cashmere sweater whose green matched and blended with the green of the airport seat. Irritation therefore compounded with frustration as we flew over the Andes to Lima. Air France was still at its gate; but I was not allowed to board because there was insufficient time to negotiate the usual bureaucracy, immigration and security, let alone airport taxes. I stood in desperation as I watched the flight take off and heard an Air France official saying to me, 'Go with these two youths'.

Ten minutes later I found myself in a taxi with two strangers who spoke no English, going through the suburbs of Lima to an unknown destination. It transpired that there were to be several destinations as I was taken from the travel agent's office to Air Fawcett's office to Air France's office and eventually to a hotel where the manager advised me to get shot of the two youths immediately. He declared them to be con men. Thank you Air France! The hotel manager proved reassuringly helpful. Airlines and agents did not, as they all refused to speak English; and nobody was prepared to take responsibility for my predicament. The nightclub in the Amazonas Hotel on the Amazon was the answer. I took a taxi and somewhere, somehow in some back street in Lima I pressed a few front bells. There were barking dogs, and a few heads popped out of windows before one helpful person told me that Maria had not returned from the Amazon but was expected the following day. I left a frantic message. Thankfully Maria arrived at my hotel the next morning. Agents and airlines wilted under her Spanish tirades. I was spared having to spend an additional week in Lima waiting for the next Air France flight. Instead, I was despatched to the Cayman Islands and thence to Miami where I was put on a British Airways flight to Heathrow. I do not know who paid for this; but I am certain that it was the dusky Maria met on the banks of the Amazon in her lycra tangerine shorts who had rescued me from an awkward travelling experience.

In the meantime I had telephoned Joyce Carter, my Secretary, from Lima to say that I was delayed. It must have been the most expensive telephone call in my life. It cost me some fifty pounds for less than one minute. 'I am here in Peru with diarrhoea (thanks to malaria tablets), flights have been missed, am alive, expect me when you see me. Hope all is well.'

I returned to the College of Arms somewhat disappointed by Amazonia. My secretary Joyce was convinced that I should not to be defeated by Latin America and thereafter presented me with various newspaper cuttings featuring Costa Rica. At the same time I was invited to become a director of a firm called Eco Safaris. I wisely declined this invitation as Eco Safaris was to prove something of a failure. However, it had contacts in Costa Rica and, in consequence, I arrived at San Jose Airport in November 1988, to be greeted by a swarthy bearded person who loaded my luggage into his car and drove me to a hotel. This was Carlos Coles. Early next morning Carlos and I set off to explore Costa Rica; and I soon became accustomed to his quiet soothing manner and gentle ways. I discovered that he was an artist of considerable note, painting everything from southern Bolivian children in trilby hats and yellow sweaters to a cheerful coati walking on clouds. On our first day together, I spotted more birds than I had seen in ten days in Amazonia. Those ornithological aces such as toucans and oropendulas came into view as we headed for Monteverde where I stayed at Pension Quetzal, named after what is supposedly the world's most beautiful bird. However, most of the quetzals I have seen have been generally rather scruffy and have lost their long emerald tail feathers.

Bob Law who ran Pension Quetzal was one of the community of Quakers who had left America in 1948 to avoid peacetime military draft and settled in Costa Rica. Nowadays tourists boost the Costa Rican economy by visits to the cloud forest above the Quaker community. Travel writers continue to write about Bob Law and the Quaker community and their teetotalism. Thankfully, I can report that Bob was very happy to sit on his balcony, drinking bourbon as we discussed Quakerism. He accepted a top-up with enthusiasm and the comment that everything should be done in moderation as we shared my bottle.

Travel writers seem to inter-relate with their own imagination. I have even argued with my own stepbrother, Gavin Young, when he wrote about Ketchikan in Alaska, talking about certain rocky peaks each surmounted by the bald-headed eagle. When I was as Ketchikan I saw only steep slopes covered entirely with coniferous forest with the occasional bald-headed eagle on the shoreline. Other travel writers have written frequently about the dreaded Bangalore/Mysore highway in India as if it were a dirt track running through a national park. They have mentioned jackals and peacocks strutting across the road. Just wait for the tiger! Travel writers are prone to fantasy. On the thirty or forty times I have travelled backwards and forwards between Bangalore and Mysore I have never yet seen anything more than pelicans on a tank outside Mysore and expectant monkeys sitting beneath the roadside banyan trees waiting for tourists to throw them bread or bananas. No self-respecting jackal, let alone deer or even tiger, will cross the road.

My first visit to Costa Rica proved to be one of many; Carlos and his wife Debbie became close friends. They had a small travel business called Jungle Trails. Debbie ran the office and Carlos took tourists into the forest. Unfortunately he was to die from stomach cancer some six years later, and only six days after I had been staying with him and Debbie in their flat in San Jose. Costa Rica has the highest incidence of stomach cancer in the world. Debbie then continued with the travel business; moving from behind her office desk she equipped herself with a pink umbrella and green wellies, leading parties into the jungle. On occasions she has been able to offload her tourists onto other guides; and I have been able to clear my desk at the College of Arms, leaving indispensable staff to cover during a two or three week absence as Debbie and I have taken off to explore further afield, including Panama, Nicaragua and the Everglades. Her blonde hair beneath her pink umbrella complemented by a yellow poncho above her green wellies have become a familiar sight as we have worked our way down muddy jungle trails.

It was with Carlos that I first experienced the Pacific. Carlos and I, together with one Francisco, had been equipped by Debbie with tents, sleeping bags, food and other necessary provisions which included a respectable quantity of rum. The three of us were despatched to a village on the bank of the River Serpente where we took a small motorboat to the mouth of the river. There we paused near the banks of mangroves and small flocks of white ibis, waiting for the appropriate moment to negotiate the tide which swirled around some alarming rocks before taking us out into the Pacific.

That first Pacific experience was serious thudding on the waves for an hour before the three of us were deposited on a sandy beach near the Panamanian border and far from human habitation. We pitched our tents, and that evening decided to treat ourselves to some of our rum. We gathered outside the entrance of my tent; and rum was poured into three plastic beakers. Francisco decided that the rum would be much improved by coconut milk. We gathered a number of fallen coconuts which Francisco sliced open with his machete. Later that night the rum and coconut milk necessitated leaving my tent for a pee. As I walked through the broken shards of coconut outside my tent, I realized that something was amiss. The flesh left in the broken remains of our drinking session had attracted most of the local hermit crab population; and the flesh of my toes proved to be rather more inviting than the flesh of the coconuts.

The following morning I discovered that my toes were in a sorry state. It was apparent that the hermit crabs had been feasting well; and I was reduced to hobbling through the forest. 'Hurry up,' exclaimed Carlos. 'I can't,' I replied, 'I have sore toes'.

Birdwatching has an advantage. If steep slopes cause breathlessness or hermit crabs cause painful toes, it is always possible to stop and pretend to see something flittering in a bush. Latin American forests are particularly good for this as the foliage is dense; and it is possible to pretend the existence of a bird, which gives adequate time to recover or to ease the painful feet.

Carlos also introduced me to the La Selva Biological Station run by the Organization for Tropical Studies. Graduates and postgraduates choose La Selva and its sister organizations for research purposes; and sometimes permit outsiders such as myself to stay there. Most of the students come from American universities, with a sprinkling from Costa Rica. One day I hope to help set up a foundation to provide for students from Oxford and Cambridge. The students study obscure subjects which I fear I tend to turn into nicknames, so that I have a Miss Fruitfly, Miss Bat One and Miss Bat Two; I am not certain that Miss Jungle Debris appreciated her name.

Mammals in Latin America are difficult, with the exception of monkeys. However, La Selva's biology laboratories are frequently frequented by agoutis, peccaries and coatis, with sloths being frequent in the trees. The river at La Selva is crossed by a suspension bridge some fifty yards long; and on more than one occasion I have started to cross to find a coati coming the other way. This causes a problem. The coati will sit and scratch, determined not to retreat. Some are sufficiently habituated that they will scuttle past and then leap into the nearest bush. Wellies are essential to guard against snakes; but it is the insects which can be troublesome. Debbie has a problem with cockroaches; and I am not an expert cockroach exterminator. On one occasion I was summoned to despatch a cockroach on the wall of her bedroom. The cockroach must have felt a movement of the air as I raised a shoe to use as a swatting implement. The cockroach flew off and disappeared. Later that night Debbie heard a clicking noise beneath her pillow. At first she thought it was in her own head; but then realized it was something else. Switching on the light, she turned back her pillow to find the offending insect. I fear I have been in disgrace ever since for not having despatched it.

On another occasion, enlisted as cockroach swatter, I aimed at the offending insect, a tiny cockroach which had somehow appeared in our car. Once again my swatting was inept. To shrieks from Debbie, the cockroach promptly disappeared behind the glass of the driver's mirror. This was in Panama; and we had to find a garage to have the whole car fumigated. It followed that Debbie's cabin at La Selva had to be closely inspected to clear out any cockroach offenders.

My artist Gillian Barlow has also paid a visit to La Selva; and her cabin yielded a paraponera or bullet ant. This horror is black and an inch long with a bite and a stinger which causes excruciating pain. The ant was removed; and Gillian remained unscathed.

This was not the case on my next visit when I stayed in that same cabin. I returned from the jungle in the evening, sweaty and well bitten by insects. Deciding to have a shower I stripped and brushed past the shower curtain. Something stabbed me in the crook of the elbow. I swore but dismissed it until I came out of the shower and again brushed across the curtain. A few seconds later I felt something crawling across my back. I reached behind me and brushed something to the floor. Looking down I saw a brown scorpion some two inches long. I zapped it with my shoe and looked at the reddening sting on the inside of my elbow. Having dressed, I went outside to my next-door neighbour who was studying snakes; but his knowledge of scorpions was non-existent. He advised me to go to the main building, where I met my friend Jane Carlson.

Jane was a biologist from Baton Rouge, Louisiana, studying the symbiosis between some bugs and nuts. I had met this pretty blonde in La Selva's laundry room. Her bugs and nuts were proving frustrating as the nuts refused to germinate. My scorpion sting provided her with a measure of distraction; and she found the whole episode a source of much amusement. The following morning the sting had disappeared; but the scorpion returned to the College of Arms, pressed between two sheets of paper. It resided on the mantelpiece in my secretary's office until one morning when I noticed tiny white shreds of paper remains. The office mouse had eaten my scorpion; and I have therefore lost the evidence for my adventure. In the meantime Jane's bugs and nuts have helped in providing her with a PhD; and she is studying protea plants in the Cape district of South Africa.

My adventures with Carlos and then Debbie perhaps provided them with something different from their usual groups of Jungle Trail tourists. I once had personal experience of such a group when Debbie telephoned me and asked whether I would like a free holiday. I could go with her for ten days around Costa Rica, helping with a party of Australian botanists. Thereafter she and I would be able to go off and spend seven days together far away from tourists. I agreed to this arrangement with some apprehension.

There were seven Australian botanists, three pairs and one singleton. One pair was rather prone to accidents. As we disembarked from Debbie's minibus on our first outing, the wife walked into a thorn or cactus and spiked her forehead; and her husband fell flat on the ground. The second pair came from the Australian outback and were so horrified at the idea of any ill-treatment to any form of animal life that they even eschewed the use of insect repellant. I found this extremely convenient. In my experience insect repellant is ineffective unless you stand next to someone who has not used it. All mosquitoes then leave you alone and attack your neighbour. This couple also had a problem with the lodges we stayed in, maintaining they were haunted by the ghosts of long-deceased slaves. The third couple consisted of a pleasant man with a wife who claimed to know everything about everything; but in fact knew little or nothing. The final member of this group was one Christine who was on her way to meet a blind date in California. I pointed out that the blind date would take one look and retreat in a hurry. A retired officer from the Australian Armed Forces known as 'Madam Lash' might terrify any would-be Californian suitor, her head being topped with a hat of monumental proportions derived from some Panamanian hat ancestry. Christine has abandoned would-be Californian suitors and turned to the dog. She is now one of Australia's leading trainers in dog obedience.

Debbie had recruited one Pablo who pretended not to speak any English. Pablo's English is in fact excellent; but the Australians were not to know this. His job was to explain the fauna in Spanish to Debbie who was to act as translator. My job was to continue walking down the trail while all the others deliberated on the nature of some plant. When I found any bird of interest, I was to rejoin the group and attempt to show the Australians what I had found. This was not entirely satisfactory, as the Australians seemed surprisingly unobservant; and would have an infuriating habit of saying, 'Look Peter there is another bird in that tree', pointing vaguely into the forest. I endeavoured to keep my patience whilst explaining that there were thousands of trees in front of us; and it might be helpful to point out which tree, whether the one with an orchid or the big-leafed one with a large branch moving to the right and then use the clock method of saying, 'Go right at six o'clock' or 'Left at one o'clock'.

Their inability to see things became apparent at our first lunch, taken on the banks of the river. I spotted an American crocodile coming down towards us. As it was swimming in the middle of the river, it should not have been too difficult to see. I tried to point out that there were three logs in the middle of the river; and if they looked at the middle log they would see it was moving and passing the others. In despair, I remarked, 'Do not mind, it is only a clockwork crocodile which the Indians in the village on the far side of the island have wound up for me. I dare say it will come round again.' To my astonishment, some five minutes later another crocodile appeared and swam down the river past our lunch party.

This time some of them were able to see it; and to the others I explained that it would not come down again as it was now wound down. It would take the villagers too long to wind it up. Although some of the party seemed slightly sceptical, I am certain that there were others who actually believed this.

That evening, we arrived at a lodge. Pablo and I decided that we needed a drink, leaving Debbie to sort out the room arrangements where there were further problems with the ghosts from bygone days of slavery. By this time, we had introduced Christine to a special drink. We called it 'toucan's blood'. In fact, it was a spiced-up bloody Mary; but round the corner on the dining verandah there was a real toucan. Now the Australians had been particularly anxious to see a toucan. Although I had spotted several toucans, they had flown off before the Australians had been able to focus their binoculars on them. This toucan was a tame toucan which I was able to coax into a nearby bush. I then summoned the Australians to give them a good viewing of a real toucan. Unfortunately, this particular bird had taken a liking to my green wellies. It flew from the bush and started pecking my feet, possibly thinking they were green yams. Our botanists suddenly realized that I had pulled a fast one!

Over the subsequent 'toucan's blood' with Christine and Pablo, I turned to Pablo and said, 'I have tried crocodile and toucan; but now they want to see a sloth. In my suitcase I have a brown sweater. Do you see those coconuts over there and would you like to put them in my sweater and just climb up that tree?' Pablo decided that we should put this idea on hold. He was spared putting my idea into practice, as thankfully sloths put in an appearance two or three days later; by which time I had acquired distinct reservations as to whether I had a future as a tourist guide.

I returned to this ghost-ridden lodge some few years later and, missing my toucan friend, I enquired as to his whereabouts. I learnt that he had been run over by a car in the lodge drive. He had paid the penalty for seeking human friendship.

CHAPTER 17

Mainly Nepal

A CROSS THE WORLD, I was to spend Christmas of 1994 and the New Year at Bamboo Banks. I had decided to see something of Nepal before going to enjoy a Kothavala Christmas. Christmas at Bamboo Banks was traditionally British. Zerene supervised the placing of candles in all the trees in the garden. The number of candles depended upon the year, so that at the millennium in 2000 there were two thousand white wax candles set in notches in the trees, supplemented by additional lines of night lights down the drive. Christmas with a non-Christian family did not ignore the playing of carols sung by the King's College Cambridge choir. There was Christmas pudding with silver trinkets and brandy butter, mince pies, mulled wine, turkey, crackers and balloons. I have been known to comment on the turkey. I have never seen any turkey in India; the Bamboo Banks turkey is somewhat tough; and so I have often been suspicious of the indigenous peacock. Balloons disappeared for two or three years after I despatched a newspaper cutting to Zerene. The cutting referred to the waste of British taxpayers' money sending contraceptives to India in order to keep the population in check. The newspaper went on to say that this was a useless exercise as most of the condoms were transmuted into children's toys, mainly balloons. The disappearance of balloons was shortlived. By the time of the millennium there had been a reassessment; and they had gradually returned to adorn the beams supporting the roof of the outside dining area.

The millennium dinner started after midnight, following fireworks and the spectacular lighting of candles. It is one of the few menus in my life which I can recall in any detail. Soup was served in coconuts, followed in turn by a chicken, mango and mushroom casserole, crab curry, a spit-roasted pig complete with apple in the mouth, and sheep's trotters by special request of David Tyman, a past chairman of the Ooty Club. I do not remember the pudding or puddings. My memory begins to wane because I left the table at 4.30 in the morning whilst the assembled company had embarked on a singsong. I left them singing *Jerusalem*. At the dawn of the millennium I was determined to ride a horse, so after four hours of sleep and a rather bad head, I went to the stables where I took Betty out and galloped through the jungle. I arrived back to breakfast well after ten; there was nobody else at the breakfast table. Somewhat weary family members gradually arrived, including Zerene who announced that there would be pink gins served in the summerhouse at one o'clock. I arrived at the summerhouse to watch the staff bearing bottles of gin; the bottles were eventually removed untouched. It was not until later that evening that David Tyman and myself, the two British in the party, restarted proceedings with a whisky.

My trip in 1994 to Nepal required taking a suitable Christmas present to Bamboo Banks. Siasp's grandfather had laid out all the gardens of Baroda for the Maharaja. My great-grandmother had taken easel and paintbrushes to India. She had disliked India, with the exception of Baroda where she painted the gardens. In the many volumes of her paintings I had hoped that I would find something to give to Siasp and Zerene. I stood on a chair and took down several volumes from the top shelf in my office only to realize that the Indian or more particularly the Baroda section or volume must be elsewhere in the family. On stepping down I slipped and cracked my coccyx on one of the uprights of the back of the chair.

Two days later I had to fly to Kathmandu. In an emergency it is possible to discover hitherto unknown sources of help. This help was discovered in a medical emporium where I was equipped with rubber rings to ease the disaster of my coccyx. One rubber ring was not enough; two were barely sufficient; but three were passable. I flew with British Airways to Kathmandu, clutching my three rubber rings as take-on luggage. It was the days before each seat had its own individual mini television. There was one large screen; and, as luck would have it, I was placed bang in front of it, sitting on my three rubber rings. There were numerous complaints from behind as my raised figure concealed the sight of the film from my fellow passengers. I was removed to the side, where I enjoyed the company of my first Nepalis, Gurkhas returning home.

My coccyx slowly recovered; and I was gradually able to discard my rubber rings, one every two or three days. It was in Bardia

National Park in the west of Nepal that I was able to sit comfortably in the back of a jeep with only one ring. I was accompanied by my ex-Gurkha guide, Thule; and we were making for the grasslands of the Terai, having left our tents early in the morning. After my recent fall from my office chair, I was not anticipating any similar mishaps. However, the first mishap of the day came when the tailboard of the jeep was let down for me to descend. I stepped on the tailboard which promptly collapsed, and I fell head over heels onto the sandy dirt road. Largely unscathed, I pick myself up and was able to spot a crested bunting perched on a tall blade of yellow grass. Thule and I then crept through undergrowth following the explosive cheeps of a tesia, a diminutive bird skulking near the ground. We were able to spot it within a few inches in front of us as we lay flat on our stomachs.

The next mishap involved a tree trunk which stretched across a river adjacent to a small Nepali village. Children were scampering across the tree trunk with an alacrity which I had failed to achieve on the crossbeam in the gymnasium of my prep school. Logs, stepping stones and tree trunks fill me with dread; and on this particular occasion I held on to Thule's shoulders. Half way across I wobbled, we wobbled and together we descended into the river to much mirth and hilarity from the Nepali children. The water was waist high; and my canvas bag containing camera, bird book and other necessities went beneath the surface where my camera, which had just taken good photographs of the Indian rhino, emitted a certain mysterious whirring. We struggled to the far bank. Thule had arranged a picnic lunch; everything was dried out, and somehow he managed to stitch together my Indian bird book, which has done splendid service ever since.

Having taken a toss from the tailboard of the jeep and fallen into a river, I was not expecting the third adventure of this particular day. Thule and I took an elephant; this was a forest elephant used by the forest wardens and the occasional tourist. The mahout sat in front with his ankus, the metal spike or goad used to jab into the elephant to direct her and keep her under control; I sat behind on khaki cushions in a makeshift howdah which thankfully had two upright wooden poles on either side of me. Thule was behind me; and so we, elephant, mahout, Thule and I progressed through the forest and grassland of the Terai. Riding an elephant is far removed from the horse or even the camel. It lumbers along giving the impression that for every two steps forward one step is taken backwards. I found this easy lumbering was suddenly interrupted by the elephant's ears flapping back against my feet. I withdrew my feet, whereupon the elephant lifted its trunk and trumpeted. Suddenly afterwards she began tearing up the vegetation with her trunk and spinning in seemingly irrational circles interspersed with sudden short but very rapid tangent dashes. Thankfully my makeshift howdah allowed me to grab hold of the two upright poles which were also grasped by Thule.

Our elephant, after several minutes of tearing up vegetation and trumpeting, then set off at a gallop down the trail. The mahout with raised voice and stabbing ankus was unable to impose any control. The problem with galloping animals, whether horse or elephant, is that they make allowances for themselves but have no consideration for the people that they are carrying. Heads, and in the case of a galloping elephant through the forests of Nepal, the body have to be lowered. Disobeying this fundamental rule risks being swept off by an overhead branch; and I am aware of at least two deaths being caused in this way. Elephants blow up quicker than the horse, so eventually this particular elephant came to a stop. Everyone said that her name was 'Speedo'; but I suspect that this was simply a name applied for my benefit. Nonetheless, Thule later confided in me that he had been very alarmed by the bolting elephant; and certainly I was relieved to return to my tent that evening without further incident. It is thought she had been frightened and angered by the presence of a tiger or snake.

It was from Bardia that I went to Birethanti. Birethanti is reached down rocky slopes and a suspension bridge composed of wooden slats across a turbulent mountain stream where I met, coming from the opposite direction, a galloping donkey. We met midway with the bridge swinging violently as the donkey barged past me. It was not good for the vertigo.

Birethanti had been chosen by my travel agent Abercrombie and Kent, that upmarket company sited off Sloane Street. My choice of Abercrombie and Kent was a mistake; and I had already been irritated by the arrival of their pretty employee at Heathrow Airport to wish me 'Bon voyage' and present me with a pigskin wallet. Although I enjoyed the company of the pretty girl over a drink, I did not

consider that the obvious expense of girl and wallet was a necessary
addition to my travelling costs. At Birethanti, I found trekkers were
using Laksmi Lodge as a night stop after a full day of looking at their
feet and sheep droppings. Both they and I were given soup and bread
for supper and a bed with a flock pillow. Trekkers were paying some
twenty dollars to Laksmi Lodge; and I was spending many times that
amount thanks to Abercrombie and Kent. When I complained,
Abercrombie and Kent merely excused themselves by saying that I
had told them that I was prepared to 'rough it'. I do not expect to
'rough it' in a basic trekkers' lodge with my transportation back to
Kathmandu consisting being sardined into a local Nepali bus and then
being charged the equivalent of a three or four-star hotel with
personal taxi and driver at my disposal. I dispensed with the services
of Abercrombie and Kent; and when I arrived at Bamboo Banks Siasp
replaced them with a Parsee travel agent in Bombay, Kavas Jehangir.

I have subsequently travelled frequently with Kavas in the
Himalayas. We have pitched our tents in buffalo fields or high on a
platform in a tree. We have been entertained by members of princely
families and the poorest of hill farmers. There have been dancing girls
whirling at dusk and long religious discussions between Hindu,
Muslim, Parsee and myself, as a titular Christian, around a bonfire late
into the night. We have consumed vicious millet-based drinks
through a hollow bamboo out of a bamboo beaker with disastrous
consequences for the bladder, and lunched off an entire chicken
when we accepted an invitation in a mountain village in Himachal
Pradesh. The unfortunate bird was placed alive into a pot of boiling
water. After a few minutes the skin with feathers was removed; but
everything else was chopped up. I seemed to receive the neck and a
leg washed down with a most disgusting and revolting drink. I have
imbibed millet, rice and sugar-cane concoctions in many parts of the
world; but this wheat-based drink was undoubtedly the worst. My
driver Tapa also imbibed and was last seen violently vomiting in the
corner of a paddy field. Kavas and I had to abandon him and clamber
up the mountainside to the road before walking through the late
evening as the occasional twinkling light broke out high on the
Himalayas.

Malt whisky has compensated for some of these dreadful drinks, as
Kavas and I have sat on tartan rugs, being served Glenfiddich whisky

to the astonishment of passing European trekkers who seem unaware that there can still be a strong bond between the British and Indians after more than three hundred years of contact between the two peoples.

Down on the plains and into Rajasthan Kavas introduced me to such as Devi Singh with his crocodiles, goat-eating leopards and striped hyenas. Devi is the Thakur of Bera. We drive in a jeep, the inhabitants namaste before him, that is to say they bow with their hands pressed together. Devi places his hand on his heart; and I, where appropriate, raise my hand and say, 'Hi'. With this strange rigmarole we have processed through Bera and out of one of the gates of the town walls and into the rocky and rugged countryside.

After my university experience with goats, I have retained a soft spot for this perky animal; and I have never been happy for the trussed up goat in Devi's jeep knowing that it would soon be tethered to a tree for the leopard to come in and take it. The goat was trussed; the legs were bound; and it was tied to a sapling. Ten minutes earlier we had made friends in the back of the jeep. Now the poor goat began to bleat desperately as we withdrew some twenty yards and waited for the leopard. It was one of life's happier moments when the leopard let us down; and the goat came back into the back of Devi's jeep unscathed. Goat and I had a chummy reunion as we returned home. Unfortunately, I suspect the goat was sent out in the next day or so as leopard fodder and fed the two cubs which I was lucky to watch with their mother the next morning.

CHAPTER 18

Garter

IARRIVED BACK AT MY DESK at the College of Arms after my 1994 trip to Nepal with Christmas at Bamboo Banks. The internal telephone rang; and I was summoned by Conrad Swan who had succeeded Colin Cole as Garter in 1992. I had mixed feelings as to what was coming. My old friend Rodney Dennys, Somerset Herald, who had the ear of the Earl Marshal as a trustee of Arundel Castle, had long dropped hints, as had Miles Norfolk himself over our turtle viewing in Austin, Texas.

I was not therefore surprised when I sat on Conrad's sofa, and we had discussions on general College of Arms matters, before he said that the Earl Marshal would like me to take on the Gartership. I was aware that Conrad was under a degree of stress and that he was finding it increasingly difficult to continue in his position. I was also aware that I was not in any hurry to succeed him. I said that I would consider the matter but wished to see the accounts of Garter House.

Garter House is a section of the College of Arms consisting of five storeys with its own front door and a central staircase, carpeted in Garter blue. The staircase and Garter's own impressive room with its high pedimented bookcases is wallpapered in dark red covered with a motif consisting of the blue garter itself with the golden words *Honi soit qui mal y pense* alternating with two crossed golden garterial sceptres and the golden crown of a king of arms which is composed of golden acanthus leaves. Garter House is also colloquially the term for Garter's practice; and the crown exists in a battered tin box in the vaults of St James's Palace.

Several weeks passed; and the accounts of Garter House did not appear to be forthcoming. I was again summoned; and this time it was both Miles and Conrad who confronted me. I started laying down conditions, the first being permitted sight of the elusive accounts and the second being that any acceptance of the Gartership would not in any way obstruct my pursuit of obscure wildlife down remote jungle trails. In turn I gave an assurance that the jungle would

213

be restricted to August, Christmas and Easter, when state and government matters tend to be less pressing.

Garter can always appoint a deputy who can stand in for him in an emergency; and many matters can be dealt with over the telephone. Some ten years later I was able to direct operations from my sick bed in Bamboo Banks where I was on drips and continuous day and night nursing, having contracted some virulent bacteria. The bacteria was not of Indian origin. It had been traced to New York; but it was probably prompt Indian action which saved my life; and the College of Arms continued to function thanks to the daily telephone conversation which I had with my secretary, Jennifer Long.

My acceptance of the Gartership depended upon the Garter House accounts. They arrived. I looked at the accounts. Later that evening I wrote a letter to Miles and put it through his letterbox in Clabon Mews. I had rejected the Gartership.

Miles always had a habit of ringing early in the morning; but on this occasion the telephone went well before seven p.m. There was a hastily convened meeting in Garter House at ten. I gave way on the condition that I would hold the Gartership on a temporary basis in order to help the College of Arms as a whole. I also insisted that I would be able to return at any time to my previous position as a Herald with life tenure. This was agreed.

The accounts were then discussed in some detail. There was a garterial honorarium which had been negotiated with the Treasury by Anthony Wagner. It was set at four thousand pounds. Colin had refused to be interviewed by the Treasury as he regarded it as an impertinence for Garter to be interviewed by a Treasury employee. I do not know why Conrad never took it up. Miles and I agreed that this was the way forward. I was not prepared for work for four thousand pounds a year, employing staff to advise the Crown Office on peerage and baronetcy successions, deal with applications for trade marks which might be considered armorial and which were coming in at a rate of two or three a week, interview all new peers and introduce them into the House of Lords, advise the state and government on matters of precedence and a multitude of other somewhat esoteric subjects.

Unlike my predecessors, I was prepared to undergo the Treasury interview; and in consequence Garter's honorarium was considerably increased, making it possible for me to accept the Gartership. I was assessed at the level of a High Court Judge, but without a pension.

On 5 October 1995, I became Garter King of Arms. On that morning I chaired my first chapter meeting at the College of Arms, consisting of all the officers. Later that afternoon I summoned all officers and staff to a meeting in what we call the waiting room to ask for their general support. As I looked around the room there were apprehensive faces; there were even bloody-minded faces; and there were faces to which I could not put a name. Thankfully, after fifteen years some of the bloody-minded faces have yielded great support and friendship; unknown faces have now made themselves well known; and, alas, others I have had simply to sack.

5 October 1995 brought with it not only the Gartership but a trail of other positions. I became an officer of the Order of the Garter, Genealogist of the Order of the Bath, Honorary Genealogist of the Order of St Michael and St George, Genealogist of the Order of St John of Jerusalem, Inspector of Regimental Colours, Inspector of Royal Air Force Badges, Member of the Royal Mint Advisory Committee, Fellow of the Royal Society of Antiquaries, Liveryman of certain City Livery Companies thanks to past squabbles between Heralds and City of London craftsmen, not to mention patronage of red squirrels and water voles with the Wildlife Ark Trust based in Northumberland.

My first week as Garter was not concerned with inoculating red squirrels against squirrel pox but rather introducing my furniture into Garter House, revitalising my uniform and making myself known to various heads of state and government departments, which included a lunch in the House of Lords with Edward Jones, Gentleman Usher of the Black Rod, and David Hawkins, Yeoman Usher, two persons who were to play a major role in my life during the next few years.

In the office the telephone started to ring. My first official telephone call as Garter came from Downing Street. Sir Alec Douglas-Home had died; and the Prime Minister wished to know how to write to his son David. Etiquette dictated that he should not be addressed as Lord Home until after his father's burial. Further enquiries came in from the Welsh. Alfred Pryse-Hawkins, the incumbent of St Benet's Church opposite the College, keenly interested in heraldry, advised me that prayers had been said for my welfare in Wales over that first weekend. I do not know whether this was true; but there were certainly enquiries as to what I was going to do about incorporating the Welsh dragon in the Royal Arms. Constitutionally Wales is a principality within the kingdom of England. It is therefore covered by the three lions originating with the Plantagenets. Wales has long been a special part of England; and, as such, was covered by the Act of Union in 1707 setting up the United Kingdom. These arguments are not well accepted in certain Welsh quarters; and I learnt a number of Welsh swear words during my first week or so as Garter. I am grateful that the other fourteen realms and territories of which The Queen is sovereign are not all jostling for a position in the royal arms.

A new Garter was also an opportunity for the Roman Catholic dioceses to plead yet again for their own grants of armorial bearings. This overlooks the fact that there is still an established church. If disestablishment occurs in the future, then doubtless Roman Catholic dioceses will line up for their grants of arms, and perhaps Muslim mosques and Hindu temples will follow suit.

On Wednesday, 18 August I introduced my first new peers into the House of Lords, John, Lord Cuckney, chairman of the Thomas Cook group and the Port of London Authority, and James, Lord Blyth of Rowington, chief executive of Boots. I lunched with John Cuckney, and towards the end of lunch took him and his two supporting peers to the Robing Room where we met Black Rod for a rehearsal. I had only once seen the Introduction Ceremony and that was some thirty years previously. It was a complicated procedure dating from 1621.

The ceremony in 1995 began with the formation of a procession outside the Chamber led by Black Rod with his rod in his right hand and held over his shoulder. He was to clear the way for Garter King of Arms, wearing his tabard, with his gilt sceptre of office in his right hand and the new peer's patent of creation in the left. It is Garter's job to introduce the new peer into the House of Lords on behalf of the Crown. In 1995 Garter was followed by the new peer with two existing peers of his own rank acting as supporters or sponsors. The junior supporter was in front of the new peer and the senior behind. All were wearing their parliamentary robes and carrying cocked hats in their left hands or firmly on their heads if lady peers. The new peer carried his or her writ of summons in the right hand.

This procession entered the House. The bright lights and the glitter of the House of Lords, as everyone craned to see the new Garter and the new peer, reminded me of a first entry onto the stage beneath the spotlights in a school play production.

On reaching the bar of the House, each in succession gave a head bow to the throne before processing up the temporal side with bows repeated as each person reached the reading clerk's table and the judges' woolsacks. Edward Jones and I prided ourselves in our bowing synchronization. Although he was some paces in front of me, his bow at the woolsacks would coincide exactly with my bow at the reading clerk's table. On reaching the Lord Chancellor the new peer would kneel and present his writ, while I would present the peer's patent. It was not long before I discovered that many peers claimed to suffer from arthritis in the knee; and requested exemption from this section of the ceremony. In the meantime, I had thrust my sceptre beneath the mace laid on the woolsack behind the Lord Chancellor while presenting the peer's patent.

It so happened that on the occasion of my first Introductions, I had not yet received the garterial sceptre from The Queen. Accordingly, I made use of my wand as Lancaster Herald. This was a round wand made of ebony topped with the red rose of Lancaster. Unfortunately, at the rehearsal its roundness did not allow it to be held in place on the Lord Chancellor's woolsack; and it rolled on the floor, landing with a resounding crash on the brass grilles covering the central heating. During the ceremony itself I made certain that this was not repeated. I thrust my Lancaster wand firmly under the woolsack; and the Lord Chancellor, Lord Mackay of Clashfern, seemed to lift slightly at the impact. All then turned towards the table where the reading clerk read out both the patent and the writ with the new peer taking the oath of allegiance and signing the Roll of the Peerage. The reading seemed to continue for a good five minutes; and I was relieved to be able to steady myself slightly by gently resting my calves against the cross bench before moving around the Chamber, bowing again and conducting the peer and his or her supporters to the barons' bench. There the three peers were lined up and instructed by me to 'Sit'; 'Hats on'; 'Rise'; 'Hats off' and 'Bow to the Lord Chancellor'. They put their hats on automatically after bowing. This process was repeated three times and after the third bow I gave the instruction,

'Keep your hats on and follow me'. The process of bowing to the Lord Chancellor consisted of sweeping from the waist, removing the hat with a left-handed backhand tennis stroke. Lady peers kept their hats on; and I always waited with some apprehension for a hat to fly in my direction. Happily, this never happened. The procession then passed once more up the temporal side of the House, bowing at the same places, before the Lord Chancellor shook the hand of the new peer; and all passed out of the Chamber.

Perhaps inevitably there were problems. Barbara, Lady Castle of Blackburn flatly refused to wear a hat. She was a supporter or sponsor on a number of occasions; and we developed something of a routine in admiring each other's legs. We would compare our shapeliness while sitting respectively in tabard and peer's robes in the Moses Room, waiting for an introduction. In fact my legs became something of a national institution; and their supposed 'elegance' was reported on more than one occasion in the national press. I had not previously been aware that I had such an asset!

Denis, Lord Healey enjoyed hamming up the situation. He always made deliberate mistakes in rehearsal and would start to process in the wrong direction. His distinguished career in the army convinced me that he knew exactly what he was doing. He was merely trying to tease, and always got it right on the occasion itself. Another well-known government minister was not so lucky. The process of sitting and rising with hats was complicated by pillars which jutted out from the wall. The hat was a bicorne. This meant that leaning back against the pillar would catch the hat and bring it forward over the nose. On this particular occasion, our peer was already greatly alarmed at the thought of the ceremony. I promised that we would nurse him through it gently. All went well until we reached the hat doffing. I then realized that his hat was on back to front. Worse still, the black cord which tightened the hat on the inside had come undone; and each time he bowed to the Lord Chancellor and put his hat back on, the visible cord grew bigger and bigger so that something like a large spider appeared to spread out across his face. Some of their more jocular lordships had taken to marking these proceedings out of ten. This particular introduction was a low scorer.

Many peers overcame their nerves and enjoyed the occasion, particularly as it followed a good lunch. Roy, Lord Jenkins of

Hillhead Chancellor of Oxford University and sometime Chancellor of the Exchequer, was frequently chosen as a supporter by peers of the Liberal Democrat party. Unfortunately, his conviviality at lunch made it difficult for the House of Lords doorkeepers to persuade him to come to a rehearsal. For extraordinary reasons he would then refuse to sit and watch the video presentation which Edward Jones and I had set up to show peers and supporters prior to their rehearsal. I am afraid that Roy behaved rather like a spoilt schoolboy and stood tut tutting in a corner while his seat remained empty. I once endeavoured to remonstrate with him; but he merely replied that he had done it all before and knew it well. I replied, 'You may have done it, Lord Jenkins; but the peer being introduced has not'. I went on to add that he was supposed to be a supporter and that his job was therefore to support. This had little effect; and shortly afterwards I stood side by side with Edward Jones, Black Rod, as the Lord Jenkins of Hillhead bore down towards us through the Royal Gallery. Edward saw my frustration and whispered to me, 'Do not start a war you know you cannot win!' It was a wise comment and one which I have had cause to remember on many subsequent occasions. Thankfully, Roy was an exception and in stark contrast to such as Margaret, Lady Thatcher who was impeccable in her behaviour towards the House of Lords staff. She always made a point of returning and thanking everybody personally for their attention and the part they had played in the proceedings.

In 1997 I introduced ninety-one peers into the House of Lords. It was decided that the ceremony was too long. In addition, there were some who considered that the hat doffing was becoming reminiscent of Gilbert and Sullivan. I have always been in favour of adaptation and allowing ceremonials to evolve; but the select committee deliberating on the ceremony of introduction to the House of Lords began, in my opinion, to take matters too far. This was not helped by Miles Norfolk who went to be interviewed by the committee saying that he considered 'everything was a load of nonsense'. Miles in his disarmingly brusque manner was sometimes prone to voicing opinions at variance with his position as Earl Marshal. Bertie Denham came out and said I had been 'torpedoed by the Earl Marshal'. The select committee decided that I should be axed, regardless of the fact that I was acting on behalf of The Crown. The matter was subsequently debated in the House of Lords; and I briefed Miles as to what to say. This time he gave me full support, as did a number of other peers. I sat in Black Rod's box; and at the end of the debate the Lord Chancellor did not even call for a vote. It was clear that there was general approval that I should be retained. Many of the peers cheered and looked in my direction as I gave a gentle wave and smile to their lordships. I felt such a wave might just be within the strict decorum of the House of Lords.

The new ceremony was to consist simply of Black Rod, Garter and the peer with the two supporters. On entering the chamber all bowed in turn at the bar before Garter presented the patent to the reading clerk. The patent was then read out, an oath or affirmation made by the new peer who then signed the peers' roll. All three peers then returned to the centre of the chamber and on a signal from Garter bowed to the cloth of estate before leaving the chamber. Margaret, Lady Thatcher confided in me that she considered the new ceremony 'just adequate'. It has greatly shortened the time taken; but still has a measure of dignity and occasion.

Before any introduction takes place, the new peer comes to Garter House to discuss a number of matters, particularly the title to be taken. There is what is known as the *nomen dignitatis* or the title itself and then there is the territorial designation. A title may be the name of a place; but I object to a county or a large city, which I consider to be the perquisite of a duke, marquess or earl. Nor do I consider a small pond or muddy lane to be appropriate. These are beneath the dignity of the peerage. Most new peers choose to incorporate their surname in their title. If this has not already been bespoken, it is used on its own. If there has been a previous peer of the same name then it must be qualified by a place name. This is not the territorial designation which in fact serves little purpose other than to fix the peer with the name of a place in the United Kingdom and allow him or her to become a peer of the same. As with the ceremony of introduction, problems can arise. Some peers did not know how to spell the name of the village in which they lived; others did not know their county. There have even been some peers who were uncertain of their proper name; and on such an occasion we have even put in a telephone call to mother. Generally matters are conducted in good humour as explained by Greville, Lord Janner of Braunstone in his recent autobiography:

My first job – to choose an appropriate name. I attended at the office of Garter King of Arms, or 'Garter' as peers refer to him. 'Well, by what name do you wish to be known?' he asked me.

'How about 'Lord Janner'?' I asked.

'Sorry,' he replied. 'That was your father's name. You must be Lord Janner of . . .'

'All right, Garter,' I replied, cheekily. 'I will be "Lord Janner of . . ."'

'No, no, no,' said Garter, shaking his head. 'You must be Lord Janner of somewhere . . .'

'Very well,' I replied. 'Then I will be "Lord Janner of Somewhere".'

Garter looked at me and shook his head. 'You know perfectly well what I mean,' he said. 'You must choose a place.'

I did. I chose Braunstone, which was the most underprivileged area and estate in my constituency, where I had spent the most time with those who needed the help the most.

Garter nodded. 'Lord Janner of Braunstone, it will be,' he said, smiling. It is a name which I remain proud to bear.

I have often been asked my opinions on a particular individual. In general I either enthuse or remain silent. Some peers such as Greville are natural entertainers and will suddenly perform conjuring tricks during serious lunches at the House of Lords. Greville has two white rabbits as supporters to his shield of arms. One supports the shield with one paw and holds a sword in the other, the sword being an allusion to law. The second rabbit also supports with one paw but holds in the other a red top hat.

Other peers such as the chirpy Tony Banks who became Lord Stratford kept us both involved in a hilarious conversation about fox hunting for far beyond his allotted time in Garter House. Tony was, of course, notorious in his opposition to fox hunting. Nonetheless he chose to have a fox for his crest. The choice of the fox and Tony's antipathy to fox hunting was coincidental. He was an admirer of the eighteenth century politician Charles James Fox; and collected Foxiana. This included a portrait of Charles James Fox by Romney. He took possession of this painting on the morning that he came to see me at the College of Arms. This was the inspiration for his fox crest.

Greville and Tony are two among many who have been memorable and fun.

Garter's encounters are by no means confined to peers of the realm. I recall meeting Benazir Bhutto, previously Prime Minister of Pakistan, and nearly mentioned to her that I was a frequent visitor to the subcontinent, meaning India. I had not really taken in who she was; but something rang a bell in time, and I avoided a gaffe. I met Henry Kissinger, the American statesman, but I found our conversation was far less interesting than that of our mutual host, Conrad, Lord Black of Crossharbour, who has since acquired some unfortunate notoriety.

After my first two peerage introductions, I changed the next day from tabard into the white silk mantle with scarlet lining of an officer of the Order of the Bath. The five officers of the Order with The Queen in attendance processed the full length of Westminster Abbey with a pause in the choir before entering the Bath Chapel or the Chapel of Henry VII for a dedication of a new stained glass window. Yesterday the House of Lords, today Westminster Abbey and tomorrow Buckingham Palace. I was beginning to wonder what Miles had persuaded me to accept; and I am sure it is no exaggeration to say that, during our seated pause in the choir for prayers or other ecclesiastical matters, I thought of my pith helmet hanging on its hat stand in India with the Mawari Arabs in the stable. They seemed a long way away; but I am quite sure my thoughts were triggered by The Queen as the Sovereign Head of the Order, sitting directly opposite me. It occurred to me that if The Queen could ride in Windsor Great Park and elsewhere, my pith helmet and Arabs would survive. They have!

As Genealogist of the Order of the Bath, I am responsible for arranging for the carving and painting of the wooden crest above the stall of the knight in question, together with the preparation of a banner of arms and a brass stall plate of his full armorial achievement. These are all to be seen in Westminster Abbey.

Every five years The Queen attends a Bath Service where the ceremonial is highly complex, not helped by rickety stairs leading up to the stalls and the ageing bones and arthritis of some of the knights. It is many years before a stall is made available to a knight. Age can sadly play its part; and during one particular service the senior knight was supposed to draw a sword. I was standing on his immediate left, near the altar, and had to move aside and duck as the sword swung in my direction. Decapitation was not part of the ceremony. At the next meeting of the executive officers, it was decided that fitness rather than age would be the criterion for the drawing of the sword in future services. At the next Bath Service I made quite certain that I positioned myself so that I was able to move aside rapidly if such proved necessary. Field Marshal Sir John Stanier was the sword bearer. I had briefed John emphatically, so he left me unscathed and undecapitated.

The Order of St Michael and St George has also involved meetings, receptions and the arrangement for banners and stall plates in the chapel of the order in St Paul's Cathedral. As my position in the order is 'honorary', I am spared another set of ceremonial robes. I merely sit in the front at the annual St Paul's service where I can observe proceedings and pass comment at the next officers' meeting. Some of the processing knights choose girls to act as their esquires. They are possibly granddaughters holding aloft grandfather's armorial banner. The knight processes with blue silk mantle over a morning coat. Granddaughter is not always quite so correctly dressed for the occasion. I consider jeans and trainers to be most inappropriate, as can be the behaviour of some smaller grandchildren of knights flinging hassocks across the aisle during the solemn reading of the names of last year's deceased. The annual meeting of the officers of the order are well used to my comments on these matters; and I am glad to report that a measure of greater dignity has now been restored to the service.

Certainly I did not wear jeans and trainers when I went to Buckingham Palace the morning after the window dedication in Westminster Abbey. The Queen handed to me the Garter sceptre with its square end which would ensure no further rolling off the Lord Chancellor's woolsack. In addition there was the Garter chain of office and the Bath chain of office, together with my letters patent of appointment. The boxes were somewhat reminiscent of Christmas; but I was now fully established as the thirty-sixth Garter King of Arms in succession to William Bruges who had been appointed by Henry V at the time of the Agincourt campaign of 1415.

A few days later I was back in Buckingham Palace where I attended the appointment of Michael Scott-Joynt, Bishop of Winchester, as Prelate of the Order of the Garter, a position traditionally

held by the Winchester Bishops. I handed the chain in its box to Her
Majesty. The three of us considered what we should do next.
'Ma'am', I said, 'we should put it around his neck'. Her Majesty
agreed. I opened the box. Alas I had not checked the three chains of
gold which tangled together before they ended in a link from which
the prelate's insignia was suspended. The three chains were typical of
all such chains including my own as Garter or Genealogist of the
Bath. We struggled and Her Majesty commented about playing cats'
cradle.

The Order of St John also holds an annual service and procession
in St Paul's. I knew little about the Order until I was suddenly
appointed its genealogist, made a knight of the Order and presented
with a long black robe, known as a sopra vest, and a black mantle.
My experience of medical charities had been restricted to my
disastrous wartime Red Cross efforts with Diddles, my Shetland
pony. Now I was to learn of the enormous debt that we all owe to
St John, its Order and its Ambulance Service, not to mention
almshouses and the Eye Hospital in Jerusalem. As genealogist, I am
responsible for heraldic matters. Knights of grace can be upgraded to
knights of justice when certified by me as being properly armigerous
or entitled to arms. This may sound a somewhat limited and esoteric
duty; but I have tried to take a wider interest in the Order, attending
investitures, county visitations and various Order functions. The
presence of St John at a local agricultural show or the Olympic games
is apparent to everyone; but my personal gratitude to the Order has
been to provide me with many new friends. When speeches or
sermons or investitures become tedious, there is always a friendly face
to alleviate the situation. Sir John Wheeler, as Chancellor of the
Order, would read the names of those being invested. I had spotted
the difficult ones in advance, particularly the Tamil or Ceylonese.
John would look over his shoulder with a wry grin to see if his
pronunciation was correct. He did a good job; only once or twice
did I glare with disapproval, but he never merited the thumbs-down
sign.

During John's proclamation of those being invested, Peter Nott,
the prelate and formerly Bishop of Norwich, would gently close his
eyes as he reclined in his central seat facing the audience. Suddenly
aware of his lapse towards slumber, his eyes opened and instantly

swept right to catch my own. The two of us stayed awake! However, both of us might have willingly exchanged our position for a river bank in Norfolk. We have shared fishing experience with Gurneys; and I have fished with Peter the morning before he presided over a Gurney wedding.

After parrying those attacks from the Welsh and Catholics during my first few days as Garter, I was then confronted by the Scots and the Registrar of Trade Marks. The Napoleonic wars had greatly involved one of my predecessors, Sir George Nayler, who was appointed the first Inspector of Regimental Colours; a position which does not necessarily attach itself to the Gartership. The Inspector of Regimental Colours, the Adviser to the Admiralty on Naval Badges and the Inspectorate of Royal Air Force Badges can be held by other officers of arms, or even non-officers; but since all the records of the Army and Royal Air Force and knowledge of what has been done in the past are retained by the College of Arms it is clearly both wise and practical to continue with a two-hundred-year-old procedure. The Navy retains its own records. As luck would have it, the first of my duties as Inspector of Regimental Colours involved the Scots Guards and the preparation of their new colours.

I am confident that the Scots and the three successive Lord Lyon Kings of Arms in Edinburgh that I have known during my Gartership will agree that relations between the two heraldic authorities are far improved on those of our predecessors. Nonetheless the Scots Guards was an opportunity to test the new Garter. Lyon made a move; but the answer is simple, English, Scottish, Irish or Welsh Regiments there may be; but there is only one British Army and the British Army has one Inspectorate. The Scots Guards remained under my authority.

The problem with the Inspectorate of Regimental Colours and the later Inspectorate of Royal Air Force Badges is that serving officers in the Armed Forces do not necessarily have great design skills. Worse still are retired generals with possibly nothing to do except write letters, which are both literate and forceful, on the proposed design for regimental badge or colour. The ghost of my stepfather Gavin has returned in this guise; some of the letters could well have been his; and so I knew how to reply. The amalgamation of regiments into new super regiments caused many headaches. The headaches descended on the Deputy Inspector, David Rankin-Hunt. I was often grateful for his skill in managing the various interested parties in such design questions. Any complainers may not have known the facts; but the Ministry of Defence does and has always provided me with total and unreserved support.

Such has not always been the case with the office of the Registrar of Trade Marks. Attempts by corporate bodies to register bogus heraldry as trade marks results in an ongoing and frustrating battle. The Registrar and his trade mark examiners submit all designs to Garter for comment if these are considered to be heraldic. The laws of arms dictate that no armorial bearings (arms, crests, supporters) may be self assumed as they are conferred as a dignity by the Crown. The Crown in turn delegates that authority to the Kings of Arms. To bring a court case would be risky. Corporate bodies have long devised their own armorial bearings. It is a practice dating back to the Middle Ages, and changing that practice would not be easy. The laws of arms are enforced by the Court of Chivalry which is separate from statute or common law. If the court decided against a company seeking to register bogus armorials as a trade mark, any pecuniary fine, let alone imprisonment, would be difficult to enforce. Members of such as the Heraldry Society press for cases to be brought in the Court of Chivalry; but I fear the national press might relish the reporting on 'mediaeval anachronisms', 'strange men dressed in tights and each wearing a carpet', and other tiresome comments. I sense that help will eventually be forthcoming from Europe where protection for armorial bearings is set to be strengthened.

However, when the winged dagger of the SAS was submitted for registration by a firm of plumbers, I suggested that plumbing vans displaying this well-known emblem had the potential to pose a serious security risk. The Ministry of Defence reacted. The winged dagger had never been registered with the Inspector of Regimental Colours. Within a few days the relevant and definitive painting had been prepared by one of the Herald painters at the College of Arms, sent to the Queen's Private Secretary for Her Majesty's approval and signature and returned to Garter House, thus enabling me to send the relevant stiff letter to the Registrar of Trade Marks. The Ministry of Defence and I with my deputy, David Rankin-Hunt, have endeavoured to ensure that all regimental badges and sundry insignia are now properly registered. The Inspectorate of George Nayler's Napoleonic days is not only active but has expanded. I believe it to be of considerable importance. Apart from the security issue with plumbers' vans, badges and colours provide all that sense of dignity and identity which is an essential part of our Armed Forces.

My first garterial week of Buckingham Palace, the House of Lords, Westminster Abbey and a few slightly lesser establishments left me mildly bewildered. It was frankly an obstacle course. My desk was equally demanding. There were departmental badges of new government organizations. Were they properly constituted? Were they actually official departments? Did they or did they not merit the use of the crown? The Home Office would suddenly decide that it wished to logo, digitalize or somehow update the Royal Arms, and decisions had to be taken as to where dignity, frivolity and practicality could be reconciled. Then there was the Royal Mint and even the last remnants of Empire. Perhaps history will record me as the last Garter who provided heraldry for the colonies, for example a blue and white lozenge suggesting an island reflected in the ocean has its sides swept by flying albatrosses counterchanged in blue and white. This is Tristan da Cunha; and this shield of arms is supported by two golden spiny lobsters.

The Royal Mint with its Chancellor of the Exchequer's Advisory Committee was one of a number of unexpected garterial positions. It was chaired by Prince Philip, Duke of Edinburgh; and we met in the Chinese Room at Buckingham Palace. As a Herald, I had long been acquainted with Chinese dragons; but as I sat during discussions on the attributes of Roger Bannister's leg destined to appear on the fifty pence coin commemorating the four-minute mile, I glanced upwards and wondered why the principal dragon in the Chinese Room in Buckingham Palace was distinctly western and not oriental.

The committee deliberates on the design of our national coinage. A dozen or so of an eclectic but delightful mix from the museum and numismatic world meet and decide on coin designs. The results of our deliberations are well known as they appear in everyone's purses and pockets. Some designs I have supported; others I have not. The hand of Queen Elizabeth I was shown resting on an orb; and I commented that it looked as if the hand was stabbing a plum pudding. Three hundred years on, Queen Elizabeth II was depicted on a horse. The horse was not a good English thoroughbred and to much apparent amusement I said it was far too 'Hanoverian'. Thankfully the British public has been spared these designs.

Later I was invited to be a member of a sub-committee, consisting of four, to consider the new designs for the basic rather than commemorative coinage. The familiar penny and its fellows were due for a new look. Established artists and coin designers were commissioned from the United Kingdom and from overseas. In addition the general public was invited to submit ideas. I and my fellow committee members then examined over four thousand two hundred designs.

I became aware that coin design is not one of the United Kingdom's great abilities. I also learned much of the public's idea of our current national icons. The cup and saucer possibly proved the most popular, but hardly suitable to replace royal heraldry or insignia. I viewed the Angel of the North from every angle, and became aware that Britain's 'national bird' was not the English robin, Scottish golden eagle or even the Irish wren or Welsh red kite. It was the puffin.

We pruned that four thousand two hundred down to about one hundred. The five pence is a somewhat absurd coin demanding a frivolous and fun design. I and others of the full committee fought a battle for Lewis Carroll's white rabbit in heraldic tabard as in Tenniel's well-known drawing. Although Heralds have never blown trumpets except metaphorically, Robin Porteous and I gave the white rabbit a good run. The misconception of Heralds and trumpets stems from Shakespeare's Henry V where 'a Herald enters with a trumpet'. The 'trumpet' was a trumpeter and not a musical instrument held by the Herald himself. I have had to process and proclaim in my career as an officer of arms; there have been plenty of spine-chilling blasts from state trumpeters; but I have certainly never felt any inclination to seize one of their trumpets and take over. I can think that none of my garterial predecessors would have different thoughts from my own.

Comments on our decisions on coinage design have not always been complimentary. Apparently we have sacked Britannia, which has caused great offence. It is gratifying to learn that British citizens

still appreciate their age-old emblems and symbols. Britannia has not
been sacked; she is merely having a rest until an artist can depict her
in such a way that she does not look like a Glastonbury hippy or Posh
Spice in a Star Wars helmet. I personally find Posh Spice attractive;
but she is not Britannia.

We did not join the Euro, but our committee had to submit
designs. The brief was that each country was allowed its own symbol
on one side, provided it was combined with the European circle of
stars. Such as the French complied with their figure of Marianne
surrounded by the necessary stars. The Dutch were slightly suspect as
Queen Beatrix's profile featured with a tiny circle of stars suspended
in mid air somewhere below her nose. Comments as to where was
her handkerchief were soon forgotten when the British submissions
were seen. Where was the circle of stars demanded by European
regulations? Her Majesty's profile was there; but apparently no stars.

Look carefully at the British coinage, and you will see the Queen's
profile is surrounded by such abbreviations as Reg.F.D. meaning
Regina (Queen) and Defender of the Faith. Plenty of full stops,
replaceable by stars, enabled us to abide by European regulations,
showed typical British enterprise and infuriated European partners.

On the reverse side of this new European Euro there were three
possibilities; European buildings, European men or women of
historical importance and then a general theme of love, charity or
democracy. This last filled me with gloom as I thought of yet more
clasped hands in friendship or fluttering doves with or without the
olive branch.

Buildings were not particularly controversial; the French possibly
enjoyed scoring over the British with the Eiffel Tower, which was
rather more modern than Stonehenge. This last seemed to have been
the British allocation with the occasional vote going to Big Ben or
Tower Bridge.

Personalities were much more tiresome. Although no European
country would deny us Shakespeare, it was the French and Germans
who squabbled over whether they could have one or two or even
three national figures and who they should be. Beethoven and
Voltaire seemed to be acceptable; but we in Britain became more
concerned over the Greek submission. This was not Homer or
Pericles; it was Melina Mercouri. Forget about the French and

Germans with their composers and philosophers, here was a living Greek with an overriding ambition to see the return of the Elgin Marbles to Athens.

We ignored all European regulations, submitted a charming set of Celtic animal designs, did not join the Euro and have subsequently seen a thoroughly uninspired and dreary set of Euro coins, that simply confirms my thoughts that coin design is seldom easy, but mixed with European and national sentiments the result is a forgettable nothingness. Even the white rabbit would be an improvement!

The Christmas of 1995 was exceptional. I spent it in England with my cousin Georgina and her family. To say that I have never since spent another Christmas in England has nothing whatsoever to do with my affection for Georgina which is considerably improved from the time she knocked down my bricks in Banny's nursery or stuck Banny's hatpins into my bottom, when two nice little children should have been 'seen and not heard' in the back seat of the car and indeed anywhere else. Bricks, hatpins and other horrors aside, we speak frequently on the telephone about the various adventures of younger members of the family.

In the meantime, this older member of the family returned to Garter House and became immersed in heraldic design, and the vetting and approving of applications for grants of arms.

Tabarded or mantled appearances, apart from House of Lords introductions, had diminished over that winter. An exception had been my first State Opening of Parliament. As Garter I took my place in The Queen's procession from the Royal Gallery into the Chamber of the House of Lords. In 1995 it was my job to set the procession in motion when the doors of the Robing Room at the end of the Royal Gallery were opened. State trumpeters trumpeted, and I judged The Queen's position before turning and giving a double flourish with my sceptre. The whole procession of Her Majesty, the Prince Philip, members of the Royal Household and state and government officials and other dignitaries, moved down the Royal Gallery, across the Prince's Chamber and into the House of Lords.

This ceremony should be relatively easy. However, there were two problems on my first Opening of Parliament. The Queen is greeted; and preceded by the Heralds, the Earl Marshal, the Lord Great Chamberlain and the Lord Chancellor, is conducted to the Robing

Room. The royal procession forms up in the Royal Gallery. In 1995 Garter and Black Rod stood side by side immediately behind Miles Norfolk and David Cholmondeley, the Lord Great Chamberlain. The Earl Marshal and Lord Great Chamberlain can move around and chat to guests in their respective boxes next to the Robing Room doors. Lesser mortals such as Garter and Black Rod are roughly rooted to the spot; those behind are not permitted even our measure of relaxation. The Queen's time in the Robing Room is a five or ten-minute affair; so television coverage makes up by interviewing relevant people about the ceremony and the House of Lords in general. Edward Jones, Black Rod, and I, standing on ceremonial duty, were confronted by a television screen in the Queen's Gallery. The screen showed Edward continuously eating biscuits. The more biscuits he ate, the greater became the chance of a serious British ceremonial losing all dignity with Black Rod and Garter sustaining convulsive attacks of the giggles.

We managed to keep our behaviour under control until the Robing Room doors opened; I turned and gave my specialized flourish with the garterial sceptre. All should have been easy; but I then became aware of another problem. Immediately behind me and in front of The Queen was Miles Norfolk. This should have presented no difficulty if the historical evolution of the ceremony had not dictated that the Earl Marshal should process walking backwards. It had somehow become the lot of Garter to stage-manage the procession down the full length of the Royal Gallery, through the Prince's Chamber and into the House. Processing forwards, knowing that the Earl Marshal behind is processing backwards, is in my view a thoroughly bad factor in British ceremonial. As Garter, I found it most unnerving having no idea whether Miles would cannon into me from behind or whether, in anticipation of this, I should speed up the procession so that unseemly gaps would appear. The Queen was undoubtedly the key figure and could indicate to Miles by her own speed whether he should slow down or speed up.

Miles was always determined to walk backwards in front of his Sovereign. He was adamant. His son Eddie succeeded as Earl Marshal on the death of Miles in 1992. To my great relief he obtained The Queen's permission to process walking forwards. He now does the flourish, and I can spend my last few years as Garter unworried, standing by my gilded pillar in the chamber and for the first time in nearly forty years actually attempting to listen to The Queen's speech.

That was 1995 and my induction as Garter. I had given the Gartership the 1995 Christmas break; but for Christmas 1996 I was not prepared to forgo horses, butterflies and adventure. I have always managed to stay in touch with Garter House with written letters, sent faxes or latterly e-mails during my absences. Time off promised to me when I accepted the Gartership.

CHAPTER 19

Letters home

S IX MONTHS AFTER BECOMING Garter, I was off after toucans and
weird birds such as oropendulas, and endeavouring to improve my
skills at humming bird identification. A selection of Latin America
experiences gave some amusement to Garter House and so I offer
them as a snapshot of my Latin American experiences in Venezuela,
Ecuador and Brazil.

To choose letters from the many that I have sent to Garter House
from Latin America is not easy; but three, one from each of the three
countries, may perhaps give some indication that my life has not been
entirely restricted to the College of Arms and the official duties of
the Gartership.

The first comes from Venezuela in August 1996, ten months after
my appointment and written to my personal staff. I am not certain
why I seem to have ignored the men!

The Llanos 21 August 1996 – the grasslands of Venezuela
My dear Margaret, Jill, Judith, Gillian, Hedgehog and the Hen,
With faxes at $10 a shot please consider yourselves lucky! I shall
make my writing even more illegible than usual by trying size
reduction to fit more in. This is El Cedral on the Llanos – an excellent
place. As you will all have learnt in school geography lessons, the
Llanos are the great grasslands north of the Amazon forest –
cowboys/gauchos and the wretched cow (bar the human, the world's
most disastrous animal), compete with capybara – the world's largest
rodent the size of a pig. What is not grass is water complete with the
straggly bits of forest – the wildlife is reminiscent of Bharatpur for
those of you who know that admirable place. Herons, ibis, storks, etc
– also 2 types of macaw and the sun bittern (a bird that has hitherto
remained elusive in Central America etc). I am now on approx 200
birds, but mammals are somewhat disappointing – plenty of crocs and
iguana and DAMN GNATS! I arrived last night to dine on piranha
heads (you eat the cheeks and the top of the head). Pause – it is so
hot that I shall take my beer and flop into the swimming pool before
lunch. I have been up since 5 and done much walking in my wellies

this morning. The lodge has a pleasant Spanish couple staying but I am mildly alarmed by what has just appeared. Ye gods. They are fatties from Boston – a dozen or more of them with bellies pouring out of tartan shirts, baseball caps and a variable assortment of binoculars, cameras and telescopes. I am definitely keeping my distance from this nightmarish horror. Happily they have brought their own Venezuelan guides who seem to have them under control. I hope that control continues! I have encountered a large anaconda – we both survived the experience. The sunset here is spectacular particularly when scarlet macaws are flying against it. There is not time for a shower and dinner where I suppose I have to try and be polite to the fatties from the US. UGH! I hope they do not discover the swimming pool – they will dislodge all the water!

2 days later. The Yankees happily remained under control and I retained the swimming pool for myself. Left El Cedral at 4.30 a.m. (was woken at 3.45) drove in the dark over pot-holed roads and obstacles included crocs/caiman to a bridge which had been swept away by floods. I crossed by motor boat which the lunatic driver who drove into a bush in midstream. My neighbour, the somewhat bulky Venezuelan woman with baby and umbrella deposited baby in my lap and damn near poked my eye out with her umbrella spokes. I was supposed to have been met on the far side – no such luck – so I eventually bargained a deal with a rascally cab driver – two in fact – and was driven for 6 hours up into the Andes where I eventually got back on course with my travel agent. I am now in a charming hotel which was originally a 17th century monastery – Gregorian chants are played from the belfry. Chilly and misty and definitely sweaters are called for. Up at 5 this morning with the son of the deputized travel agent in this area and the guide. The son believe it or not has just left Rugby and is about to start at London University! At 6.30 we were down into the tree line and scampered/slid/slithered through the jungle to catch the Andean cock of the rock – 5 males displaying – one of the world's great birds – the size of a small chicken brilliant red and black with a magnificent repertoire of belches and gurgles. Walked the highlands this afternoon – hard work as the altitude makes the ups and downs somewhat breathless. It is now 10 p.m. I am feeling extremely stiff after all this activity, I shall have a bath, suck the sweets which have been put by my bed and then retire to that splendid four poster with its rose-coloured curtains to be woken at 5 for a 5.30 departure – the Andean condor is on tomorrow morning's schedule. Tomorrow Night I shall be in Merida which is the capital of the

Venezuelan Andes where there is a fax – so I will send this. That will be your lot as I then leave for the cloud forests with all those splendid orchids and epiphytes and bromeliads etc. I think that I shall need a holiday when I return to recover from all this hectic exercise.

Hope all is well and no major problems.

Love

Garter

I am sorry that I was critical of the American bird watchers; but I have to add that the following morning I found an anteater lying out across the branch of a tree. Seeing the Americans two hundred yards away, I walked across and drew their attention to my find, thinking that an anteater must surely be of interest. 'We are only interested in birds', said one of the leaders of the group. My anteater, the tamandua, was totally ignored!

Quito 22 August 1999 – the capital city of Ecuador

My dear Everyone,

I doubt whether this will arrive before I return; but herewith nonetheless. It has been impossible to write since my last letter as I have been in the wilds of Amazonia in the company of pesky insects – the little devils have been hellish particularly at night and I swear they find some way through the mosquito net. Thankfully no chiggars – they are the worst and itch like fury for days. Post simply does not exist.

Tourists do not see jaguar – forest guides and guards are lucky if they see them once a year. This intrepid traveller has just see three! A most spectacular view of them on a sandbar – one stood and stared at me and my canoe paddler for at least two minutes only 50 yards away. I even managed to remember to take their photographs!

Tourists should not expect to see tapir, I spotted one five minutes after the jaguar and watched it wade across a river. This and the jaguars were real goodies and made the trip to Amazonia well worthwhile in spite of the insects.

Amazonia is difficult – I walked for hours down trails – but as before the forest always seems dead except for insects including some delicious butterflies (not all insects are nibblers!). I eventually managed to add 63 birds to my list – mainly the large and spectacular such as toucan, exotic fruit crow and macaws – I simply do not know where all the small birds lurk. Yes – agoutis and marmosets – but not a coati in sight (Costa Rica produces coatis every day!). The macaws were much in evidence – especially the blue and yellow which was spectacular and I have never seen it before. The scarlet macaw – an old friend – was also much in evidence. The bird count now stands at 313 and it was a relief to have a guide whose spotting and identification was on my level and this has somewhat restored my confidence after the amazing and humiliating abilities of the remark-able Pancha (my previous guide).

Returned to Quito today after 3½ hours (boring) in a speed boat 1½ hours bus ride and ½ air flight. Am back in my civilized hotel which I note in my guide book heads the five star list – so much for telling Metropolita Travel that I would be happy with three star. It is on Avenue Amazonas – the 'grand' street of Quito – and I set off this afternoon to explore. I cannot quite place Quito – apart from uniform guards with guns outside every bank it seems remarkably easy and placid. Contrary to all reports, the traffic cruises gently and it is far easier than London to cross the main streets. Pedestrians amble and seem totally relaxed. It is quite different from Caracas with its sense of fear, Mexico City with its crazy traffic, Lima with a touch of both fear and mad traffic – perhaps it is more akin to San Jose in Costa Rica but Quito is far larger, more sophisticated and there is much more street vending. I shall know more tomorrow when I spend the day pottering around the old part before heading off south and the coast.

I had to spend last night on the river in what is called a flotel – an awful crowd of tourists on board, including – alas – British. Bermuda shorts over which beer bellies sagged, children with souvenir Indian blowpipes, and sweaty English (unfortunately) girls clearly having one night stands with members of the crew. Ugh! I know we disagree, but I really do not think I could ever face going on a group tour! I am afraid I remained somewhat stand offish and was regarded with some awe as a solitary traveller and was pointed out by the crew as the man who had seen jaguar and tapir! Otherwise the 2 camps I stayed in previously were unoccupied except by me and the staff (and the wretched mosquito).

I am now finishing my gin and tonic and shall move to the dining room in my Quito hotel. Tieless and coatless but I shall doubtless pass. At least my nose seems to be on the mend and its disastrous experience less apparent!

The dining room – I am looking out at the 15 mph traffic and Ecuadorian girls. Some are quite pretty but I do not understand why the pretty ones so often go in pairs holding hands? The dining room is empty except for a Japanese couple and a solitary male at the table behind me – outside ethnic Indians pass by with trilby hats, shawls and bundles on their backs – these must be street vendors packing up for the night. I shall now attack some seafood helped by gin and tonic (wine is, I understand, revolting unless an exorbitant price is paid for the imported).

I shall not be bringing back any ethnic presents – they are not worth bothering about! Bad luck!

With love

Peter

More fatties; but worse still was the total and incomprehensible absence of binoculars in the possession of any of the flotel tourists. What I wondered was their reason for going to Amazonia. I lent my spare pair to a German couple and discussed impossible tourists and the sleeping habits of river dolphins with the chief guide, Isabel, who was full of her sighting of a harpy eagle, one of Latin America's star turns. I then said to Isabel, 'What do you think I have seen?'

'You didn't did you?' she replied. There was only one thing to trump her eagle; and she knew it.

'Oh yes,' I said, 'not one,' as I raised my finger, 'not two,' as I raised a second finger, 'but three,' as my third went up. She was aghast; even the guides do not expect to see jaguar. 'And then,' I went, 'guess what?'

'Oh no,' said Isabel.

'Yes,' I said, 'a tapir.'

The reference in my letter to my nose was my failure to make a proper application of sun cream on the Papallacta Pass some thirteen thousand feet up in the Andes. I had been more concerned about altitude sickness, which did not appear to affect me. The flesh fell off much of my nose and required medical treatment in Quito. I was bright red with plasters across the damaged area causing considerable amusement to the band in the foyer of my Quito hotel. Sondheim wrote a song called *Send in the Clowns*, which the band struck up every time I made an appearance.

Quito itself was not so peaceful as my letter suggests. Two days later there were some good-natured and seemingly harmless demonstrations outside the Presidential Palace. The Army appeared. I sat in the square watching until there was a sudden outburst of gunfire; panic set in; and people ran out of the square in all directions. I rose from my seat, becoming aware of a stinging sensation in eyes and nose. It was tear gas. I refused to join the fleeing Ecuadorians but walked in stoic British manner out of the square and took a taxi back to my hotel. I am not certain why there has been such an over reaction to what seemed to me a perfectly friendly group of people trying to express their views without any sign of anger or resort to violence. That perhaps is just Latin America.

Caracas, Brazil 25 August 2005 – Botanists' paradise north west of Rio
Dear Everyone,

I am in my cell in this monastic institution which seems to be under the protection of St Vincent de Paul – that 17th century saint who was connected with or befriended by Anne of Austria. His statue and pictures compete with those of the Virgin Mary. My cell only has a crucifix above my bed and no other furnishings. The building is dominated by a Gothic church where I have attended mass. The whole place has a mediaeval monastic feel with cloisters and stone passages and curious medicinal smells. The food is very reasonable except for breakfast, which I had to cook myself, but I do not seem to be able to manage any passable fried egg – I will try again tomorrow. I can obtain beer in the refectory and even wine made by the priests/monks which is a cross between cough mixture and cranberry juice – I am sticking to the beer. It is cooler here with montane vegetation that would thrill any botanists – the birds need working at – but current count is over 200 with about 90 totally new to me – plus 2 new species of monkey and the maned wolf which is a magnificent beast. Food is set up in the courtyard after evening mass (chicken legs and raw beef) – the wolves mount 14 steps (not unlike those at the College) up into the courtyard. They did not come last night probably because I was having an earnest conversation on Japanese heraldry with a Canadian and his Brazilian wife! I did see the wolf the night before last and will wait up again tonight but will probably give mass a miss. Iguazu had a lot of water and a lot of tourists – but better I think than Victoria Falls and certainly better than Niagara. I was on the Argentine side – the Argies were charming and unlike Brazil I was allowed to cash travellers cheques. The hotel had a forest of foreign flags outside – all nations of note were there except the UK – a statement perhaps!

P.

PS The wolf has just been – it came after mass when I read *Harry Potter and the Half Blood Prince* in a back pew. However I have endeavoured to compensate for such irreligious behaviour by straightening the crown on the head of Our Lady of Fatima and checking the halos on the heads of the ubiquitous statues of St Vincent de Paul.

I never achieved much success with the fried eggs. Armed with two spatulas and a hot plate the size of a large dining room table, I seemed incapable of keeping eggs under control. The hot plate appeared to slope in such a way that eggs would slide towards the edge and in spite of my efforts to prevent their increasing momentum, they would inevitably plop to the floor.

It was in Brazil that I became reacquainted with the Amazon, spending my nights slung in a hammock in villagers' wooden houses tethered to the riverbank and eating piranha and casserole of tortoise. Our large tortoise had lurked in the bottom of our boat for several days. It was not a happy animal; and I was relieved when Mrs Sid eventually casseroled it and served it up as a delicious meal in its own shell. Mrs Sid was the wife of my guide Sid; and we all slept in those slung hammocks with Amazonian families whose children must be among the most deprived and sad in the world. They have nothing; to play at the back of the house runs the risk of being lost in the forest; to play at the front risks falling into the river with its currents and piranhas. Throw a piece of meat on the end of a string and bamboo cane into the water and it would boil with piranhas. I watched two little girls aged about four and six with nothing to do except walk from one window to another. They were literally bored to tears, hugged each other, broke down and wept.

In another house there were half a dozen children. The youngest, another small girl aged about six, had acquired something to play with, six pieces of offcut from a wooden door made by her father. She kept the pieces in a plastic bag and arranged them in various shapes and patterns. Her great delight was to find a nail, and she attempted to join two pieces of wood together, only to be told by her mother to stop making a noise. Such emptiness of life is so very different from children in India playing marbles, jacks, hopscotch, stick and hoop and generally having a fun-filled time. A little self-initiative might bring some joy to Amazonian children; but I fear this may not happen.

The Americas and India were not the only sources of adventure and wildlife during these years, as two sample letters sent from Uganda in August 1998 demonstrate.

The Impenetrable Forest
8 August 1998

My dear Everyone,

I did write 3 days ago, but I am not over trusting of the hotel where I was staying. The chances of my first letter arriving may be slim – I hope I am wrong! All has been well except for my guide Elias who has been suffering from toothache. However I have dosed him up with paracetemol and threatened to take him to the dentist. This combination of treatment (I suspect mainly the fear of the dentist) has seemingly sorted him out.

We came here from Kabale where the hotel was fine except for the food and mosquitoes. Goat stew was the speciality – not to be recommended. Apart from being exceedingly tough, I have a soft spot for the perky goat and do not like the idea of eating him. The mosquitoes were not good. They inspired a witty ditty in the middle of the night

The mosies through the night they come;
I am tired of their incessant hum;
They bite their way from thumb to bum;
I try in vain the pests to kill;
Instead I have to take my pill;
And pray I do not come home ill!

At Kabale I took to a canoe so narrow I could barely fit in. Sitting on a makeshift cushion of dried grass I was paddled across Lake Bunyoni to an island where Elias and I chalked up our 112th bird and 13th Mammal (the 13th was the black rat!). One bird (the white-tailed blue monarch) is stated in the bird book to be so rare that the chances of ever seeing it are 'negligible'. This excitement was somewhat dampened when I saw it elsewhere the next day! The bird expert of the Impenetrable Forest confirms that my identification is quite correct; but the bird book is wrong. In fact the new bird book on East African Birds seems to be rather full of errors.

I have now spent 2 nights at a rather primitive lodge on the edge of the Impenetrable Forest – Tin huts – outside loos – shower in a canvas bag ordered 5 minutes in advance and then suspended from the ceiling. WELL the so-called Impenetrable Forest was penetrated yesterday. IT WAS AN EXPERIENCE! I set off in a party of 5 at 7 o'clock. 2 young Americans, 2 Aussies aged about 30, hardened by trekking in the Himalayas, and Garter King of Arms. The Americans packed it in after 1 hour or less. Quite unbeknown to me Elias (who did not come) had succeeded in overriding the forest authorities who stated that nobody was allowed on the trek over the age of 30 unless they could prove fitness ability! Elias argued that I was a hardened forest expert! If I had known what was in store, I would not have gone. 12 hours of horrendous slog – it was not the time, but the impossible terrain – up and down hillsides often with nothing resembling a track. On a number of occasions I had to climb up through the forest on all fours. The object of the exercise was to find gorillas, which we did. Gorillas in the wild are as lugubrious as they are in a zoo. I spent three-quarters of an hour with them – a troop of about 24 – and then a 5 hour trek home. I could hardly make the upward slopes through the undergrowth – they were killers. I had to stop frequently for breath, my feet felt like lead and my knees ached something terrible. Arrived back at base 7.30. I remember once in school corps having to carry a bren gun throughout the night over the Marlborough Downs; but that was nothing compared to this little jaunt. 12½ hours!! What I find somewhat extraordinary is that apart from a number of scratches and a slight stiffness I seem to be none the worse for my adventure this morning. I was able quite happily to spend 8 hours on a well-maintained track roughly on the level gently bird and bug watching. With the help of an excellent bird guide assisted by Elias the bird total has now reached 172. The butterflies are numerous and excellent and I chalked up a good new monkey.

I am now drinking Nile beer – I shall finish this and order my canvas bag shower before dinner. Last night was spaghetti à something (minced goat?)

Hope all is well and no major problems

Peter

Julia – Do not be put off gorilla trekking. There are 3 groups in the neighbourhood. 2 are readily accessible but get booked up by Abercrombie and Kent. I drew the short straw and had the group furthest away and deeper into the forest. Those going to the near groups were back after ¾ of an hour not 12½!

Ndali Lodge
15 August 1998

My dear Everyone,

I am the only guest here – nothing new about that. But this is an admirable place down-up-down two ruts and set on the edge of a crater lake. Very attractive and may even merit a photograph. I suspect that the owner one Mr Mark Price is English – but he is abed with a fever so I have not encountered him only his greetings! The Field, Country Life and sporting prints suggest he might be civilized. My cabin is delightfully elegant – four poster beds *with* (for the first time) mosquito netting, flowers by the bed etc, all beautifully maintained and a half dozen lanterns that actually work (no electricity here). All in contrast to the dreadful Mountains of the Moon Hotel in Fort Portal last night – a really run down sleazy place. Elias got food poisoning – I was wise enough to be suspicious and smuggled most of mine out to flush it down the loo. I survived on biscuits until I offered one to a dusky maiden who promptly gobbled my entire packet (she must have eaten about 30). However I am now catching up and having an excellent dinner. The only advantage of the wretched Mountains of the Moon Hotel was CNN News and the newspapers so I could catch up on the weather in England (ugh – bad luck) and nice snippets of local news such as the enclosed.

> ### Sons refund bride-price
> *Sam Aisu and James Okolang of Olungia village in Kumi meted out the perfect punishment to their father for battering their mother – they 'bought' her from him.*
>
> *The sons, disgusted by their father, Faiso Ouma's behaviour gave him back the 18 heads of cattle he paid as bride-price for her in 1970.*
>
> *Ouma said he would use the cattle to acquire a new wife.*

This – CRUMBS – as I wrote 'This' – there was an earthquake! I am not joking. It lasted for 4/5 seconds and everything rattled and shook but no damage. In fact this has been the third today. The first was early this morning when I was in the forest there was this rumble like thunder and the whole earth beneath my feet heaved. It was an extraordinary and rather intriguing experience. The second was an hour ago just after I arrived here, a fairly mild tremor I suppose. I am not an earthquake expert, so I do not know. This last was considerably bigger and staff here seem alarmed. I think I prefer to be in the forest and not in a building with all this going on. There are rather a lot of beams above my head which would crash down if the quakes get more dramatic. I do not remember from my schoolboy days in geography lessons that Central Africa was an earthquake-prone area – obviously I am wrong!

Earthquakes aside, the mammal count improves – I saw no less than 7 species of monkey today. Note for Julia – black and white colobus about five times today but also red colobus and sex among the chimpanzees.

The elements are playing merry hell this evening – since the earthquake 5 minutes ago a wind has come rushing in and there are flashes of lightning. The only consistent element seems to be the cacophony of frogs. I shall pause for a few minutes, order a Nile Beer, eat my fish casserole and then report back. I think this is going to be a disturbed night!

5 minutes later – wind dropped – lightning seems to be confining itself to the main Ruwenzori range and my pancake pudding has arrived. I shall gobble the same, have some coffee, retire under my mosquito net; be prepared to dive under my bed if there are further earthquakes and bid you all goodnight.

Peter

Unbeknown to me, two Europeans had mysteriously disappeared at Bwindi shortly before my arrival. Not long afterwards a settlement there at the entrance to the Impenetrable Forest was attacked, and the Europeans staying there taken into the forest and macheted.

Physical exhaustion may have been caused by gorillas leading me from Uganda possibly across an undefined border into the Congo; but in ignorance I probably encountered greater physical risk on the Luangwa River in Zambia. I had already been in close contact with wildlife in the form of a marauding hyena who had made a nocturnal visit to my small ablution tent. The tent had sustained a measure of destruction. However, nothing was missing except for my soap. I was led to believe by my guide Bob Svenstadt that hyenas were partial to soap. I wondered what soap did to hyenas' digestion and whether they subsequently blew or farted dramatic bubbles from one or other end. Whatever the hyena's problems may have been, Bob decided next morning to drive to the local village some miles away to provide extra provisions and acquire a bottle of whisky. In the meantime he advised me to cross the River Luangwa which was heavily infested with crocodiles and hippos. I asked Bob where was the boat. There was no boat; and I would have to wade. As sizeable crocodiles were very apparent, I naturally posed the query as to how I might avoid these reptiles which had already acquired a certain notoriety for being among the most dangerous in Africa. Bob's answer was to provide me with a bamboo pole and instruct me on how to cross the Luangwa River, avoid the crocodiles and reach the other side. I should place the pole in front of me; and using it like a pogo stick jump up and down, make a lot of noise and make certain that I did not allow the water to rise above my knees. I duly took off my safari boots, strung them around my neck, took two or three strides into the water and plunged in my stick and jumped up and down.

To my alarm there was a sudden great splashing. My thought was on something crocodilian; but it transpired to be two large four or five pound fish who were as equally alarmed as I. I then proceeded across some fifty yards, putting my pole into the water and jumping up and down to reach the sandbar in the middle of the river. I looked across and was about to take off across the second half of the river only to see on the far bank a pride of lions, three lionesses and five cubs of assorted ages. The lions, somewhat astonished by my pogo stick activities, rose from their siesta and moved off. I had waded across the Luangwa, where I put on my socks and safari boots before wandering off through the bush. I soon re-encountered the lions a hundred yards or so in front of me, and once more they lazily rose to their feet and moved on. I found little except a warthog, a bushbuck and then put up the lions for the third time. I decided that lions and crocodiles were probably sufficient for one afternoon, so I retreated.

When I arrived back in London, I encountered Peter Moss, one of the directors of Eco Safaris, and told him that I had crossed the Luangwa River on foot. He was horrified. As a ranger in the Luangwa River Valley, he expressed the view that I must be one of the few people who ever crossed the Luangwa River on foot and survived. It is certainly true that the Luangwan crocodiles have taken a number of people. I suspect that Bob's advice was not unsound; but possibly lions and crocodiles on this particular occasion may have been a slightly risky experience. Bob did not seem to be unduly worried that evening when he returned with his provisions. All you could do is draw on your own common sense and experience and depend upon the advice of the local experts and guides. I can only say that I was not taken by a crocodile; and the lions clearly did not consider that I was suitable edible material. Crocodiles I would not trust; but with lions I feel it is possible to gauge their mood and appetite. I did not for one moment think that these lions were aggressive or that I was on their menu.

CHAPTER 20

The Queen Mother's Funeral

IN 2001 I INTRODUCED FORTY-THREE new peers into the House of Lords. My tabard was becoming well used. The annual Garter Service and the State Opening of Parliament came and went. At our first Garter Service Edward Jones and I prided ourselves on our synchronization. Her Majesty requested we summon the new Knights Companions of the Order of the Garter for the investiture ceremony. Edward and I came and stood before Her Majesty, bowed and turned about to process the length of the throne room in Windsor Castle. Edward banged on the far door with his black rod. Our synchronization was such when a large piece of paint dropped to the floor we both in harmony together muttered 'Oh shit!' Sir Simon Cooper, Master of the Household, was reputed not to be too pleased as he gave instructions for repair work. He threatened a brass plaque to take the blows of future Black Rods.

I had little part in the funeral arrangements following the untimely death of Diana, Princess of Wales. The decision was taken that it should be a private rather than a state occasion. I took a proclamation up to Buckingham Palace on the Monday after her death; but it was not required. I also took the depositum or Latin inscription for the coffin plate. I had wondered whether a simple English inscription might be more in keeping with the last decade of the century; but precedence was followed. I worked on the Latin phrases early that Monday based on the depositums of past members of the Royal Family. The crowds in the Mall were extraordinary and once or twice I had to receive police help to see me through from St James's Palace to Buckingham Palace. The Queen Mother's funeral was very different; and a proclamation was required. Both proclamation and depositum had long been prepared.

The Queen Mother died on 30 March 2002, the day before Easter Sunday. I was staying at Bawdeswell when Francesca, the au pair girl of my godson Robert Gurney, found me in the garden and broke the news. I put in a telephone call to Buckingham Palace so that the Lord

246

Chamberlain's Office would know my whereabouts in case any query involving such as heraldry might arise. It is a well-known fact that the Queen Mother's funeral had long been planned. Nonetheless, in spite of such meticulous preparation, unexpected events occur; and a little bit of enterprise and initiative is sometimes required. The funeral was not a state occasion. This means it was the responsibility of the Lord Chamberlain's Office and not the Earl Marshal assisted by Garter. The Earl Marshal was skiing; but the Prime Minister and government started muttering about a state funeral and interfering in long-laid plans. It would have been a disaster; and thankfully I was able to tell Eddie Norfolk, the Earl Marshal, that he could remain skiing and I as Garter would not have to act as his number two. Sir Malcolm Ross, Comptroller of the Lord Chamberlain's Office, would stand for no alteration; and he and the relatively new Black Rod, Sir Michael Willcocks, with responsibility for the lying in state, ensured that the Prime Minister was kept at bay.

All plans remained on course; and I had merely to concern myself with my own part which was to proclaim the styles, titles and dignities of the Queen Mother towards the end of the funeral service. I had already inherited from my garterial predecessors the form of the proclamation. However, this left out any reference to her style as Queen Mother. The original proclamation simply termed her the Queen Dowager. Technically this may have been correct; and her own wish to be known as the Queen Mother, which she had expressed in 1953, was arguably unofficial. However, it had been used in all printed ceremonials since 1953; and more importantly she was known as the Queen Mother by everyone in the United Kingdom and the Commonwealth. I had therefore had this inserted so that she was described in my proclamation as both 'Queen Dowager' and 'Queen Mother'. I left out the Order of Canada, which caused a flurry the day before the funeral; but this was done because she was only an honorary member of that order. I also omitted Lord Warden of the Cinque Ports and other positions which she had held. These included 'sometime Empress of India'; and my omission of this also caused offence in certain quarters. The proclamation was long enough; and if I was to recite every position and office that Her Majesty had held, then I might have taken up a quarter of the entire funeral service at Westminster Abbey.

I was happy with the content of the proclamation itself. I was less happy with ensuring that I had it with me at the right moment in the service and that I would be able to deliver it properly. I had the proclamation typed out with double spacing and pasted onto a board of black card. I was not prepared to allow any steward or verger in Westminster Abbey to place it on my seat. I dreaded the idea of arriving at my chair to find that no proclamation was there. I probably knew most of it by heart; but it was not a risk I was prepared to take. On the other hand, carrying a board in my hand in the procession up the aisle might be undignified. My board needed to look more resplendent for the occasion. I therefore took the black ribbon from my knighthood insignia of the Order of St John and cut it up. As the ribbon was black, I was able to attach two three-inch long and one-inch wide black tags to the bottom of my proclamation board. Whether or not anyone was to notice this on television I do not know; but at least I felt I had a rather more official looking prop.

Having settled the proclamation, I became concerned that I might just find the occasion of the Queen Mother's funeral an opportunity for nerves. This would not do. My first lecture in America had found me with my mouth and hence voice drying up. On that occasion I had a carafe of wine. Clearly I could not produce a flask of whisky from beneath my tabard when proclaiming the Queen Mother's styles and titles. The drying up of the mouth is only one problem. Nerves can also produce a certain twitching. I was aware that my proclaiming would be televised throughout the world; and at the same time I would be holding my sceptre. A slight twitching in the knees would probably go unnoticed; but twitching when it reaches the sceptre could become exaggerated by the sceptre's two-foot length so that the television screen might be subjected to my face hidden by the sceptre behaving like a clock's pendulum. None of this would do.

I went to see my doctor; and was somewhat surprised to learn that most actors or actresses, not to mention racing car drivers, take pills to quieten the nerves before they perform. I had no problem in being armed with two lots of pills and told to try them out and see whether or not they had any drowsy effects. I had two or three days before the funeral took place. I tried out the pills; they might have been pink sugar. I was not aware of any difference whatsoever either mentally or physically. The day before the funeral we had a rehearsal in

Westminster Abbey. I stood and proclaimed, taking about two or three minutes. I had no idea of the Abbey's acoustics; I had no idea whether or not I would be heard in the Abbey, let alone around the world by millions on television. I also had no idea as to whether I had spoken too fast or too slow; but the rehearsal continued; and nobody commented on my part except the Lord Chamberlain's Office querying the Order of Canada which I did not consider to be a problem.

The next morning Robin Blair, Lord Lyon, came to Garter House. The court tailors also came, and we were duly robed in our tabards. Black sashes were provided; and I had agreed to wear white gloves, which were part of the uniform of Scottish officers of arms. The English Heralds do not wear white gloves; but on this occasion I made a quick telephone call to the Adjutant of the Life Guards, and I was duly provided with assorted sizes and so resolved that particular problem.

Robin and I set off in a government car to Westminster Abbey. Parliament Square was packed; and there was no way in which the car could reach the Abbey by that route. We negotiated various detours and back streets, eventually reaching the Abbey doors where I took Robin into the Jerusalem Chamber. Anyone entering Westminster Abbey might just notice an insignificant wooden door on the right-hand side. This is essentially a private door which leads into the Jerusalem Chamber where Henry V was born. It is also a chamber which is used by the Order of the Bath for its annual meetings and is full of glorious and splendid history. In the Jerusalem Chamber were gathered the clergy and other somewhat esoteric officials such as Sir Roy Strong, High Bailiff of Westminster, and Lord Hurd of Westwell who was the High Steward of Westminster. I know Roy well; but I have never yet fathomed what the High Bailiff is, does or why he exists. Nonetheless he and Douglas Hurd were both dressed in ceremonial garb. After coffee in the Jerusalem Chamber we needed to move out into the aisle. At this point, just in case, I took the opportunity to swallow my pink pill. I went out into the Westminster Abbey aisle with George Carey, the Archbishop of Canterbury. George and I cast our eyes over the congregation where the women were all dressed in black except for one who was wearing a shocking pink hat. George and I embarked on a somewhat frivolous conversation about that hat when I suddenly discovered that my wretched pill had lodged itself in the corner of my throat and had not gone down. It was too late, we all set off. I held my proclamation board with its St John's tags and I held by sceptre upright. I tried gulping to get rid of my wretched pill; this did not succeed. It was not until sometime later that, to my relief, it dissolved. I am not certain what would have happened had my proclamation come at the beginning of the service.

I eventually arrived past the Royal Family and took up position in a chair at the top of the steps leading to the altar. Her Majesty The Queen and the Royal Family were immediately below me. I made note of this, being aware that any television camera focussed on The Queen would show me in the background. It was essential not to bite the nails; which I could not do because I was wearing gloves provided by the Household Cavalry. I have since seen a video of the service and I can confess to only one feeble yawn during the course of George Carey's sermon.

George's sermon eventually ended; there followed anthems and prayers until finally there was the last post played by the State Trumpeters. The last post is an agonizing piece of music; because every time you think it has finished, it then begins again. Eventually I went out, stood in front of the Queen Mother's coffin and proclaimed. I had reminded myself that this was to be no more difficult than reading a lesson in the church of St James in Long Burton in Dorset. Of course it was; and I was much relieved to return to my seat, where I looked across at the Lord Lieutenants who were gathered below the altar steps in a series of pews. Some of them were slight or even close acquaintances; but there was nothing except a deadpan expression from them all. I sat in my chair and thought, 'Oh hell, what have I done?' Perhaps my fly buttons were undone; but then I realized that my tabard would have covered that misfortune. I wondered whether I had said that Her Majesty the Queen Mother was of the 'Star of India' rather than the 'Crown of India', the Star of India being one of my favourite curry houses in Chelsea. What else could I have done? I was not very happy until I started to process out of Westminster Abbey and somehow I caught the eye of Prince Philip, Duke of Edinburgh. There was something about that eye which has a certain twinkle which comes through even on serious occasions. I knew that my fly buttons had not been undone and that my curry house had not been erroneously inserted. I was confident that I had done a reasonable job. Robin Blair and I then returned to Dean's Yard in Westminster Abbey and waited for our car. There was a car problem caused by congestion in the area; and a group of four of us gathered, Robin, myself, the Duchess of York and Derry, Lord Irvine of Lairg, the Lord Chancellor. I have often thought that this was a somewhat incongruous combination after the Queen Mother's funeral. However, our car arrived; and Robin and I departed to the House of Lords. The reason for this is that my tabard and sceptre are stored there in Black Rod's office since their main use is for introducing new peers.

Barriers were up; and nobody was being allowed through. However, tabarded figures were sufficient for the barriers to be dismantled for Garter King of Arms and Lord Lyon King of Arms. We went into the House of Lords. Although I am not a lord, I think by now I was regarded as something of a mascot. I went straight to the Peers Guest Room where I was sure I would be able to buy both of us a drink. This proved unnecessary as we were caught by Melvin, Lord Bragg, who immediately bought us a bottle of champagne. We shared the champagne with the Errolls. I have a certain affection for Isabelle Erroll ever since she and I started an evening of dancing in a Polish town hall in upstate New York when the Errolls were doing something Scottish with tartans, kilts and reels and I was being a trifle less exciting on a lecture tour for the English Speaking Union. Melvin and the Errolls, accompanied by champagne, provided the desired relaxation after a somewhat eventful morning.

CHAPTER 21

Bamboo Banks

FOR TWO WEEKS AFTER THE Queen Mother's funeral I seemed to become something of a national celebrity. I went to a restaurant in Chelsea; and everyone in the restaurant rose to their feet and clapped. I was mobbed by three or four pretty blondes at the Earls Court Underground Station; and even approached by people on the train itself as it jolted along between Blackfriars and Earls Court. Ten days later I went to Arizona to ride Bart in the mountains. The staff of Bellota Ranch had all watched the Queen Mother's funeral on television and recognized me immediately. I do not think I wanted to be a celebrity. Thankfully, by the time I flew back from Tucson, I had returned to relative anonymity. Such anonymity is not always possible to obtain. It was only recently that I sat on a train going from Delhi to Lucknow when I was confronted with the tiresome enquiry as to my occupation. I always find it very difficult to explain the Gartership. I try to say that I am interested in royal heraldry or history. On this occasion my neighbour on the Indian train suddenly perked up and said, 'Are you Garter King of Arms?'

The funeral was at the beginning of 2002. At the end of 2002 it was half time in my Gartership. Somehow the College of Arms had survived my first seven and a half years; and I was able to take off once again for India. Three days after reading the final lesson at the College of Arms Carol Service, 'In the beginning was the Word . . .' I found myself lying on a thin mattress, covered by a blanket well-eaten by sundry insects, on the baked sand of an island in the Brahmaputra River.

There was a strong whiff of buffalo dung as the large herd of village buffalo was concentrated at night on the edge of the village where my tent was pitched. The village was composed of buffalo dung huts with thatched roofs, scattered somewhat haphazardly along the riverbank. Fish and buffalo were the livelihood of the villagers whose only means of transport was by boat or on foot.

I was sharing my tent with my old friend Kavas with his endless

252

packets of Charm cigarettes and cracking finger joints. He was in good form, having relaxed everyone around the campfire the previous evening giving excellent renderings of Boy George on a guitar, wearing his new prized possession, a round Muslim-type cap embroidered in black and white. In the next-door tent was Hermanta. Hermanta and I had greeted each other as long-lost friends since I had known him from his days as assistant manager at the Wild Grass Resort in Kaziranga National Park in Assam. Poor Hermanta had a terrible night sitting in a crouched position suffering the snores of his tent companion, a stranger who synchronised his snores with arm gesticulations. Nights on the Brahmaputra yielded good singalong camp company, spectacular sunsets and a reminder that star-lit skies continued to exist, even if seldom seen in polluted London or overcast England.

We were on our way to Arunachal Pradesh, the easternmost state of India, bordering Burma, sparsely populated by a seemingly mixed grouping of people: Burmese, Nepali, Nagas and Bangladeshis. Although I was not aware of any political difficulties, the area was restricted with special permits necessary. It seems that other non-resident Indians were excluded; but foreigners were allowed in, provided they constituted a group of at least four. My step-brother Gavin was remembered by some of the Nagas I met who continue to recall him with affection. He spent time among them during the Naga insurrection as a foreign correspondent for the *Observer* and was still regarded as something of a hero.

The restrictions allowing us to go into Arunachal Pradesh and into the large reserve of Namdapha presented no difficulty; Kavas and I did not even have to resort to some tall story of my non-existent party of four having missed a flight connection. Kavas as a wily Bombay Parsee had fixed everything. The authorities at the border, the police control and the forest authority were, without exception, friendly and welcoming. The forest director was particularly charm-ing; and Kavas and I were subsequently able to entertain him to dinner at our base forest camp in the park where he explained that Indian tourists were excluded because of their disturbance to wildlife. Since every leaf and mosquito must be preserved, I rather wondered why I spotted him the following morning fishing for mahseer, the prized game fish! I did not press this point.

The purpose of visiting Namdapha was to find birds endemic to the north east hill states, especially the white-crested laughing thrush. This large bird, of chestnut brown with a white head and crest and black eye-stripe, I was determined to see; and Hermanta informed me that it was a speciality of Namdapha. Our expedition, consisting of Kavas, Hermanta and myself, together with our cook and driver, was equipped with everything from food and blankets to portable loo and was full of hope and expectation. It was therefore disappointing that the first birding parties encountered were the all too familiar birds of the Indian plains, orioles, minivets and drongos.

The camp in Namdapha was even worse. Most camps attract a fair cross section of the local birdlife; but this camp yielded only a resident whistling thrush and a Burmese shrike. The terrain was hardly that of the hills, being thick tropical forest at a low elevation with the last snow-capped peaks of the Eastern Himalayas apparent in the distance before they fanned out into the hills of China and Burma. To reach higher elevations would have required weeks of trekking which was clearly not a possibility.

A local forest official, with his infectious smile and impossible accent made his appearance. I was never able to catch his name properly. It sounded like 'bushmouse' so I duly named him 'Mr Bushmouse', which he seemed to find acceptable. The first evening Mr Bushmouse and I left the others and set out on the dirt road leading to the camp. After ten minutes an elephant emerged from the bushes some fifty yards in front of us. Mr Bushmouse, two yards in front of me, turned and signalled me to run. Happily the road had a corner, and looking back the elephant was out of sight. With some relief I was able to reduce my sprinting to a hurried walk and discovered from Mr Bushmouse that the elephant was supposed to be a domestic elephant. It was only half trained and had somehow become detached from its shackles. The following day the elephant was removed to a camp some five miles away for further training; but not before Mr Bushmouse and I had been forced to take a short cut up a forested hill. As evening descended we were on a precipitous and slippery slope, where I fell over at least once, feeling an idiot. What I was doing? Never certain on my feet, I was wondering whether old age was eventually catching up. My concern increased when we reached level ground and seemed to walk on for miles.

Here I was in an obscure part of the world with a total stranger being led through the jungle to what? Thoughts of being taken hostage or disappearing for ever into the bush were beginning to cross my mind when the lights of the forest camp came into view. I was deeply relieved; and my faith in Mr Bushmouse was restored.

Three days in Namdapha yielded little. It is part of Project Tiger; but signs of tiger were non-existent, as were those of any potential tiger prey, apart from the sound of a barking deer. I saw the spore of a pack of wild dog, so presumably some prey must have existed. There were a few primates, the hoolock gibbon, the Assamese macaque and the capped langur, all to be seen after considerable effort. The birds were equally disappointing; and we had been turned back by leeches. The plan was to load the camp elephant, Raj Mullah, with tents and bedding while Mr Bushmouse, Hermanta, myself and a runner set out at five in the morning. By ten o'clock the runner was to return with our decision as to whether or not to proceed. If we were to proceed, the elephant with mahout and Kavas, in his Muslim hat and cigarettes, were to come forward and all were to spend the night in a clearing further into the forest.

However by nine our advance party was in difficulty. The trail was easy to walk but was heavily overgrown, particularly by ferns which harboured leeches; and our leech guards, impenetrable canvas leggings, were proving ineffective. Scores of leeches covered my safari boots and at every bootlace eyelet was a veritable queue of the wriggling horrors. These were not a problem as they would have been blocked by the leech guards. Far worse were the leeches which attached themselves above the leggings and as I plucked one from my hand another two or three immediately took its place and latched on. We decided to turn back. Continuous leech plucking made searching for other wildlife impossible. Of all my encounters with wildlife over the years, this was probably the most unpleasant, albeit harmless. The bearer was sent back to base and our elephant released from duty. The elephant had been in a bad mood; and Kavas had been doubtful about further nights of roughing it in the jungle. Whilst I was disappointed, Kavas and elephant Raj Mullah made general peace by means of sugar cane and apples. I would have liked to add that Kavas played her the guitar; but unfortunately the latter had been left behind.

I had been denied my white-crested laughing thrush, and we left the Namdapha camp with a degree of disappointment. As so often happens with wildlife, a birding party was spotted by Hermanta on the side of the road back to civilization. It was to keep us occupied for an hour or more and made up for several indifferent days. Fruiting bushes had attracted various kinds of laughing thrush which have an irritating habit of cackling loudly for half a minute and then remaining elusive and silent. The fruiting bushes were full of necklaced laughing thrushes; and there were other interesting hill state birds in the adjacent trees.

Whilst looking at these adjacent trees, but keeping my eye on the fruit bushes, Hermanta suddenly exclaimed, 'Peter Sahib, there he is'. I turned my binoculars back to the laughing thrushes, saw Hermanta's bird and said rather crossly, 'No Hermanta, that is the white-headed shrike babbler'. This is another bird with a white head and chestnut body. I knew it well because I had found it seven years before in Kazaranga where it had been added to the National Park bird list. Whilst it was a good bird, it was simply not the white-crested laughing thrush. Hermanta was very disappointed but agreed. As binoculars were again trained on the fruiting bushes, within a minute or two the required bird hopped out. Hermanta did not see it immediately; but it reappeared after two or three minutes and gave both of us a good view. The Namdapha mission was accomplished; we stood on the track, shook hands, embraced, danced a jig and embraced again. It may sound strange behaviour. Those that go to India hoping to see a tiger in one of the game parks and leaving disappointed would have known how I felt about leaving Namdapha without seeing my laughing thrush.

The return to civilization allowed for a much needed bath and change of clothes at a tea plantation bungalow in Dibrugarh before a morning ride on a good mount that was an Assamese Rifle ceremonial horse. I galloped down the banks of the Brahmaputra, something which evoked childhood memories when I had to name the Brahmaputra in prep school geography lessons. It also stirred up past memories of horsemanship as I crossed an Indian main road with a skittish horse. My advice to anyone crossing an Indian road is never do it unless you hang onto the tail of the sacred cow. Indian traffic is something totally alien to the western world and negotiating it with a nervous horse is probably not a good idea.

Riding along the Brahmaputra was followed by a day in Calcutta before returning to my Indian home at Bamboo Banks. In Calcutta Kavas and I stayed at the exclusive Tolleygunge Club before visiting one of Mother Theresa's hospices, which was alarmingly depressing (Kavas fled after two minutes), and a Kali Temple where goats were still ritually sacrificed and the whole compound was full of cheerful and enthusiastic worshippers. I could not help feeling that this was somewhat better than the mournful and flagellating manifestations of Christianity which I have encountered in Latin America. At least the Hindus seemed to have a sense of fun; although the poor goats might not agree.

One day in Calcutta yielded entries in the card indices in the library for my great-grandfather Sir Richard Harrison and my step-brother Gavin Young. I noted that any reference to my own books was absent. St John's Church with the obelisk of those who died in the black hole of Calcutta had a framed patent of arms to the See of Calcutta granted by my predecessor as Garter, Sir Isaac Heard in 1810. The Verger was delighted when Kavas explained I was Heard's successor; and I was taken into a small lobby and allowed to sit in the chair of Warren Hastings for a photographic session. Memorial inscriptions in the church harked back to the British Raj, to a subaltern, for example, returning home from a dinner party when he and his horse were struck dead by lightning. We merged with a Catholic wedding, attended a prayer session in a multi-storey Muslim mosque, where I covered my head with a small rush hat, and we visited a Jain temple where the garden of meditation incongruously contained statues of Aphrodite in various stages of undress, Hercules with his lion and Bacchus with his grapes. After our final imbibing of the grape or rather whisky, Kavas and I separated, he to Bombay and I to Bangalore and on to Bamboo Banks.

At Bamboo Banks Siasp and Zerene Kothavala were in excellent Christmas spirit. Apart from a Northern Indian couple, there were no other guests in the farm cottages. According to Siasp, this was the fault of President Bush and the threat of war with Iraq, coupled with the antics of the bandit Veerappam who continued to elude the police in spite of his sporting a set of highly distinctive whiskers. As other guesthouses in the neighbourhood appeared to have been full, I rather suspect that it was Siasp's outspoken nature that may have been the problem, not that that would worry him. Railing, as ever, against the vegetarians who ruled India, he was delighted at the recent sacking of Manika Ghandi from her ministerial job concerned with wildlife and conservation. She had recently run a chatline or correspondence called *Have a Heart* and when asked by some poor individual how he could rid himself of the rats which infested his house, she replied that the rats had a life and as much right as the owner of the house to live there; he had a duty to accommodate them. In his more expansive moments Siasp despaired of the coconut-bashing cow-worshipping veggies and claimed that the only reason why India works is on the kinetic energy built up and left by the British.

The young married couple from the North immediately encountered what I call 'Siaspisms'. Having established that the husband was half Kashmiri, he enquired, 'Are you a crook?' The husband replied, 'No, why do you ask?' to which Siasp retorted, 'Nothing grows straight in Kashmir except the poplar tree'. Radika, the wife was highly amused and more so when this was followed by Siasp's observation on the Rajputs, of which she was one. 'The trouble with the Rajputs', he explained, 'is that the blood rises up and is blocked by their moustaches; it never reaches the brain'. The great joy of his wit is that it can be taken tongue in cheek. Happily Radika and her husband did precisely that and on their return from a southern tour of India they made and fulfilled a special promise of making a detour to come back to Bamboo Banks to wish us all a Happy New Year.

Siasp announced over Christmas that he wished to become an alcoholic. Zerene, who had long enjoyed her drink, thought that this was an excellent idea. Siasp would become ever more outrageous and amusing. Siasp's attempt at alcoholism made a start but petered out after a day or so. Although my duty-free *Glenlivet* carried us over for several evenings, I am afraid it was largely consumed by myself.

Life was lazy at Bamboo Banks over Christmas and the New Year. The forest was bone dry; the elephants had upgraded their aggression; the birds and wildlife were all too familiar; the deer seemed to have vacated the area seeking better grazing where the drought was less apparent, and there had been a wild boar population explosion. My friend Pat Pradesh had encountered a boar in August. It had charged;

and Pat, running, had tripped, fallen over and found the wild boar on top of him. As this was by the side of the road, an oncoming truck blasted its horn and drove the boar off but not before it had ripped open Pat's thigh which subsequently required fifty-six stitches.

I have always treated wild boar with respect but not fear. If I see them, I generally stand still and let them move out of the way. This was not the case with the boar which Siasp and I found while out riding on the farm. It was not even in the jungle being only about a hundred yards from the front of the house. Siasp spotted it, crouched in the grass. Albert, one of the four dogs, got wind of it and lifted his nose. Suddenly the boar got up and charged. Albert ran back towards Siasp and myself. The boar saw the horses and backed off; but I would not have liked to have been there on foot. This was in a place which I have walked frequently for many years.

The elephants had also become more aggressive with the pressure of human farming and the activities of the bandit Veerappam. Veerappam had taken the ivory tuskers. There was a superfluity of female elephants who reluctantly mated with the non-tusked bulls. Non-tuskers were apparently second rate and as a result female elephants remained frustrated. A week before I arrived at Bamboo Banks an elephant had been helping itself to horse fodder from a bullock cart in a diminutive village near my friend Sunni's house in the jungle. The house was substantial and surrounded by wire fences within which she kept impossible barking dogs which include a pedigree dachshund. In addition there was a pony and an orphaned chowsingha or four-horned antelope. Sunni may have been the squiress of the village and well protected, the villagers were not. The elephant during its feed discovered that there were two villagers sleeping underneath the cart. It tossed the cart some ten yards away and then trampled on one of the sleeping villagers. The second villager, by now wide awake, ran; and the elephant charged him through the village, caught up with him but unfortunately did not complete the job. The poor fellow had a severed spinal cord and multiple smashed limbs. The hospital discharged him as keeping a dying person would cost the family money; the last I heard is that the poor fellow was at home waiting to die.

My other elephant confrontation was thankfully limited. I woke one morning to hear noises in the form of trumpeting behind my cottage Stone House. The forest authorities had telephoned through a warning. We were advised not to go out into the jungle. Instead we rode the horses on the farm; but that evening Siasp and Krishna and I went down the nearby Moyar road, which had previously yielded little except a few elephants, endless peacocks and a pair of bears.

Although the bears were good viewing, we decided to continue and took the road to the village of Singara. There was not much happening as the dry forest had driven away spotted deer; only peacock and wild boar were conspicuous. However elephant were about and Siasp spotted a herd in the bushes as we turned round to go home. It was whisky time and the sun had set. It was dark; some five or six elephants were only a few yards from the road. Siasp stopped the car, one elephant trumpeted and made it clear that it was coming at us, or at least that is what I thought because I said to Siasp sharply, 'Move!' There was a certain pause with further elephant agitation and I reiterated to Siasp soundly, 'Move!' We moved. I have seen enough elephants not to muck around with them; and to have a sighting of elephants in the dusk on the side of the road is not the greatest form of wildlife viewing.

I left Bamboo Banks and returned to London where it was snowing for the first time in twelve years. It was back to my second seven and a half years as Garter.

CHAPTER 22

Life continues

I TOOK THE OPPORTUNITY to write a few brief notes as to a week or two weeks in the Gartership on my return to snowy London from Namdapha. There was the design for panels in the Chapel Royal. The original panels had been designed by Holbein; but there were three which had been grilled, presumably for overhead ventilation or central heating. It had been decided to replace the grilles by three new panels; and I was asked to provide these panels based on Holbein. I looked at the other panels on the ceiling and decided that the three panels, to represent The Queen, Prince Philip and the Prince of Wales should contain badges or motifs taken from their armorials. Rather more interesting was the rococo scrollwork which Holbein had used to surround the armorials. This scrollwork tended to terminate in seahorses, griffins or fanciful animals. In consequence of this, I designed rococo corgi heads for the Queen's panel. I understand that this has caused some considerable amusement and enjoyment. Tim Noad, the artist I worked with, was given firm instructions that the corgi heads were to look like corgi heads and not foxes' masks. Tim and Holbein now happily blend on the ceiling of the Chapel Royal. I hope I can take a little credit for the corgi heads!

My notes now continue as follows:

Two trade marks, one of which bears some resemblance to the Arms of the Milk Marketing Board, the other, for Tamworth Football Club, being the Arms of the Borough of Tamworth with a horizontal fess bearing the Crest of the Borough of Tamworth and the Stafford Knot. I intend to raise objections to both.

A letter from the Department for Constitutional Affairs requesting my advice as to the flying of the lion rampant as displayed in the Royal Standard from the mast of the sailing dinghy of some Lancastrian. The Department claims that it has no objection provided the double tressure is removed; the Lord Chamberlain's office also has no objection; but this overlooks the fact that the Arms of other

261

individuals may be a red lion on gold. The Army has become involved claiming that the Colonel of the Scots Dragoon Guards was given the right to fly a lion rampant by King George VI. Again this overlooks other Arms with lions rampant. The situation will need to be resolved.

The processing of the Royal Warrant for the revised Armorial Bearings for the Duchess of York continues with a deadline.

Two Peers, Lady Tonge and Lord Chidgey, are introduced. Lord Chidgey is kind enough to give me lunch and to inform me that he wishes to proceed with a grant of Armorial Bearings. I had a chatty conversation with Shirley, Lady Williams of Crosby, about western saddles and neck reining. We both agreed that riding on a loose rein creates difficulties and can be nerve-racking.

The constitutional changes involving the abolition of some of the duties of the Lord Chancellor, the creation of a new Speaker for the House of Lords and sundry legal appointments requiring a new Order of Precedence to be submitted by Garter for The Queen's approval. Some disagreement over this and discussions with the Earl Marshal as to further meetings.

The Scottish Regiment requires a new Badge. Some feeling by the Scots that this is a Scottish matter but I have to insist that there is only one British Army and that although Lyon is consulted it is ultimately a matter for the Inspector of Regimental Colours. The Ministry of Defence has failed to send through the proposed design which has now been agreed by the Regiment and work must begin tomorrow.

The Advisory Committee to the Royal Mint has encountered difficulties over its proposed design for the fifty pence piece to commemorate the Victoria Cross. This shows a soldier carrying a wounded colleague in the sights of a machine gun. The Chancellor of the Exchequer claims that it is 'too gloomy'. A meeting of the Advisory Committee has been summoned which I am unable to attend; but my comments are required.

The Office of the Auditor General for Wales has petitioned for a grant of Armorial Bearings; and I need to work out a suitable design.

Flags for Ascension Island – in 1999 the Ministry of Defence issued regulations concerning the Flags for overseas territories. There is some doubt as to the authority and wisdom of this; and I am now advising the Foreign and Commonwealth Office as to what might be done for Ascension Island leading up to the appropriate Royal Warrant. The matter revolves around the use of a white disk on the Blue Ensign. The Ministry of Defence has promulgated that the white disk should not be used in future, seemingly ignoring the fact that Armorial

Bearings where blue predominates will not stand out on the blue background of the Blue Ensign. A white disk overcomes this problem.

A discussion with Alan Dickins (Arundel Herald Extraordinary) on the question as to whether or not the Freedom of Information Act is applicable to papers relating to the setting up of the Canadian Heraldic Authority. Alan Dickins thinks it is not; but as correspondence contains nothing controversial its content could be released. This query came from the Canadian Heraldic Authority itself, on behalf of a Canadian scholar.

Coloured working drawings were sent off to the relevant craftsmen in respect of Stall Furnishings for the Order of the Garter, the Bath and St Michael and St George. Afterwards I realized that John Stanier's griffin's head had been turned into that of an eagle. Thankfully I spotted this and was able to rectify this error before the craftsmen set to work.

That is simply on one day, namely Monday the twenty-seventh of June 2005.

The Garter Service that same June was memorable as the Garter Service of The Queen's Golden Jubilee year. Sovereign heads of state who were members of the order were present. It was seldom that I have given firm instructions to a sovereign head of state, namely the King of Norway, not to move and to do as he was told, this being at his installation in the St George's Chapel as a Knight of the Garter.

I refrained from reminding the Queen of Denmark that we had once been disastrous dancing partners. This had been in 1958 when she had come from Benenden School to Wellington; and I had been detailed to dance with her. We did an energetic Charleston to the then popular tune of *Happy days are here again*. She tripped over my feet and fell flat on the floor. She picked herself up, and we carried on. However, this incident had been noted; and the Master of Wellington's wife, Ruth Stainforth, had somewhat cuttingly said to me, 'You realize that that was the King of Denmark's daughter'.

Norway and Denmark apart, there were further problems at The Queen's Golden Jubilee Garter Service. I arrived immediately before Her Majesty to take up my position in the Quire where The Queen's ceremonial service sheet was placed on my seat in order for me to put down my sceptre, cross into the aisle, bow in front of Her Majesty and give her the service sheet. There was a problem. The

Queen of the Netherlands had occupied my seat. Rapid thoughts crossed my mind; we could do the installation of the King of Norway; I glanced to see where the Queen of the Netherlands should properly be seated so that I could then occupy her place without having to stand in solitary state in the middle of the aisle. Thankfully, the Queen of the Netherlands suddenly realized that she had made a mistake; and with a firm English accent she muttered something like, 'Crikey, I'm in the wrong place' and dashed across the aisle.

As my Gartership draws to its end, I am often surprised to find myself a bachelor living in London rather than a countryman with children in the local pony club. It took me years to adjust to London life; but it is largely thanks to Ginny or 'Miss Texas' that I had become more familiar with my London surroundings. Advantage of this, and the absence of children of my own, was taken by others including my friend Louise Wells and her sister Georgina who were placed in my charge for two or three days when they were approximately eight and six. Friends were somewhat amused at the idea of my looking after two small children; what on earth would I do with them?

Undeterred by sarcastic comments, we set off happily with a loaf of bread to my first destination, St James's Park, where we fed the sparrows by hand. Unfortunately, Louise was wearing frilly white socks; and the Canada geese mistook these frills for extra pieces of bread. Having extricated Louise from pecking geese, we made our way to Westminster Abbey. The Abbey is full of heraldry and royal effigies. I showed them griffins, wyverns and lifted them up to see fat Queen Phillippa of Hainault and the forked beard of King Richard II. The heraldic animals enthralled. Unfortunately there was a sudden silence and an announcement of prayers. This silence was broken by the shrieking voice of Louise, 'Peter, there's a cock' as she pointed to a carved cock above the stall of a knight of the Order of the Bath in the Henry VII Chapel. We travelled through and around London, taking in red and green men on the traffic lights; and the 'gobbling machine' which took and released their tickets in the underground. 'Please may we do that again?' said Louise. 'No,' I said firmly.

The next day Georgina, Louise and I started down an escalator at Victoria Underground Station. Georgina promptly fell over and took up a sitting position in the middle. It was one of the steepest escalators

I have ever encountered; and it was also the rush hour. I looked back, only to find that Louise was suffering from a bout of nerves and the escalator frightened her. She stood at the top as her sister in a sitting position moved downwards. I rushed up against the tide of descending travellers, grabbed Louise and somehow managed to get both of them off at the bottom. They were given firm instructions as to where home was. I did not exactly tie a label round each of their wrists; but I did tell them that if they ever got lost they should go into a shop; and I gave them my address and telephone number. The escalator was one problem; but the trains themselves were another. In pushing one child onto the train, I found it essential that the second child was not left behind.

Worse was to come at the zoo when I bought both of them choc ices. A large slab of Louise's choc ice fell to the ground; and she endeavoured to pick it up. I suggested that this might not be a good idea, only then to discover that Georgina had somehow hopped over the barrier and was making faces at a monkey. The monkey was harmless enough; but I was beginning to realize what it was like to be an acting father for two or three days. There were certainly some compensations for being a childless bachelor. They went to the ladies' loo; and I was not certain whether I should accompany them or whether I should stand outside and hope that they would reappear. They did reappear; and shortly afterwards Louise suddenly became very serious and announced, 'Peter I would like to give you a present'. I replied, 'How very nice and kind.' 'Unfortunately Mummy says there is a recession.' I have been waiting for my present ever since!

Louise had a tortoise called Henry; and Henry also came to stay, living on my balcony. He brought with him five pounds a week pocket money. This was supposed to be spent on fresh fruit and vegetables together with roast pheasant. I am afraid that Henry did not have fresh fruit and vegetables every day; he had a lettuce and a tomato once a week and a piece of roast chicken. The change was considerable; and I kept it as rent. The day came when Henry laid an egg in the Wells home. He was a free-range tortoise; and the egg seemingly appeared on the drawing room floor. This caused great delight; and the egg was placed in the airing cupboard to hatch. Expectations were somewhat shattered when I pointed out that the hatching of an egg depended upon fertilization by a male. Henry may suddenly have changed sex and become a female; but there was not a male tortoise in the household. Henry's feat has always struck me as being rather strange, as I thought that tortoise eggs came in sizeable clutches.

Louise and I have retained a strong friendship; and today she runs an organization called 'Fishnets Lingerie' in Prague. My visiting Prague and some of Louise's other enterprises can cause the unjustified raising of an eyebrow by the more conservative members of the College of Arms.

Educated by Ginny in my London surroundings before she returned to Texas to become a notable classicist, I had then been polished by small children and therefore considered myself well qualified to conduct tours of London for American friends. Perhaps the climax of these tours came with Ashley, the daughter of my old friends Leon and Eleanor Bradshaw from Salisbury, North Carolina. I took Ashley and her husband Bays to the House of Lords. Being something of a mascot at the House of Lords, I was able to show them around without any official or staff questioning our presence. On the contrary, we were all greeted as if popular members of that establishment. On leaving the House of Lords, we encountered Denis, Lord Carter, the Government Chief Whip. I introduced Ashley and Bays to Denis who told me that I must take them to the Chapel of St Mary Undercroft, beneath Westminster Hall. I was not familiar with the House of Commons, but I took Denis's advice and arrived at the entrance. The House of Commons was in recess; strict security was in force; and the official on duty informed me that 'Nobody, not even the Prime Minister himself, is allowed in'. I meekly said, 'What about Garter King of Arms?' There was a pause; the official then said, 'That is a different matter.' We were allowed in. I have to admit I was somewhat impressed; and Ashley was totally dumbfounded. We left Parliament, and she rang her parents in Salisbury, North Carolina, immediately. 'Mo-o-om,' in her long Southern drawl, 'Guess what!'

Showing friends around London or guiding them through a tropical forest is one thing; but being a tour guide for strangers is another matter. My stepbrother, Gavin Young, started all his books with reference to worm-eaten volumes of Conrad, Stephenson,

Kipling and other authors from the days of Empire and adventure. *Lord Jim*, *Treasure Island* and *Kim* were stored in the attics of his grandmother, Maggie. Most of these books which also inspired me are now in my flat in Harcourt Terrace. These books now beckon. Like Bilbo Baggins the hobbit I can close the door and go on adventures. Friends and relations all have children who go on 'gap years', which they consider particular to their own generation. I am announcing that I too shall shortly be going on a 'gap year'. Initial astonishment changes in such a way that I am gradually becoming the 'gap year guru'. I do not know what form my own 'gap year' adventures will take, with or without those sundry friends or relations; but I am sure that the horse, birds and butterflies and a pretty girl will feature. It is to my special pony Fly, my goose Louise and Ophelia the hamster that I owe so much enjoyment in life. Some of the pretty girls have their own special dedication at the beginning of this book. Life when my Gartership ends on my seventieth birthday will certainly continue.

died 21st August 2010

Index